SOCIAL ANTHROPOLOGIES OF THE WELSH

Royal Anthropological Institute

The RAI Country Series

Series Editor: David Shankland

A series of publications celebrating the traditions of anthropology in different countries. Not assuming any essential national identity, but rather – noting the pragmatic reality that anthropology may follow markedly different trajectories in different places – exploring how the discipline has taken shape, being both influenced by its wider social, cultural and intellectual setting and helping to create it.

Social Anthropologies of the Welsh

Past and Present

EDITED BY W. JOHN MORGAN AND FIONA BOWIE

The RAI Country Series, Volume Five

Sean Kingston Publishing
www.seankingston.co.uk
Canon Pyon

First published in 2021 by
Sean Kingston Publishing
www.seankingston.co.uk
Canon Pyon

British Library Cataloguing in Publication Data
A catalogue record for this book is available from the British Library.
The moral rights of the editors and authors have been asserted.

ISBN 978-1-912385-33-1

Foreword

One summer's day in 1995, whilst working in Turkey at the British Institute of Archaeology at Ankara, I saw an advertisement for a lectureship in anthropology at the University of Wales, Lampeter, and, having asked various senior colleagues for their thoughts, applied. On the day of the interview, I went for an early morning walk in the town and was very courteously greeted by those whom I passed on the road. Thinking that such a pleasant community would be an ideal place to work, I was delighted to be offered the post.

Anthropology at the University had been started by Fiona Bowie, who with Oliver Davies, had moved to Lampeter to teach in the Department of Theology and Religious Studies. Over the next few years, a flourishing Department of Anthropology came into being. The friendly welcome that I had received in the town was mirrored by that within the university, presided over by the late Keith Robbins. A superb Vice-Chancellor; polite, engaged, interested in his staff, he regarded the audit culture dispassionately, as something that no doubt had to be followed, but without in any way permitting it to interfere with the workings of academic life. It is a matter of some sadness to me that he passed away before this project came to fruition, and at least now I can pay some small homage to his memory.

The essays in this volume show just how fruitful a country Wales is for anthropology, whether looked at in historical perspective through the early writings of Gerald of Wales, or in terms of industrial and post-industrial change, as Chris Hann writes in his evocative piece on South Wales. There is also no doubt in my mind that anthropology can contribute something absolutely distinct when looking at contemporary society. This is perhaps because as anthropologists we tend to look at the connections between different aspects of social life, whereas other disciplines, almost by definition – whether history, politics, or economics – privilege one particular strand and begin their considerations from that. For this reason, any discussion concerning a specific region can be enormously enriched by including anthropology in its inter-disciplinary mix.

Yet, curiously, even though anthropology as an academic discipline in Wales has on many occasions experienced exactly that favourable beginning that we enjoyed in Lampeter, there has not emerged a major, stable department that has reached critical mass. As the editors write in their Introduction, anthropology has featured in Aberystwyth, where Fleure and then Daryll Forde created a distinct strand, combining anthropology and geography together. Likewise, it has been started with success in Swansea, only later to fall by the wayside. We are faced with the situation that despite the enormous contribution to intellectual life that has been made by anthropologists from Wales, and the extraordinary fieldwork that has been conducted in Wales, the discipline has not quite managed to establish itself in the way that, given its early beginnings, one would expect.

Thus, though in this series we have conventionally traced the way that anthropology has come to be founded then grown within a particular region, in this case we are faced with the opposite situation: initiatives start successfully, even expand over a period of some years, then contract again. Though on the inside of this endeavour in the 1990s, I have no clear idea of why this should be the case; though I would certainly like to know the answer. Whatever conclusion we may reach, this volume, as well as offering in a taste of how extra-ordinarily fruitful anthropology has been and could be in the future, is at the same time a plea: that a discipline that has so much to contribute should be a major part of intellectual life in Wales, in whatever form that might take.

David Shankland
Director, Royal Anthropological Institute

Acknowledgements

We thank the Royal Anthropological Institute, the Learned Society of Wales, the Honourable Society of the Cymmrodorion, Cardiff University and the Wales Institute of Social and Economic Research, and Data for the generous financial and administrative support that made possible the symposium at which the papers that comprise this volume were first presented. We thank individually Professor David Boucher, Yr Athro Paul Chaney, Rev. Professor Douglas Davies, Yr Athro Meredid Hopwood, Yr Athro Ian Rees Jones, Yr Athro Prys Morgan, Professor Nigel Rapport, Dr David Shankland and Dr Lynn Williams. We thank especially Mrs Jane Graves and colleagues at WISERD, Ms Amanda Vinson and colleagues at the RAI and Dr Sarah Morse and colleagues at the Learned Society of Wales for their invaluable support in organizing the symposium. Finally, we thank the two anonymous readers who commented helpfully on the manuscript.

W. John Morgan and Fiona Bowie

Contents

Introduction

W. JOHN MORGAN AND FIONA BOWIE

The chapters in this book have been developed from papers given first at a symposium on 'Social anthropologies of the Welsh', co-sponsored by the Royal Anthropological Institute, the Learned Society of Wales, the Honourable Society of Cymmrodorion and the Wales Institute of Social and Economic Research, Data and Methods, Cardiff University, which hosted the event. The symposium was introduced with a public lecture entitled 'Horizons of comparison' by Professor Dame Marilyn Strathern, FBA (née Evans, of Welsh heritage in North Wales), and Honorary Fellow, the Learned Society of Wales. This was on the 1 May 2019, the symposium itself held on the following day.

The symposium was inspired by an attempt by one of the editors, ultimately fruitless, to find a printed version of the late Professor Eric Sunderland's presidential address to the Royal Anthropological Institute on anthropologies of the Welsh. Himself a Welsh-speaker, Sunderland, a distinguished physical anthropologist, had also been principal and then vice-chancellor of University College of North Wales (later Bangor University) between 1984 and 1995), president of the University of Wales, Lampeter, between 1998 and 2002, and a founding fellow of the Learned Society of Wales.

The institutional context of anthropology in Wales

Eric Sunderland played a significant role in the development of anthropologies in and of Wales. In some ways his career and influence mirrored that of his illustrious predecessor, Herbert John Fleure (1877–1969), who at Aberystwyth held the first chair in Wales with 'anthropology' in its title. If one is looking for ancestors, then Fleure is a founding father. Born on Guernsey, he was largely self-educated due to poor health as a child. Free of disciplinary constraints he developed a holistic and enduring interest in all aspects of his homeland – its natural history, geology and geography, its archaeology, history, people and culture. Although focusing on a small community and setting, an island bounded by water, Fleure's world was vast in its appreciation of geological and evolutionary time, and in the complexity of the interconnections he saw in all aspects of life, particularly human life.

Fleure's breadth of vision combined with an unshakeable belief in the potential of education for developing peace and understanding among peoples. The community studies that flourished in Aberystwyth under Alwyn Rees in the second half of the twentieth century reflected Fleure's discovery that looking in depth at one community is not the same as seeing it as an isolated entity. To fully understand any place and the human cultures that develop there, it must be seen in terms of location, history and environment, synchronic and diachronic. There is nothing static about these processes, and understanding how and why change occurs was central to Fleure's outlook.

After undergraduate studies in geology and zoology at Aberystwyth, Fleure was introduced to physical anthropology while studying at the Zoological Institute of Zurich from 1902 to 1904. He accepted a lectureship in the Department of Botany at Aberystwyth on the understanding that he could develop his broader interests. As Garnett (1970:257) points out in her informative biography of Fleure, his anthropological interests were evident in his ambitious University of Wales anthropological survey of the Welsh people in 1905, which involved visiting all parts of the principality, urban and rural. Fleure came to know and love Wales, and was equally at home speaking in chapels and village halls as in university lecture theatres. His travels were reminiscent of those of Gerald of Wales, described by Huw Pryce (this volume), but rather more scientific in ambition. Fleure was ahead of his time in regarding the widespread assumption of 'racial' differences between the Welsh and English as oversimplified. When looking at morphological data or blood groups, for example, he insisted that the relationship between people and place needed to be considered. The history of settlement in a valley could be quite different from that of neighbouring moorland communities, each environment giving rise to contrasting cultural and physical characteristics.

In 1917, Gwendoline Elizabeth Davies and Margaret Sidney Davies of Gregynog endowed at Aberystwyth the first and only chair in Great Britain of geography and anthropology, to which Fleure was duly appointed.[1] In accepting

---

1   Miss Gwendoline Elizabeth Davies and Miss Margaret Sidney Davies of Gregynog Hall (formerly Plas Dinam, Llandinam), near Newtown in Powys, bequeathed their home to the University of Wales. They acquired the building in 1920 and

the chair, Fleure expressed the hope that 'universal mutual knowledge between peoples of different environments ought to be an element in education for peace' (ibid.:260). Fleure moved to Manchester in 1930, which created links between what was then known as the Victoria University of Manchester and anthropology of and in Wales. Although anthropology has not survived as a separate discipline at Aberystwyth, there is still an annual Gregynog lecture, endowed by the Davies sisters in 1936, for 'the encouragement of the study of music, geography and anthropology'. Both Fleure and Eric Sunderland shared with the Davies sisters a love of music as well as the conviction that anthropology and geography are natural companions (see O'Connell, this volume). It is timely that the next Royal Anthropological Institute's biannual conference is to be held jointly with the Royal Geographical Society, once again uniting two of Fleure's life-long passions.

Eric Sunderland shared Fleure's interest in human origins, morphology and blood groups, and emphasized the leading role of demography in physical (biological) anthropology. Rather fittingly, I. Morgan Watkin, former director of public health medicine at Aberystwyth, recognized in a short article the similarities between the two men (Watkin 1994). Linguistics, history, politics, religion, geography, physical anthropology and surnames are all covered in a few pages, finishing with a section concerned with Wales' contribution to peace and justice.

That the search for peace and harmony among people, disciplines, and nations occupied much of Fleure's life has already been mentioned. Eric Sunderland too had a keen sense of civic duty. He served as honorary secretary of the Royal Anthropological Institute, and between 1989 and 1991 was its president. He served also as secretary-general of the International Union of Anthropological and Ethnological Sciences. On retirement, he was appointed high sheriff and lord lieutenant of Gwynedd, and was returning officer of the Wales devolution referendum in 1997. He was a member of the Gorsedd of Bards, an honour given at the National Eisteddfod, in recognition of his contribution to Welsh life and culture (Sillitoe 2010). Sunderland, like Fleure, possessed a charismatic personality. He was a kind and encouraging teacher and mentor, as well as a skilled politician and administrator. He had

---

rescued it from ruin, turning it into a splendid centre for the arts. The building housed the Gregynog Press and a distinguished fine art collection, hosted musical performances, and the extensive grounds were managed with the natural history of the area in mind. In addition to hosting the first meeting of the League of Nations in 1922, for many years the hall was the centre of conference activities for the federal University of Wales, and is now a conference centre run by the Gregynog Trust.

an exceptional memory, recalling the names of former students and the year in which they studied, following their careers with satisfaction, and assisting whenever possible.

Despite scholars such as Herbert John Fleure and Eric Sunderland, anthropology struggled to gain a permanent foothold in Wales. Individual anthropologists of distinction have worked in each of the constituent institutions of the University of Wales, and have left Wales to build illustrious careers elsewhere, although not always within a department of anthropology. The significant role of community studies at Aberystwyth under the leadership of Alwyn D. Rees, as well as studies conducted at Manchester University by Ronald Frankenberg and colleagues, have had an influence far beyond Wales. These are mentioned in several chapters of this volume, although the context of discussion and argument is different in each case. We are also mindful that readers may focus on individual chapters rather than the volume as a whole.

At Bangor (with distinguished gerontologist Clare Wenger) and at Swansea, links with sociology and medical anthropology were particularly strong. Between 1964 and 2004 there was a flourishing department of sociology and anthropology at Swansea, with anthropologists appointed also in development studies. As Gareth Rees's chapter in this volume illustrates, Swansea, together with Aberystwyth and Manchester, could be said to comprise a distinctive 'school' or approach to anthropological studies in Wales, one that drew on both sociology and anthropology, with a joint chair for both disciplines (first held by W.M. Williams).[2] The most significant study of Wales to emerge from the department in the 1960s combined the expertise of a sociologist, Chris Harris, and an anthropologist, Colin Rosser, in their study of kinship in the 'urban villages' of South Wales (Rosser and Harris 1965). Nickie Charles, Charlotte Aull Davies and Chris Harris continued this collaboration between disciplines in the 1980s, with their study of families and kinship (Charles *et al.* 2008), which emphasized the continuing importance of family ties in South Wales despite the considerable economic and social changes of previous decades.

Several doctoral students of the Swansea department focused on ethnography in Wales, particularly in urban areas, complementing the largely rural studies conducted at Aberystwyth. Other areas of the world were not neglected, with (among others) Margaret Kenna writing on Greece and Felicia

---

2   Reginald Byron (1944–2017) who was later appointed to a chair, was head of department at Swansea from 1991 to 2006, seeing the department through both good and not such good times. A specialist in the anthropology of Northern Europe, Byron was also instrumental in helping to establish anthropology as a subject area at Lampeter.

Hughes-Freeland on South-East Asia. When W.M. Williams contributed a chapter on the history of sociology and anthropology at Swansea to a volume celebrating the twenty fifth anniversary of the department (Williams 1990), the future looked bright. Nevertheless, the university closed the department in 2004, despite protests internally and from the wider anthropological community. It is therefore encouraging to note that Martin Stringer, who came from Birmingham University to be pro-vice-chancellor in 2015 is an anthropologist with a strong record of ethnographic work, particularly in the anthropology of religion.

Established in 1822 as St David's College, Lampeter boasts that it is the oldest university in England and Wales other than Oxford and Cambridge. In its early years, its mission was training for the Christian ministry, although never exclusively so. As the University of Wales Lampeter in the 1990s, it became a broad-based humanities college, and two appointments in 1993 (Penny Dransart in archaeology and Fiona Bowie in theology and religious studies) provided the nucleus of a new venture in anthropology. The latter was encouraged by the then pro-vice-chancellor, D.P. Davies, to set up a department of anthropology, which admitted its first undergraduates in 1995. The aim was to be as inclusive as possible with opportunities for students to have a broad base in cognate disciplines, either through shared modules or joint degrees. The first member of staff appointed to teach the new anthropology degree was David Shankland, followed in succeeding years by Keith Brown, Dimitrios Theodossopoulos, Veronica Strang, Elisabeth Kirtsoglou and Angels Trias i Valls.

By the late 1990s, the department, with five full-time and four part-time staff, and with contributions from anthropologists in other departments, including archaeology and theology and religious studies, probably had one of the largest groups of anthropologists of any institution in Wales (although still small by most other standards). It offered single, joint and combined-honours undergraduate degrees, an MA in social anthropology, and M.Phil and PhD supervision. Changes in university funding, particularly the end of the mature student grants at the beginning of the 2000s, saw a decline in provision at Lampeter as well as at Swansea. A few anthropology staff moved to Bristol University in 2002, while the remainder joined the archaeologists to form a new joint department, now led by Luci Attala, one of the first undergraduate intake in 1995.

Social anthropologists have consistently been appointed to teach religious studies at Lampeter (although the institutional framework for the subject has changed frequently), including Bettina Schmidt, who works on religion in Brazil and is director of the Religious Experience Research Centre founded by Sir Alister Hardy at Oxford in 1969. There are also social anthropologists as tutors on the online MA in the study of culture and cosmology taught through the Sophia Centre, headed by Nick Campion, within the Faculty of Humanities and Performing Arts at what is now the University of Wales Trinity St David.

Cardiff University has never aspired to create a separate department of anthropology. However, as the contributions to the symposium and volume show, there are scholars who have produced ethnographic and anthropological work, particularly within the social sciences, but also in arts and humanities departments (such as Geoffrey Samuel, an expert on Tibet and Indic regions, whose work bridges anthropology and religious studies). Sara Delamont's ambitious book on social anthropology in Western Europe (Delamont 1995) illustrates the fruitful coalescence between sociology and social anthropology. This volume has benefitted from Gareth Rees's knowledge of Welsh community studies. He is the former director of the Wales Institute of Social and Economic Research and Data (WISERD) at Cardiff.

Identity and place: comparative themes

We turn now to the present volume. Finding common themes in an eclectic and to an extent interdisciplinary collection of essays can sometimes present a challenge, although the variety of approaches and topics in the volume was intentional. There are however two interwoven strands that run through most if not all the contributions. The first is the notion of what it means to be Welsh, including the role of language in identity formation. The second is the importance of place. The two themes are connected. We are considering those people connected to, living in and identifying with a place, the Principality of Wales.

Identity: Who are the Welsh?

When I. Morgan Watkin (1994) asked the question 'who are the Welsh?' he was covering familiar ground. In answering this question, authors sometimes, as in Watkin's case, turn to the notion of race and the etymology of the word 'Welsh'. The twelfth-century Norman-Welsh chronicler Gerald of Wales suggested that the Anglo-Saxons referred to strangers/foreigners as Wallic (Welsh), but, as has often been pointed out, if this were the case one would expect the term to be applied to the Scots and Irish as well.

More likely is the explanation that the term 'Welsh' in various forms was used by the Teutonic tribes to refer to Romanized Celts, a term applied to Celtic tribes in many parts of Europe, surviving to this day in several local languages and dialects.[3] The old English Wealas was applied to those under

---

3   For a summary of the origin of the terms 'Welsh' and 'Wales' and '*Cymry*' and '*Cymraeg*', see Davies and Bowie (1995).

Roman jurisdiction (which was why it was not attached to their fellow Celts in Ireland and Scotland). The Welsh called themselves the 'kinsmen', or 'those from the same country', the term *Cymry* embracing both the inhabitants of Wales and the Brythonic areas of north-west England in what is now Cumbria (Watkin 1994:53).

What is known is that the inhabitants of much of north-west Europe and Asia Minor in the Bronze and Iron Ages belonged to a collection of tribes and language groups generally referred to as Celtic. They included the people of Gaul (whose Gaulish language was once spoken throughout what is now France) and Britain. At some point the Celtic languages spoken in the islands of Britain split into two families, Brythonic (giving rise to Welsh, Cornish and Breton) and Goidelic (Scots and Irish Gaelic and Manx). Given the considerable population movements in Europe at the end of the last Ice Age (around 10,000 years ago) and over succeeding millennia, notions of any discrete 'race' of people who could call themselves 'Celts' or 'Welsh' needs to be treated with great caution. Fleure was rightly suspicious of the notion of 'race', which is an ideological and cultural rather than a scientific notion.

The borders of the modern Principality of Wales have been as fluid as its population and the geographical reach of the Brythonic language/s. The Mercian king Offa built an earth dyke some 150 miles (240 kilometres) long in the eighth century (*Clawdd Offa*), which coincided for part of its route with a fifth century AD Roman earthwork, used to delineate the border between the southern part of Wales and his Anglo-Saxon kingdom. In 1536, the modern boundary followed much the same route, leaving some largely Welsh-speaking areas of Cheshire, Shropshire, Herefordshire and Gloucestershire on the English side of the border.

The status of Monmouthshire in the south remained fluid until the twentieth century, being considered part of England for some purposes and Wales for others. It was only when the Local Government Act of 1972 created the Welsh county of Gwent, which included most of Monmouthshire, that it was unambiguously considered part of Wales (changing its name once again to Monmouthshire in another local government reorganization in 1996). Not surprisingly, the sense of being Welsh or English along the border can be somewhat ambiguous, and some people on both sides of the border often identify with their immediate locality rather than the labels 'English' or 'Welsh'.

The inhabitants of Wales when the Romans arrived were in no sense isolated, trading with Ireland, continental Europe and beyond, as well as with the Anglo-Saxon tribes to the east. There were cultural and linguistic distinctions between the Welsh and Anglo-Saxons, as both Tacitus in the first-century CE and Gerald of Wales in the twelfth century noted (see Pryce, and Bowie, this volume). One difference still evident today is the patronymic naming system in which a child takes the given (Christian) name of their father or mother, prefixed by *ab* or *ap* ('son of', from the Welsh for 'son', *mab*) or *ferch* ('daughter of').[4] So, for example, one might find Iwan ap Owen (shortened to Bowen) or Rhodri ap Harri (Parry). This system has been revived by some of the more educated, culturally nationalist Welsh-speakers of recent years. In the fourteenth century, between 50 and 70 per cent of the population followed this practice, although place names and nicknames – often describing appearance – could also be used.

It was the Laws of Wales Act of Henry VIII in the sixteenth century, which absorbed Welsh into English law, patronymic surnames were discouraged, and in Protestant Wales the pool of Christian names narrowed as Roman Catholic saints names were avoided. The patronymic names became surnames, sometimes with the addition of a final 's', giving rise to the large number of people with surnames such as Jones and Evans (from various forms of John/Iwan/Sion/Evan), Thomas (Tomos), Hughes/Pugh (from Huw/Hugh) and Davies (from the many forms of David/Dafydd/Dai).

Welsh surnames, therefore, do not denote descent in the way that is often the case in Scotland, Ireland and England, and are therefore of little help to genealogists. Locating an individual in terms of residence has remained a characteristic feature, at least in rural Wales, where people may be known and introduce themselves by the name of their farm or some other distinguishing feature of the locality (see Forde, this volume). This necessary linkage of names to specific geographical places of origin has remained a cultural trope in contemporary Wales, giving an impression of shared origins and kinship, which is still highly valued (as in Scotland and Ireland).

Most chapters consider language and identity in one way or another. At first it may appear that someone who speaks Welsh and lives in Wales is unambiguously Welsh. They have access through the Welsh language to a literature and culture that is hard to appreciate through the medium of English. Those born and brought up in Wales who do not speak the language may be apologetic about their 'Welshness', or lack of it (see Hann, this volume) and experience their lack of bilingualism as a loss. As several contributors point out, there are nuances and tensions concerning speaking Welsh, learning Welsh, with being Welsh and with the implication that the majority of the population who do not speak Welsh are somehow less Welsh as a result. Some authors prefer to look at class rather than ethnicity, focusing on the

---

4   I. Morgan Watkin included a section on Welsh naming practices in his article on the Welsh (Watkin 1994:59). Apparently a census of landowners on Anglesey in 1873 lists 196 landlords whose names begin with the letter 'J', every one of which is 'Jones', still the most common Welsh surname.

social and structural features of a locality that are often shared with other parts of the United Kingdom or Europe, and to de-emphasize the role of language. There is no reason in principle why scholars should not look at both class and ethnicity, although the divide between a sociological and a cultural/social anthropological approach sometimes precludes this in practice.

An attachment to place is also seen as a way of being Welsh. Elen Phillips (this volume) shows how Iorwerth Peate's aim of gathering collections for the National Museum of Wales may be seen as shifting gradually from a desire to capture a representative image of the people of Wales as they really are – with their dialects, work tools, buildings and customs – to a rather nostalgic preservation of a rural way of life typified by his boyhood in Montgomeryshire. Iwan Rees's study of the Welsh in Argentinian Patagonia (this volume) draws out the ambiguity of Welshness for a population, most of whom have never set foot in Wales. The revival of the Welsh language in Patagonia has followed the revival of Welsh-medium institutions, including schools and the media, within Wales. Gerald of Wales in the twelfth-century was already writing the obituary of the Welsh (Pryce, this volume), but as Dafydd Iwan, a Welsh folk singer, put it in the chorus of one of his most popular songs, '*Ry'n ni yma o hyd*' ('we are still here').[5]

For Dafydd Iwan, the Welshman who turns his back on his language and culture in order to succeed in England (the Dic Siôn Dafydd referred to in the song) is as much of an enemy as 'Maggie and her crew' (Margaret Thatcher, the prime minister of the UK who, in the 1980s, was responsible for the closure of the coal mines and loss of industrial jobs in Wales). It is the role of the folk singer to link myth, history and contemporary events, and the impact of modern social, political and economic changes are discussed in the second part of the volume.

In many ways, the industrial areas of Wales are no different from other parts of Europe that underwent similar changes. There are characteristics, however, that are typically if not exclusively Welsh. Chris Hann (this volume) cites Samuel Strong's study of Blaenau Gwent, one of the most deprived areas of the de-industrialized South Wales Valleys. The inhabitants have strong attachments to the place and to family and friends, which in the absence of

---

5   Dafydd Iwan's song, which is something of a rallying cry for Welsh nationalism, is entitled '*Yma O Hyd*'. It gives a brief sketch of Welsh history, with the chorus repeating the words 'We are still here, despite everyone and everything, we are still here'. Simply to survive as a people who have preserved their mother tongue is presented as a significant achievement. There are few Welsh-language speakers (including learners) who were alive in the 1970s and 1980s who are not familiar with the song.

alternative opportunities tie them to the area. For Strong's interviewees, being Welsh is synonymous with being an inhabitant of Blaenau Gwent. Living in an area where generations of their family had also lived did in a sense make it unique, at least from the individual's viewpoint. As Marilyn Strathern points out (this volume), it is a matter of perspective. Rees, and Blakely (this volume), also refer to the enduring role of kinship, particularly centred around the female carer role, that persists in South Wales. The stereotype of the 'Welsh mam', keeping the home together and sacrificing herself for her family, has a relevance to lived experience.

The experience of place

An attachment to a particular place, whether it be an area of the South Wales Valleys such as Blaenau Gwent, a single farm or village or a nation as a whole, is not unique to Wales – despite the oft repeated claim that the Welsh word *hiraeth* ('longing' or 'homesickness'), and by implication the sentiment expressed, has no equivalent in English. Taulant Guma and Rhys Dafydd Jones (this volume) show how some European migrants to Wales fall in love with the landscape, and try to encourage their countrymen and women to visit and get to know the Welsh countryside as a way of integrating into Welsh society. The European Union referendum result, with Wales as a whole voting decisively to leave the EU, came as a blow to such people, who had made their home in Wales. The role of migration in and out of Wales and within Wales is considered in several chapters (see below).

If the close ties of kinship and sociality, together with a lack of economic alternatives, in the relatively deprived de-industrialized areas of North and South Wales limit mobility, language is a factor for some of the more professionally mobile inhabitants of Wales. The inspiration of men like John Saunders Lewis (1893–1985), a writer and prominent Welsh nationalist who co-founded Plaid Genedlaethol Cymru (Plaid Cymru, 'the Party of Wales') in 1925 and was its first president, could make leaving Welsh-speaking Wales seem like an act of treachery for some activists. Lewis was born to a Welsh-speaking family in Liverpool, where he studied at the local university. Lewis's Welsh nationalism was inspired by his reading of the French nationalist and writer Maurice Barrès (Chapman 2014).

Many years later, in 1962, Lewis gave a radio talk about the fate of the Welsh language, in which he predicted that Welsh would all but disappear as a living entity unless there was urgent action. This sombre cultural prediction led to the formation of Cymdeithas yr Iaith Gymraeg (Welsh Language Society), the campaigns of which created a climate that led to the Welsh-medium television station, Sianel Pedwar Cymru (S4C), and to a Welsh-language and Welsh independence movement, the achievements of which include Welsh-medium schools, Welsh-medium university teaching posts and Welsh devolution. As several of the contributors point out, the role of the state and the strength of civil society at a local level can have a profound influence on people's identity, attachment to a locality and sense of belonging.

The revival of the Welsh language and the accompanying nationalist sentiment had a specific character in Wales. For example, Gwynfor Evans (1912–2005), a colleague of Saunders Lewis, learned Welsh in his teens (his mother was Welsh-speaking), and he remained committed to helping others learn the language throughout his life, founding a Welsh-learners society, Pont ('bridge') in the 1980s to encourage incomers and non-Welsh-speaking Welsh people to acquire the language, and to identify with Welsh-medium culture and causes. Gwynfor Evans served two terms as president of Plaid Cymru and was the first Plaid Cymru MP to be elected to Westminster, representing the constituency of Carmarthen in West Wales.

Evans, like other Welsh nationalist contemporaries, was a pacifist, and advocated non-violent action against the British state when it was felt necessary.[6] Others demonstrated their commitment to the future of the Welsh language by learning it (if they were not already Welsh-speakers), speaking it at home, sending children to Welsh-medium schools, and broadcasting and publishing in Welsh, despite the relatively limited audience for works in Welsh as compared with English. In many cases they turned down career opportunities outside Wales, or even outside Welsh-speaking areas of Wales. Many who took part in the movement to support and strengthen the Welsh language were in fact incomers and learners, working closely together with local Cymru Cymraeg ('Welsh-speaking Welsh').[7]

As Iwan Rees shows about Patagonia (this volume), and Elaine Forde considers in her discussion of the relationship between language and values in Wales (this volume) there can be a cultural attachment to Wales as a country and to the Welsh language that does not necessarily coincide with residence (as well as a lack of such attachment by some Welsh-speaking people in Wales, whether of Welsh or English, or some other heritage). Ifor ap Glyn, the winner of the prestigious Crown at the National Eisteddfod, was brought up in the

---

6   Direct action in the 1980s and 1990s drew inspiration from the earlier actions of Saunders Lewis (son of a Welsh Calvinist minister and a convert to Catholicism), who, together with David John Williams and Lewis Edward Valentine, set fire to a house on the Llyn Peninsula in 1936 in protest over a proposed 'bombing school' on the site. As a result, Lewis was dismissed from his teaching post at Swansea University.

7   For the contribution of Welsh-learners to Welsh-medium institutional and cultural life, see Bowie and Davies (1992).

Welsh-speaking diaspora in London, where his family have lived since the 1880s. For Ifor ap Glyn (note the use of the patronymic surname), the saying *cenedl heb iaith, cenedl heb galon* ('a nation without a language is a nation without a heart') still holds true (Ifor ap Glyn n.d.). Here place and identity merge – the land of Wales and its tongue together represent the sacred heart of the nation and by extension its people.

Wales is unusual within the United Kingdom in the valorization of poetry and literature, together with music and dance, and the system of *eisteddfodau* from the local to the national is an important vehicle for the development and performance of these arts. There is accommodation to English and to Welsh-learners within the *eisteddfodau*, but they are primarily showcases for the Welsh language and culture. Welsh-medium schools generally have a good academic reputation and are often seen as the schools of choice for the aspirant and established middle classes. Chris Hann (this volume) points out that locating these schools in areas without a Welsh-speaking hinterland can be problematic, but they have been extremely successful in maintaining and growing the number of individuals fluent in Welsh, and able to access Welsh-medium employment (see Forde, this volume).

Although there is not a separate chapter on sport in Wales, sport has been and continues to be of importance both as a pastime and at the international level as a symbol of Welsh national identity. All types of sport are popular, with some regional differences, such as football in north Wales and rugby football in the valleys of South Wales, where it has always been a community sport without the social class implications that it traditionally had elsewhere in the UK. In the twentieth century, with the development of international sport, Welsh teams and individual sports men and women are seen and supported as representing the nation. The sustained and exceptional success of the Welsh team has contributed to rugby being recognized as the national sport. However, the international success of all Welsh sports men and women is celebrated, as the victory of the cyclist Geraint Thomas in the 2018 Tour de France illustrates.

As noted above, the whole issue of language can be fraught, whether between Welsh-speaking and non-Welsh-speaking areas (see Forde, this volume), those born in Wales and incomers, or within families, where language use can split along generational lines in complex ways. Earlier generations of migrants, whether of Italian or Polish, or one of the many nationalities who arrived in Cardiff docks since the mid nineteenth century, have generally been absorbed into their local communities and in some cases have become fluent in Welsh, identifying with both Wales and their non-Welsh heritage. Cardiff Bay was one of the most racially mixed areas of the UK in the nineteenth and early twentieth centuries, but as Guma and Jones (this volume) remind us, anti-immigrant sentiments can surface or resurface. The link between attachment to place, and even the sanctification of nature and of the landscape, and forms of nationalist sentiment, are often painfully intertwined in Wales as elsewhere in the world, influenced by complex factors. Fleure's aspirations for anthropology to create peace and understanding between nations and individuals is a continuing project.

An outline of the chapters

The symposium and the chapters of this volume illustrate the development of social anthropology, past and present, both in and about Wales, from the perspectives of both national and international scholarship, with contributions from both distinguished scholars and from younger, emerging academics.

Chapter 1 is a revised version of Marilyn Strathern's public lecture for the Learned Society of Wales, which preceded the symposium. This provides an intellectual and anthropological context for the chapters that follow. It is pointed out that focusing on a country's anthropology summons all kinds of comparisons; and that, if they resonate with self-consciousness about intellectual practice, there remains something to say about the embedding of a discipline in local institutions. This has meant in turn that anthropologies differ in the attention they pay to their hinterland, and here aspects of Welsh scholarship are intriguing. Strathern concludes that, as far as the aims and scope of study are concerned, anthropologists in general may find kindred scholars in Welsh ventures beyond their own time and ambitions.

Chapter 2, by Huw Pryce, is an account of Gerald of Wales as a medieval ethnographer of the Welsh. The chapter traces Gerald's life (*c.*1146–*c.*1223), education and ecclesiastical career. It points out that Gerald had to negotiate a world marked by ethnic difference and conflict, and shows how his acute awareness of such differences helps to explain his remarkably precise and perceptive observations on Welsh society. The chapter examines how, and why, Gerald described the Welsh in his *Description of Wales* and other writings, and assesses the significance of his approach in the context of modern scholarship on medieval ethnography.

In Chapter 3, John O'Connell focuses on the study of Indian music undertaken by the Welsh polymath Sir William Jones (1744–1794). The chapter explores the significant contribution that Jones made to comparative musicology and ethnomusicology. Comparing music and language in the Celtic lands, the chapter shows how Jones helped musicians and writers alike realize an Orientalist register in expressive culture. The Irish poet and songwriter Thomas Moore (1779–1852) is shown to be of especial interest.

Chapter 4, by Elen Phillips, explores the collecting and recording activities of Dr Iorwerth C. Peate, the first curator of the Welsh Folk Museum at St Fagans (now the National Museum of History/Amgueddfa Werin Cymru). A former student of H.J. Fleure at Aberystwyth, Peate was also an influential figure in the folk-life studies movement in Britain. The collecting methodologies practised during Peate's curatorship included Mass Observation-style questionnaires, documentary photography and, arguably most importantly, the recording of oral testimony and dialects. For Peate, folk museums were living community centres, not repositories 'for the dry bones of a dead culture'. The chapter gives an appraisal of Peate's curatorial legacy, framed within the context of current museological thinking.

Chapter 5, by Fiona Bowie, bridges the historical and contemporary chapters in this volume. Approaches to the study of religion in Wales and contemporary religious practices are seen in the light of the country's rich religious history. Anthropological themes, such as the importance of place and the natural world, emerge in the written 'Lives' of Welsh saints as well as in historical and contemporary pilgrimage practices. The main Christian religions are represented, together with other world religions. There are also new and old forms of paganism, eco-spiritualities, shamanic communities, new religious movements and forms of 'religion-like' practices. The chapter presents vignettes of these various aspects of contemporary religious life. Conversations with a variety of religious practitioners give a flavour of the continuities, as well as the differences in belief and practice that coexist in contemporary Wales.

In chapter 6, Iwan Rees considers the Welsh diaspora in Argentinian Patagonia. Drawing on earlier studies, he shows how the state of the Welsh language in Chubut was portrayed negatively in the second half of the twentieth century, during which a decline in the use of Welsh from the 1920s onwards was a common theme. He then shows how more recent sociolinguistic studies and investigations of identity construction have been inspired by the revitalization of the Welsh language since the 1990s. Rees draws on recently collected data, illustrating how linguistic developments in Chubut's contemporary varieties of Welsh vary with language use and other social factors.

Chapter 7, by Gareth Rees, provides a review of community studies and twentieth-century social change and how these studies offer perspectives on Welsh society. Such studies constitute a principal element in the anthropological and sociological analysis of modern Welsh society. Rees looks at the pioneering studies of Alwyn D. Rees and colleagues based at Aberystwyth before and just after the Second World War. He also considers other important examples of community studies, such as those of Ronald Frankenberg and Isabel Emmett, associated with the Manchester School of anthropology, and the work of Tom Brennan and others in Swansea, including Colin Rosser, Chris Harris and

Nickie Charles. Rees compares the methodological and analytical approaches of these studies, including the ways by which researchers engaged with 'their communities'.

Chapter 8, by Robin Mann, David Dallimore, Howard Davis and Marta Eichsteller, presents the results of fieldwork at Rhosllanerchrugog, a deindustrialized village near Wrexham in north-east Wales. The authors argue for a place-based understanding of civil society at local levels. The researchers investigate local civil society ethnographically, analysing four inter-linked components of place. These include sites of participation; the role of individual agents in leading and running local civil society groups and organizations; the presence of local civil society organizations themselves; and opportunities for association and collective action through events. These components, it is argued, are integral to understanding civil society practices across a range of socio-spatial contexts. They emerge out of the process of embarking on ethnographic fieldwork and the initial analytical reflections on how a broad range of civil society activities take form over local socio-spatial terrains.

In Chapter 9, Helen Blakely considers welfare reform in the South Wales Valleys from the perspectives of history, community and kinship. The contention is that through a fine-grained analysis of local complexities and particularities of social relations it is possible to develop a commentary relating to the social world more broadly. Such an analysis is adopted here to consider the everyday interactions of a group of welfare-reliant single mothers, the 'Lifeline girls', with the pervasive mechanisms of street-level welfare governance in a single community of the South Wales Valleys, known here as Valleyside. By situating these encounters within a local social and economic structure, and a wider institutional context of market and state, their significance for social relations may be grasped.

Chapter 10, by Elaine Forde, explores the role of models and asks, how socio-cultural models may assist comparison. In anthropological research, and given the absence of any earlier objects for comparison, it is often such models – abstractions of everyday observable phenomena – that emerge as comparative focal points. In this case, models do the work of foregrounding certain issues while eliding others. Models by their nature can only be fleeting representations, abstractions from real complexity, and should not be expected to endure. However, some models do. Such is the case of Denis Balsom's 'three Wales' model, which is examined in the chapter. This is a spatial representation of the map of Wales depicting interrelationships between language and national identity.

Chapter 11, by Taulant Guma and Rhys Dafydd Jones, considers issues of participation and belonging from the perspective of EU migrants. It contributes to the literature critical of what Hall calls the 'migrancy problematic' (Hall 2015). This overlooks migrants' roles as active participants in the social, cultural and economic life of the 'host' society, and ignores experiences of attachment and belonging in the new country. Focusing on the agency and experiences of EU migrants living in Wales, Guma and Dafydd Jones illustrate forms of civil society participation and belonging that tend to be overlooked or rendered invisible by a preoccupation with the 'migrancy problematic'.

In the final chapter, Chris Hann takes a partially autobiographical perspective, using information derived from conversations with his father. He begins by considering issues of class, community and mobility with reference to the ethnography of Wales. He then presents empirical data before returning to these concepts in a broader framework, with reference to Hungary, Brexit, human mobility and what Raymond Williams termed the 'idea of settlement' (Williams 2006). The chapter's aim is to pose questions with respect to Wales that have wider British, European and global implications.

It is hoped that the present volume will reinvigorate anthropological research in and teaching about Wales, as well as anthropology as an academic subject at its universities, colleges and schools. Despite the focus on social anthropology in this volume, the variety of disciplinary contributions we present echoes the far-sighted view of Herbert Fleure:

> living things and their environments together form a unity and ... if we separate life and environments, and contrast influence of environment on man with man's very doubtful mastery over nature, we are in danger of losing the idea of educational holism and the fullness of truth.
>
> (Freeman 1987:42)

Anthropologies in and of Wales still have a clear and vital message concerning the nature and role of human beings as cultural and biological animals, in all their complexity and specificity.

References

Bowie, F. and Davies, O. (eds). 1992. *Discovering Welshness*. Llandysul: Gwasg Gomer.

Chapman, T.R. 2014. 'LEWIS, JOHN SAUNDERS (1893–1985), politician, critic and dramatist'. *Dictionary of Welsh Biography*: biography.wales/article/s10-LEWI-SAU-1893 (accessed 20 November 2020).

Charles, N., Davies, C.A. and Harris, C. 2008. *Families in Transition: Social Change, Family Formation and Kin Relationships*. Bristol: Policy Press.

Davies, O. and Bowie, F. 1995. *Celtic Christian Spirituality: An Anthology of Medieval and Modern Sources*. London: SPCK.

Delamont, S. 1995. *Appetites and Identities: An Introduction to the Social Anthropology of Western Europe*. London: Routledge.

Freeman, T.W. 1987. 'Herbert John Fleure, 1877–1969'. In T.W. Freeman (ed.), *Geographers Bibliographical Studies*, Vol. 2, pp.35–52. London: Bloomsbury Academic

Garnett, A. 1970. 'Herbert John Fleure, 1877–1969'. *Biographical Memoirs of Fellows of the Royal Society* 16:253–78.

Hall, S. 2015. 'Migrant urbanisms: ordinary cities and everyday resistance'. *Sociology* 49(3):853–6.

Ifor ap Glyn. n.d. 'Heart of the nation'. *This Is Wales*: www.wales.com/about/language/heart-nation (accessed 28 October 2020).

Rosser, C. and Harris, C. 1965. *The Family and Social Change: A Study of Family and Kinship in a South Wales Town*. London: Routledge and Kegan Paul.

Sillitoe, P. 2010. 'Eric Sunderland 1930–2010'. *Anthropology Today* 26(3):28–9.

Watkin, I.M. 1994. 'Who are the Welsh?' *International Journal of Anthropology* 9(1):56–68.

Williams, R. 2006 [1960]. *Border Country*. Cardigan: Parthian.

Williams, W.M. 1990. 'Sociology and Anthropology at Swansea, 1964–1989'. In C.C. Harris (ed.), *Family, Economy and Community*, pp. xx–xx. Cardiff: University of Wales Press.

1

Horizons of comparison

Marilyn Strathern

Introduction

Focusing on a country's kind of anthropology summons all kinds of comparison. Whether or not they resonate with self-consciousness about intellectual practice, there will always be something to say about the embedding of a discipline in local institutions. Such location has meant in turn that anthropologies differ in the attention they pay to their hinterland, and here aspects of Welsh scholarship are intriguing. They afford, among other things, reflection on what may be involved in the act of comparison.

One evident horizon of comparison is the place that rural studies undertaken in Wales had in the origin of British rural sociology and twentieth-century ethnographies of the British Isles. In their invitation to think across communities and national boundaries, those studies had their own horizons, which in turn are impossible to scan without also recalling specific institutional histories. As a way of bringing this material into the present, I also introduce an altogether earlier horizon, that of the Welsh Nonconformist Enlightenment. Its internal diversity was intensely comparative, both through proselytism and denominational ambition and through those practices of interpretation within and beyond the text that characterized early modern biblical study. It might be asked what kind of comparison lies in relating this unlikely pair. Yet perhaps there is something to be gleaned from juxtaposing the world(s) summoned through biblical exegesis and the way local ethnographies seem – as we shall see – to be at once about everything and about very little – or rather, only about something. Instead of assuming that the anthropologist's purchase on comparison is transcendent, I shall try to conceive an interplay between diverse ways in which views come in and out of focus. Here it is helpful to start with a scholar who has been deeply involved in studying expressions of things Welsh.

The art historian Peter Lord offers a comparison of two portraits of families by the same artisan painter made within eighteen months of each other; it leads him to comment on an intersection of values, importance and quality. The 'importance' of the first in capturing the tenor of the times is set beside the fact that he also sees in it a certain 'quality'. I refer to what he calls 'the finest Welsh painting of its period' (Lord 1996:70), Hugh Hughes's *The Family of John Evans at Breakfast* (*c*.1823), which he compares with its sequel, *The Family of David Charles of Carmarthen* (*c*.1824–5).[1] He does not see the same quality in the second; in his view, the former has a directness and structural integrity that has been dissipated in the spaced-out fineries of the latter. What he says about the way he compares the two is interesting.

The question of what makes for comparability, he observes, cannot be answered easily. Lord rejects categorizations that demean local significance, even though one cannot avoid evaluation (of quality), since 'the comparison of adjectives is built into the grammar of every European language and therefore into the structure of thought of western people' (ibid.:66–7). Comparison is indeed interwoven with the very way such people articulate their conception of things, so one might well wonder why social anthropology has been so committed to its comparative method as though it were a distinguishing feature. In fact, anthropology reproduces the difficulties that the art historian voices. For similarity and difference – or as he puts it 'more like' and 'less like' – unavoidably combine and separate phenomena of any order (Candea 2019; cf. Gagné *et al*. 2019).[2] At the same time anthropologists' commitment to the comparative method comes from an impetus comparable indeed to his concern about importance and quality, though hardly expressed in those terms.

On the one hand, every social or cultural context has its own integrity, and the anthropologist takes care not to categorize or evaluate entities in advance; on the other hand, certain features of social and cultural life inevitably seem more noteworthy or diagnostic of larger themes than others, inviting contrasts both internal and external. At any rate, when Lord says of *The Family of John Evans at Breakfast* that it 'is the most important early nineteenth-century

---

1   The first is reproduced in Lord (2016:155, fig. 162), and both appear in Lord (1990:figs 8, 109), as well as in Lord (1996). The paintings are, as far as I can ascertain, in private collections.

2   See Lord (1996:67). A commentary on the vernacular terms 'similarity' and 'difference' is developed in Strathern (2020).

Welsh painting because it is an epitome of a central aspect of the evolution of culture in that period' (Lord 1996:68), he goes on to acknowledge the role that its quality plays in holding the viewer's attention. If the painting was 'a conscious celebration of the achievement of the Nonconformist middle class' (ibid.:64), one of its effects was a boyhood memory recalled years later by a visitor to the house where it hung, the then twelve-year-old having been mesmerized by the cups and saucers on the breakfast table. Yet Lord worries that he allows his judgement of its importance to be influenced by his judgement of its quality.

This analogy cuts across two apparently distinct domains of scholarly discourse – rendering one (the art historian's musings) in terms of another (a brief reference to anthropology's comparative method). There is a bit more to it than a common denominator of analytical intent: each is potentially illuminated by the particularities of the other. As a kind of comparison itself, it is one I propose to pursue on a rather larger scale.

British ethnographies

'British rural sociology might be said virtually to originate in rural Wales', observed the sociologist Graham Day (1998:237).[3] When in the late 1970s I volunteered to write up some anthropological investigations in rural Essex, the genre 'village studies' typified a small handful of British ethnographies. The list would have included Isabel Emmett's ethnography of Llanfrothen ('Llan') in Merionethshire (Emmett 1964), not far from the industrial town of Blaenau Ffestiniog, where she subsequently worked. Diverse controversies and re-examinations have occurred since. Thus, her later study in Blaenau enabled her to engage with Day's criticism of her emphasis on an ideological Welsh/English divide. What she saw as continuities between Llanfrothen in 1960 and Blaenau twenty years later (Emmett 1982b:209–11), across time and space, was comparative grist to her own theoretical position as to the social 'reality' of such a divide. The friendly debate continued to rumble on (Day 1998). An in-married resident in both places, with an intervening period in

---

3   Bell and Newby (1971:137) acknowledge Rees's study of Llanfihangel, north Montgomeryshire (Rees 1950), as '[t]he founding of what was to be a rather over-looked school of Welsh anthropology', although this image morphs into Rees as 'the founding father of the British community study' (Bell and Newby 1971:140; and see below). Rapport opens his collection on the anthropology of Britain observing that '[t]he anthropological study of modern-day Britain' was originally the province of geographers and sociologists, citing Rees's study among the former (Rapport 2002:3). Frankenberg's study of Glyn Ceiriog (Frankenberg 1957) has since acquired status as 'a ground-breaking study of [village] hierarchy' (Degnen and Tyler 2017:40).

Max Gluckman's Manchester as a sociologist writing shop-floor ethnography, Emmett had studied social anthropology at the London School of Economics and subtitled her initial ethnography 'a social anthropological study'.[4] It opened with a ringing endorsement of comparison.

'Social anthropologists', she wrote, 'wish to make comparisons and if they did not intend to do so their work would be almost pointless' (Emmett 1964:x). She quickly dismissed misleading units of comparison. Isolated details extracted from the context of general social knowledge were not 'facts'. 'It is not necessarily an advance', she observed drily, 'to try to compare one shallow study with another' (ibid.:x). She herself looked for the 'insight' that may come from comparing studies of similar depth and intensity, which will in turn have involved entwining information and interpretation. Several comparative moments appeared in her ethnography. Thus she compared Ministry of Agriculture figures for Welsh dairy farming with that from neighbouring English counties; a question about voting behaviour was prompted by one of the four studies put together by Elwyn Davies and Alwyn Rees in 1960; she criticized a generalization about chapel injunctions against singing and dancing from the same source, and so forth.

Emmett developed a more systematic comparison with Ronald Frankenberg's account of the role of 'strangers' in Pentrediwaith's (Glyn Ceiriog, Denbighshire) organized activities, here concluding that what looked like a resemblance turned out on closer inspection not to be one, a distinction she related to different distributions of English and Welsh speaking in village life. Finally, to describe the distinctiveness of Llan people's reticence in organized matters, she drew on an observation from the American Pueblo Zuni. The Zuni, she said, have trouble, like the Welsh, in putting forward leaders precisely because it is not 'Welsh' (or 'Zuni') to put yourself forward.[5] She did not elaborate the ethnography on which the Zuni concept was based, but its ultimate ethnographic contextualization was implied. In sum, for all these comparisons she was also summoning distinct contexts.

---

4   In the mid 1950s, Gluckman's department at Manchester was Anthropology and Sociology. Shortly after his appointment in 1949, Gluckman had said that he was keen to develop 'the study of modern communities in England' (quoted by Mills 2008:100). Emmett held the position of Lecturer in Sociology.

5   Emmett's source was the generalized account found in Benedict (1935). At other points, she cites Richards's study of Bemba diet, Pitt-Rivers's ethnography of a Spanish village and Colson on the Makah Indians, while within Britain a chapter on the moral code opens with a contrast with working class districts of London where she grew up (Emmett 1964:101) and she endorses Rees's observations about illegitimacy before commenting critically on some of the correlations he draws (ibid.:104–5, 108).

Sociologists Colin Bell and Howard Newby included Emmett's work in a cluster of studies stemming from 'the comparative Welsh study of which ... [Rees 1950] was the precursor' (Bell and Newby 1971:140). They then made a now familiar lament (see Day 1998:241) that any attempt to give unity to the Welsh studies 'is prevented by that bane of community studies, non-comparability of data' (ibid.:140). The very virtue Emmett was after, insight, is cursorily dismissed: Frankenberg's study was 'full of insights', they say, but almost 'totally lacking in socio-geographic data' (ibid.:140). In their view, each might have something to contribute to sociology, but – they claimed it was through an absence of common framework or theoretical position – these studies hardly contributed to any larger synthesis among themselves.[6] They seemed to be about too little. Missing was (I adduce) what anthropologists often take care to avoid: categorizations determined in advance.[7]

'Community' had become thoroughly if controversially entrenched as an analytic, and writers at the time felt they had to address it, whether to endorse or disavow. Indeed, I wonder whether that central concept (community) was not putting obstacles in the way of perceiving the common framework or theoretical position that some found lacking. One reason lay close to the surface. Frankenberg later regretted that in 1966 he had adopted a definition of community that stressed an arena of social coherence based in locality and community sentiment, rather than following Gluckman's rejection of imputations of harmony in favour simply of 'people co-operating and disputing within the limits of an established system of relations and cultures' (Frankenberg 1982:5).[8]

---

6   '[A]s a realistic, model-building sociologist', Frankenberg (1994:286) had offered his own systematic comparison of communities in Britain, ranging over several rural and urban studies on a 'morphological continuum' from the truly rural to the unequivocally urban. The more-of-this and less-of-that model was explicit in his schematic representation of the two extremes, where 'urban' might be more accurately called 'less rural' (ibid.:286). Many of the characteristics that he polarizes fall into a thoroughly theorized tradition/modernity paradigm: status 'ascribed' or 'achieved', solidarity 'mechanical' or 'organic', economy 'simple' or diverse'.

7   Thus, they say of Rees that he was starting 'almost completely from scratch with little or no a priori theoretical perspective to provide a framework for his data' (Bell and Newby 1971:137). The context of these remarks is an appraisal of just how the concept of community could be conceived, whether as object of study or methodological heuristic, or in terms of its social or 'normative' veracity.

8   Communities have something in common, so while all communities are societies not all societies are communities (Frankenberg 1994:238). We see here the hand of general social theory: from functional integration to cooperation and conflict to discordant pressures. See Werbner (2017) on internal differentiation.

In similar vein, Emmett caustically cited Raymond Williams's description of the warmly persuasive aura of 'community', a term never to be used unfavourably:

> An account of life in a place where plain matters of fact are that people habitually exchange gifts and services without money payment; [where] a strong value is put upon a life in which work, leisure and sociability merge ... is *read* and *heard* by many academics as 'romantic and nostalgic'.
>
> (Emmett 1982b:209, original emphasis)

However, to grasp other dimensions of that concept, the necessity to step beyond it will also become apparent.

For the moment, what the early Welsh studies did have in common was the extent to which the observer undertaking the study was also a participant in belonging to the community in question. Emmett might have been an outsider, yet she was so to speak an insider's outsider, typical of the few already in the locality.[9] Boundaries there were, but what relation did they have to an object of social study? And to the modes of study? In retrospect, it seems that at the time the concept of community functioned as something of a boundary object, deflecting various disciplinary differences. We might well ask about the then relation between anthropology and sociology.[10]

Although I have noted something of a characteristically anthropological care not to categorize in advance, while at the same time not ignoring diagnostic features of social (and cultural) life, I quote our Essex sociologists again for their more capacious view.[11] Writing at the end of the 1960s, Bell and Newby observed (of the studies in their book) that 'the labels sociologist and anthropologist are used almost interchangeably and tend more than anything else to reflect the institutional and academic allegiance of the social scientist' (Bell and Newby 1971:62). They pointed to a significant institutional connection: the University of Wales as the centre of British community study.

---

9   Day (1998:249) says as much. Frankenberg was the exception here, as Davies and Rees (1960:xi) noted.

10 Degnen and Tyler present the current state as interdisciplinary as far as British studies are concerned. Although 'ethnography' rather than 'community' seems to be the boundary object, they suggest that nowadays a more creative space exists between anthropology and sociology than in previous decades, 'reminiscent of a period in the 1960s' when credentials did not have to be defended (Degnen and Tyler 2017:25).

11 At the time, the new University of Essex was one of the sites for the burgeoning discipline of sociology, its great spurt of growth being in the 1960s, as Degnen and Tyler (2015:27) remind us.

They could have been more specific: the studies came out of the University College of Wales at Aberystwyth, and the Department of Geography and Anthropology as was. That said, in 1960, Davies and Rees (1960:xi) claimed that the Welshmen contributing to their well-known four-studies collection, insiders as they were and all postgraduates of Aberystwyth, were also able to write with a measure of detachment because of their knowledge from beyond, from elsewhere than Wales, and because of their general reading of 'comparative anthropology'. We might qualify our question by wondering what anthropology meant not just at the time but in that place.

Aberystwyth's anthropology

The anthropology that flourished at Aberystwyth had had a named presence there since 1917, a time when posts in anthropology were to be found in only a handful of British universities. I comment on one strand of what was being laid down in the period between the wars, at the end of which Rees was sent off to the Welsh countryside.[12]

In 1917, anthropology was allied with geography, the joint name of a new chair.[13] A lecturer in geography and head of zoology, Herbert (H.J.) Fleure had welcomed the double designation for the scope it allowed him to advance his philosophy concerning physical and social evolution.[14] Now Frankenberg was to develop a morphological continuum from more to less rural communities in order to refine accounts of social change in Britain (see note 6); a generation earlier, written at a time when central Asia was thought to be the cradle of humanity, Fleure took on no less than the development of social life itself.

---

12   Apparently this was at the suggestion of the college's principal, Ifor Evans. At that point the department was under Daryll Forde, who succeeded to the chair in geography and anthropology (as it was commonly known) in 1930. Forde was a geographer who had completed a PhD in prehistoric archaeology, including work in Wales, and went on (while at Aberystwyth) from early ethnographic work in the Americas to undertake major fieldwork in Nigeria. Lewis credits him with having 'set in train local community studies' (Lewis 1973:56).

13   The Gregynog Chair in Geography and Anthropology. The present Aberystwyth Department of Geography and Earth Sciences announced, in 2018, developing a single honours degree in sociology, to be housed within it. Its convenor explicitly recalls the degree in sociology offered in the past (between 1960s and 1980s) and the pioneering work in community studies conducted by Rees. See: www.aber. ac.uk/en/news/archive/2018/10/title-217064-en.html (accessed 7 February 2019).

14   Fleure was to be both a fellow of the Royal Society in geography (1936) and president of the Royal Anthropological Institute (1945–1947), concerning the latter in its aspect of anthropology broadly conceived, including 'physical anthropology' and archaeology.

The scope of his interests across natural and human history was crystallized in the compact ten-volume project, intended for a general audience, that he published with the archaeologist/anthropologist Harold Peake.[15] Let us linger for a moment on the first volume of *The Corridors of Time* (Peake and Fleure 1927).

Comparisons abounded, beginning with comparisons of different primates, of varieties and forms of stone tools, fossil remains, geological strata and so forth, providing the basis of diverse typologies in terms of similarities and differences, according to the normal science of the time. Evidence was assembled, sorted, scrutinized, all driven by the chronology of evolutionary change. But as a preface to the scientific story the authors began with an extraordinary first chapter, itself full of comparison although almost entirely without comment. The chapter jumped immediately into a range of creation stories – from Choctaw Indians, Bengali tribals, American Hopi, Philippine Bilaan, Nilotic Shilluk. By the time we come to the Babylonian and Hebraic accounts, these narratives seem all of a piece.

Thus they noted the earliest Jewish records of *Yahweh* (Jehovah) forming man out of dust and woman out the man's rib, as recorded in Genesis, and how subsequently the Jewish creator was no longer 'the tribal God *Yaweh*' but *Elohim*, translated as 'two Gods', male and female, who made man in their own likeness, male and female (recalling the paired divinities of Babylon). They offered a potted history of the fate of scriptural texts, with Jewish priests adding to them and early Christians adopting a number for their own collection of sacred writings. They then pointed to the nineteenth century for changing attitudes on the part of 'educated men' towards the Jewish scriptures and the composite nature of the Bible (ibid.:10). It was only after translation into the vernacular ('the vulgar tongue') during the Renaissance that people regarded the texts as written by God himself, they observed, and 'further enquiry into the origin of man was deemed not only unnecessary, but actually impious' (ibid.:10). Peake and Fleure's plan was to rekindle that curiosity through contemporary scientific research.

There is an echo here of what was already a half century or so of anthropological work on early religions; indeed their short list of books to consult was headed by James George Frazer's *Folklore in the Old Testament*

15 Peake worked independently of any university base, and his many affiliations included the Society of Antiquaries and the RAI, of which he was at one time president. Peake and Fleure's significant effort may or may not have inspired the work of Forde, including his great compendium of peoples and places, *Habitat, Economy and Society* (Forde 1934).

(1918), from which they had drawn many of the creation stories. Frazer in turn will have been no stranger to the several centuries of historical and interpretive work on the part of European scholars and divines concerned with the comparison of religions.[16] At the same time, Frazer's own immense comparative project was understood as a break from the past, the new human sciences operationalizing an old conceptual framework towards altogether new ends (Sheehan 2019:206). At any rate, the nod to comparative religion makes a thought-provoking entry into Peake and Fleure's scientifically inspired work.

There will be more to say about Fleure and Aberystwyth's anthropology, but it is helpful to enlarge the context in which to do so. I turn momentarily away from comparison in the context of communities to comparison in the context of religious debate.

Bala: the Nonconformist enlightenment

Aberystwyth had of course been the first institution to offer university-level courses in Wales, including geography from the outset in 1872, although Bangor and Cardiff were not far behind. The founding principal was described as a liberal Nonconformist, the institution non-sectarian. The import of this lies in Wales's religious history and its intertwining with education. The strand I follow here, well-known in Welsh scholarship, concerns one lineage of divines.

For the first twenty years, Aberystwyth's principal was a Calvinistic Methodist minister, Thomas Charles Edwards, with a reputation all over Wales as a fiery preacher. In this he had followed his father, growing up in the ambience of Lewis Edwards's Calvinistic Methodist College at Bala. When he finally left Aberystwyth he returned to take over the principalship of what he transformed into Bala Theological College. His father's life work had been a wide embrace of education: Lewis Edwards had devoted himself to convincing Methodists 'of the value of an educated ministry' and 'the importance of education and culture to the whole nation', himself believing 'as strongly in the press as in the pulpit' (Evans 1959:196).[17] 'He opened the windows of the mind so that the light of knowledge – literary, historical, and scientific – could come flooding in to reanimate "the queen of the sciences" [here, theology]' (ibid.:191). In this narrative of enlightenment, one might wonder how darkness had ever fallen. For Lewis Edwards was in turn following in the footsteps of

---

16   For recent discussion see e.g. Levitin (2019), Stroumsa (2019) and other contributions to Gagné *et al.* (2019).

17   Hence Edwards's several books, essays and the periodical *Y Traethodydd* (begun in 1845).

one who had had a powerful impact on the spread of literacy in Wales. His wife's grandfather was Thomas Charles, whose name, in the words of the Aberystwyth historian on whom I draw, Eryn White, 'is inextricably linked with the development of education on the Sabbath' (White 1997b:337; see also White 1997a).[18]

In the late 1990s, the old college building at Bala was maintained by the Presbyterian Church of Wales Youth Movement, and a pamphlet produced by them sketches its former history:

> Today, it is difficult to imagine a time when the Calvinistic Methodist
> did not believe in educating their ministers and preachers, and that they
> [ministers and preachers] once fiercely *resisted* any attempt to educate
> them. They believed that the only education required of a preacher was a
> thorough knowledge of the Bible and its contents, supported by any Biblical
> information which could be gleaned from the *'Geiriadur Beiblaidd'* (Thomas
> Charles's Dictionary of the Bible) and other denominational publications.
>
> (Clarke n.d., my emphasis)

It then notes how the original eighteenth-century ministry had consisted of educated men, but Thomas Charles dying in 1814 was the last. A decline in Methodist activity was attributed by the subsequent generation of leaders, the pamphlet claims, to education having got in the way of evangelism – hence their resistance. The extent to which this popular history is true is not my concern. What is intriguing is the apparent re-description of Thomas Charles's compendious *Dictionary* as being on the side of those against education.

The *Geiriadur Ysgrythyrol* (Scriptural dictionary) of four volumes, published between 1805 and 1811, should be placed in the context of evangelical publications that were to pour from local presses. (Charles himself established a press at Bala that same year.) Along with Thomas Jones, Charles pioneered a periodical publication for Calvinistic Methodists; over the following years other denominations followed suit – Wesleyan Methodists, Baptists, Independents, Unitarians and even Anglicans. Alongside ever more detailed biblical commentaries, such as the Baptist John Jenkins's comprehensive four-volume guide to Bible theology in 1811 (White 2013:127), all agreed on the importance of producing instructional literature, and thereby supporting daily

---

18 These followed Griffith Jones's circulating schools and earlier efforts (White 1997a:317, 325–7). Charles noted that imparting religious teaching in the mother tongue increased a general thirst for ideas, and often led to literacy in English (Jenkins *et al.* 1997:90).

spiritual reading and knowledge of the Bible.[19] Could the very zeal with which separate denominations sustained literacy be interpreted in terms of sectarian interests? Yet this does not seem to have been the issue over the ministers' and preachers' subsequent objection to education.

Recall Peake and Fleure's remark about those who regarded the biblical texts as written by God so that enquiry into the origin of man was deemed unnecessary. They could almost have had in mind a letter Charles wrote in 1807, in which he talked of the Book of God as a rich and inexhaustible mine of knowledge only fools would not spend their days searching within (ibid.:126), implying one needed little else. Charles adds that one must labour diligently for such knowledge – that is, to know how to know it. Hence his dictionary 'contained a wealth of information about the Bible, its content, and context', as well as being a source of systematic doctrine (ibid.:19). As the preface has it, translated into English:

> The Holy Scriptures are the treasury of all useful and essential knowledge.
> Since they are all given by God's inspiration, they must share in his
> perfection … Because of the perfection of his knowledge, he cannot mistake;
> because of the truth of his nature, he would not deceive us in anything;
> because of this, the knowledge granted us in the Scriptures, is overarching,
> sure, and complete … The lack of understanding of the Scriptures, and
> [failure of] submission to God's authority in them, is the cause of all errors
> in judgement and way of life.
>
>   (quoted by ibid.:127)

These words are not ones we associate with enlightenment – with critical endeavour, scientific experimentation and the premise of doubt. They have a different authoritative basis, derived indeed from the kind of authority the Enlightenment sought to challenge. This is not the same, however, as saying that they are in themselves 'against' education.

The claim that all one needed was the Scriptures could be used to deny the relevance of any other kind of learning. This seemed one of the imputations of the pamphlet. But that passes over the nature of the learning contained therein. Let's for a moment leave aside the question of authority; leave aside, too, some of the accompanying practices, the learning by rote that followed attempts to instil its truths, and even Charles's explicit concern that education was but a means to an end, the promotion of Christian knowledge and the saving of souls. All that aside, his scriptural dictionary also makes other claims.

----

19   'Charles also believed in the importance of regular catechizing to instil knowledge
     of the scriptures' (White 2013:126).

Macrocosm and microcosm

'The Holy Scriptures are the treasury of all useful and essential knowledge'. All knowledge. That everything you need is at your fingertips sounds like a claim to encompassment. It is as though the world were (within) the Bible, self-referential and self-signifying, and the invitation is to immerse oneself. The circumscription of the Bible (this is the Word of God) is axiomatic and unquestioned; it does not come from anything outside – it is thus that the world of the Scriptures is non-comparable and unbounded. From this perspective the Scriptures comprise, in their unboundedness, a macrocosm. One might even say that the dictionary was demonstrating the Bible as macrocosm by being itself a kind of textual analogy to it.

However, an alternative perspective also comes into play. The Bible was not after all completely self-referential or self-signifying, or the dictionary would not have been needed. As soon as one lays out the relation between the two, perspective shifts.[20] We know that Charles was sensitive to the quality of language; he was also insistent on the effort needed to benefit from what God provided. His dictionary opened up a world of internal commentary and debate, a world that required interpretation – needed diligent labour to understand – and thus a world to be apprehended through considering diverse locations in the text and different kinds of information bearing on this or that topic.[21] In short, it was a comparative endeavour of sorts. As in the very effort to translate the Word of God, the dictionary had been compiled through countless interpretive and critical moves, through painstakingly analysis, evaluation and detailed attention to sources, all of which meant bringing diverse concepts and images into conjunction with one another – that is, scholarship as usual. Here is another quotation from the preface (again in English):

> The purpose of a Scripture Dictionary is to explain words used in the
> Scriptures. This, naturally, leads to the opening up of doctrines, the

---

20 In the same way, there is an interplay or a shift between 'all knowledge' and 'knowledge of the Scriptures'; the two are not reducible to each other.

21 Peter Williams, who in 1770 produced the first ever Bible in Welsh to be printed in Wales (used by both Anglicans and Dissenters), also argued that the Book itself was not enough unless efforts were made to give guidance to readers (i.e. placing them 'outside' the text) (White 2013:122). Translations were scrutinized and criticized for their doctrinal inclinations (ibid.:123–4) and it was important to develop a language appropriate to spiritual experience (White 1997a:267).

explaining of texts, and the giving of the history of ceremonies, noteworthy
persons, or kingdoms, etc., mentioned in the Holy Writ.

(quoted in Jenkins 1910, vol II:485)

Every such scholarly scrutiny became joined to a wider endeavour, one
among many applications to the task. This was also true of the Nonconformist
denominations each producing their own scriptural literature: from this
perspective they were concerned to define what they were about, and thus
proselytized about one another. As soon as an entity is seen in relation to
others, its boundaries thus become apparent; it becomes a representative of
the world to which it belongs – a microcosm. So also, to judge the dictionary
(or the translated Bible), as I am doing here, with respect to Enlightenment
assumptions about scholarship imagines a wider world of which they are
a part. The dictionary's internal comparisons become less like those of a
concordance's criss-crossing of references than those of an encyclopaedia
bringing in matters from elsewhere to shine illumination from beyond. These
effects are (mobilized by) a common oscillation of perspectives.[22] The reader
is now immersed in the text, now positioned beyond it through making
comparisons, whether internal or external.

In an Enlightenment sense of the term, the dictionary's scholarship was
as deeply educational as it was doctrinal, and that of course touched on its
claim for the Bible itself. The sense of self-sufficiency or encompassment of
everything one needs to know works alongside the perception of how partial
or incomplete any knowledge is when comparison comes into play. Switching
back and forth between these perspectives is not unlike the experience of
immersion in a field and what happens when that is opened up to analysis
through comparative scrutiny – ethnographer turns anthropologist. Now
macrocosm, now microcosm, such switching enables people to take up
apparently conflicting stances, as in the case of those who resisted any
attempt to educate ministers and preachers on the grounds that it would
make comparable what was incomparable, the completeness of the scriptures
as education.

---

22 That is, on any scale of comprehension or apprehension they alternate, as we
    might speak of percept and concept as alternately figure and ground to each
    other. The pair macrocosm and microcosm occupy diverse theoretical registers in
    anthropological expositions, too numerous to dwell on here; in any event, rather
    than 'apply' the notions (as they are expanded in other contexts) to the material, I
    hope the material provided here will exemplify (and expand for this context) their
    analytical purchase.

A return to the beginning

Something of this oscillation has been present from the outset. Recall how the art historian Lord contrasted Hughes's two paintings. It is not incidental that the John Evans whose family took breakfast was a printer and publisher (he had founded the *Carmarthen Journal*): Hughes 'painted a situation he understood fully in a way he understood fully' (Lord 1996:65). A macrocosm? The appropriateness of the image in Lord's eyes (he had called it an epitome of the period) speaks to the sense of self-sufficiency he (Lord) was registering: it is as though everything you need to know is within the picture, down to the copy of the journal that the eldest son is reading. For Hughes himself, a kindred spirit to his principal sitter, the 'picture and the press took the place of the pulpit' (ibid.:71). Newspapers were a token of God's providence, we are told, Hughes often depicting the written word in his imagery, reading and writing being the essential agents of spiritual progress through education. Of course, it is always possible to reverse the macrocosmic effect, and analyse the painting's elements in relation to what is outside the frame – the popularity and elegance of the blue and white china, for example. That indeed seems to be the prominent mode in which Lord approaches the second painting.

Intent on self-improvement, he suggests, here Hughes was reflecting a world to which he did not really belong. (The David Charles whose family he painted was Thomas Charles's younger brother.) He seems to be saying that Hughes has depicted a microcosm, a representation of manners and aspirations beyond his own circumstances. The painter is not really part of the scene, even though within a couple of years he was to marry one of the daughters. Indeed, perhaps his impending relationship with the Charles family is intimated through the awkwardness of the composition. The references are to a milieu (Lord suggests) with which he was not entirely comfortable, registered again in the further suggestion that he came to idealize his father-in-law. In short, the painter appears at a distance from the conversation group in a way not true of his engagement with the breakfast table.

Between the paintings the same contrast also works within, at least apropos the printer's family at breakfast. It is thus that we can read Lord's play with those two intersecting dimensions, 'importance' and 'quality'. No wonder he finds them oscillating – you think you see one, and then you see the other. The contrast is between a self-referential, encompassing effect and an analytical, comparative one. In the senses in which he was using these concepts, to respond to the 'importance' of something is to allow it to take over, to occupy the visual field, and however momentary give the sense that a whole world is there. 'Quality', on the other hand, requires the comparative work of coordinating values and adjudications. As Lord says, 'the quality of the [Evans] picture is not directly a factor in its importance – as it would be had I sought to *compare* it favourably to the icons of academic art' (ibid.:70, emphasis added).

Such alternation – the thought sparked off by Thomas Charles's ruminations on the Bible – is not itself an act of comparison. It is, rather, a matter of comprehension and apprehension, an alternation of perspectives, of which comparison (with its microcosmic effect) is but one. What, then, comes of knowing this is the case?

Borders

Anthropological comparison is hardly alone in assuming that the basis of comparability must lie in shared features and common ground known in advance. That said, it is also possible to think across contexts – disjunctive comparison it might be called (Lazar 2012:351) – as in drawing analogies across apparently distinct domains of scholarly discourse: hearing an art historian's musings, for example, chime with certain anthropological concerns. So, it is not entirely out of order to wonder what might be learnt from the fleeting foray into early modern scriptural preoccupations.

Think again of Fleure's kind of anthropology. Famously, he undertook an extended study of the Welsh, a grand survey of physical characteristics and family genealogies. Recent appraisal of Fleure's work (Rees 2015, 2019) suggests his aim was to eliminate easy stories of racial and cultural superiority apropos Saxons and Celts, and to emphasize the role long played by migration and local difference in the decentralization and diversity of the British Isles.[23] The approach got away from predetermined computations of average types and advocated the meticulous comparison of clusters of traits as they occurred in specific locations.

In retrospect, the early twentieth century *Anthropological Survey of Wales* seems at once open and closed. On the one hand, the Welsh comprised, in Amanda Rees's words, 'a nation-sized laboratory that would allow [Fleure] to investigate relationships between race, language and place' (Rees 2015); on the other hand, his identification of physical types led across Britain and into Europe, where, against then prevalent views about the wholesale replacement of aboriginal populations by incomers, he advocated attention to the complexity of people's movements.[24]

---

23 A role Fleure then used to illuminate aspects of European prehistory. Fleure's initiating focus, true to his time, was how place and geography shows its mark on people.

24 A view with which Patterson (1996b:196) might have had sympathy, given her interest in showing that the roots of modernity lay as much in Celtic as in Anglo-Saxon Britain.

As his laboratory, we might say, Wales was at once macrocosm, containing within it all the ingredients required for determining the relationships in which he was interested, and a microcosm of what (in terms of those relationships) was occurring across prehistoric Europe. Macrocosm becomes microcosm, and vice versa, through what happens to boundaries. Given that Wales was a self-contained arena for building up his correlations, it was also unbounded – that is, Fleure's pursuits had no restriction. As soon as these findings are seen to extend beyond, then Wales appears bounded, a specific representative cluster whose coordinates can be specified, inviting comparison. The 'laboratory effect' works either way.

From the twenty-first-century hand of a scholar who has long worked in Britain comes the arresting observation that 'the anthropology of Britain might include and entail anything that concerns the discipline of anthropology: all human potentiality is there' (Rapport 2002:6).[25] With the inflection I have been giving these terms, it seems to me that Nigel Rapport is offering macrocosmic insight. Macrocosm is without borders: all human potentiality is there. I would not have caught the power of this statement but for the ringing tones of the cleric for whom a book could be a treasury of all useful and essential knowledge.

An anthropologist concerned with interpretations of Welsh identity opens an essay on 'Wales from within' with another glimpse, this time of the oscillation. It is an oscillation in self-understanding, between that of an unbound ethnographer to that of a bounded anthropologist, but she does not come to this by herself. Fiona Bowie writes: 'If one of the chief pleasures of learning a language and living in another culture is the privileged sharing in other people's perceptions of the world, then one of the hazards ... is to see oneself as the object of those perceptions' (Bowie 1993:167). As to the latter, just as explanations open up doctrine, consciousness of one border (the one that turns her into an object of people's perceptions of outsiders) has the microcosmic effect of multiplying innumerable others, and it appears that nothing is shared in a straightforward way.[26]

To be conscious of the effects of switching perspective gives insight into the limits of comparison, which emerges as a defining, relational, boundary-

---

25   This is proffered in the context of a claim that anthropology in Britain has the potential to provide some of the best the discipline can offer, on the grounds of familiarity and linguistic competence (immersion); individual lives are examined as manifestations of universal capacities (Rapport 2002:7, 14).

26   Bowie goes on to stress internal diversity, and the 'many conflicting and interlocking definitions of [Welsh] identity which actively compete for symbolic space and public recognition' (Bowie 1993:169).

making exercise, as in plotting an entity through its coordinates with others. Anthropology's commitment to comparison at once perpetuates scholarship as usual and acknowledges its kinship with how people compare things all the time. Yet anthropologists sometimes become less than articulate about those unbounded moments when people take their way of things as all there is, as everything that is of importance. There is nothing novel in pointing to the very paradox of articulation. There is nothing particularly Welsh here either, although perhaps some of these glimpses into certain modes of scholarly practice, stimulated by an aspect of Thomas Charles's work (to which he himself would have paid no attention), give reason to return to those formative 'Welsh studies' encouraged by Fleure's successor at Aberystwyth, Daryll Forde. Briefly, local perceptions of community might or might not have depended on logics of comparison; but when they did not, comparison might yet have been the only a way of articulating them.

Comparison at home

Bell and Newby's notorious problem with community studies was their lack of comparability. This seems in retrospect rather trivial. These studies provided ample grounds for all kinds of comparison, not least (as they themselves noted) Alwyn Rees's initial interest in an area of scattered family farms, with delayed marriage of the inheriting son, insofar as it bore 'striking resemblance to' (Bell and Newby 1971:137) a similar situation in Ireland. But what their complaint overlooked was the very way in which such studies were also dealing with the profoundly non-comparable.

Day's riposte was that there is 'a common framework which unifies the Aberystwyth studies: a shared definition of the essential nature of rural Welsh society' (Day 1998:241). He quotes Davies and Rees on the consistency of vision attributable to the fact that what are 'in detail particular to their localities ... are not peculiar to them. They are characteristic of rural communities throughout Wales' (Davies and Rees 1960:x). The 'centrality of the same basic relationships' (Day 1998:242) – kinship, neighbourliness, chapel, language – recur.[27] And Day gives us two views. On the one hand, people make judgements about and thus evaluate segments of the population in relation (say) to what is respectable or less respectable according to norms of conduct enacting a 'fundamental social division which is more or less evident in all Welsh rural communities' (ibid.:242). On the other hand, boundaries can disappear as an issue, with the interweaving of social networks that give people a sense of 'belonging both to a particular place but also to a wider culture and society' (ibid.:244); never the

---

27 Day comments that each community replicates the same basic elements ('mechanical solidarity').

same for everyone, of course, the community as network is experienced as an endless 'web of reciprocity' (ibid.:242).[28]

In other words, people are both doing comparative work (relating, creating boundaries) and suspending such work (there is no limit to the relationships in which they are enmeshed). He then in effect offers another doubling. Summing up in Rees and Davies's own words – they offered 'studies of a culture "from within"' (Davies and Rees 1960:xi) – he shows that the view from within can also be taken in two ways (as I reformulate it). After all, to imagine a view from the inside is already to take an outsider's view, so that within is the outsider's insider if you like. This implies a relation to what lies beyond; if not analysed or described, the beyond therefore seems – as Bell and Newby complained – 'missing'. However, the view that sees no boundary, where everything is part of what is in existence and has its own integrity, lies on an inside that needs no conception of an outside. Here there is neither within nor without. Such a switch of perspective is not to be settled through what kinds of groups or non-groups are at issue but allows any order of collectivity to appear to be at once about very little – that is, only about something – and (alternately) to be about everything.[29]

Crucially, Day (1998:252) encapsulates oscillations of this kind in his contrast between people's 'mental constructs' (including how they talk about themselves), and their enactment of the relationships – the local networks of interaction – in which use of such constructs is grounded. '[P]eople manage to sustain … boundaries conceptually while at the same time subverting them in practice' (ibid.:254). Emmett's equivocation in her discussion of Welsh-speaking teachers, doctors, lawyers and ministers is germane. Their social distance from working people was substantial, 'yet to outsiders, including myself, the apparent lack of such distance was and is one of the most marked

---

28 Hence Day's title, 'a community of communities'. (The claim can be broadened to include urban and industrial communities.) People have different networks for different activities and allegiances, and he makes the interesting comment (after Jenkins 1971) that this influences the place of kinship in their lives. Kinship figures in their talk about themselves, in constant reference and discussion – that is, it affords an arena, precisely, for articulation and comparison, where other networks do not form such topics of conversation. 'One has the impression that there is a community of people *who can be discussed* because their relationships are known, and that because their relationships are known they are recurrently brought to mind' (ibid.:165, emphasis added).

29 Conversely, the switch of perspectives I describe here is no substitute for social analysis and does not compete with it; it is an effect of practices of comprehension and apprehension that may produce paradoxes or lacuna that such analysis is not going to resolve.

features of the society' (Emmett 1982a:174); common language and self-presentation minimized social differentiation.

This non-performance of distance supported her own argument that, in Welsh-speaking North Wales at the time, ordinary people were waging an underground defence of their language and culture. She quoted her 1964 account: 'All their resentments as working-class against the ruling class; as country people against the towns, as ordinary people against powerful officials, are poured into the Welsh-versus-English mould' (ibid.:166).[30] In other words, it is when people *talked*, at the point of articulation, that comparison began, and one boundary came to represent many others. Professional talkers, otherwise known as cultural and political leaders of the Welsh community, were the teachers, doctors, clerics and so forth whom Emmett called its 'spokesmen' (ibid.:173–4). Day enlarges on the implications for those anthropological accounts provided from within. Very definitely, he asserts, they represent 'the views and standpoint of a local, academic, Welsh intelligentsia, who themselves are much preoccupied with the relationship between "insider" and "outsider" perceptions' (Day 1998:248). While insisting that descriptions must convey authentic insider views, clearly the standpoint from which they write (Day goes on to add) is only one among other insider versions.

I cannot resist the twentieth-century provocation that Nerys Patterson has bequeathed, for all that it may be out of place in the twenty-first. Observing that only some national identities get scrutinized, she wrote:

> The period in which English culture acquired its coherence and strength
> – the industrial revolution and the establishment of empire – also saw the
> emergence of modern thought about human societies. Crucially, the very
> concepts employed to generalize about the nature of social life rested upon
> the conceptualization of the nature of English society. Comparison was at
> the root of sociological method and at the heart of it all was the comparison
> of English culture with others.
>
> (Patterson 1996a:73)

Given the principal place that comparison holds in the anthropological delineation of relations, its analytical and microcosmic work in this sense, it

---

30   The divide is between 'Welsh' and 'ruling England', not the English as such (Emmett 1982b:219). (I run together, as she did to some extent, her two otherwise distinct studies.) Day (1998:247) quotes Emmett to the effect that communities are marked not by homogeneity but by complex differences in knowledge and understanding.

is no surprise that its practitioners are preoccupied with their own position. Nevertheless, comparative analysis characterizes scholarly activity more generally. It inspired generations of clerics to advocate the need to instruct in Welsh. Just like the anthropologist who strives to give an authentic insider account, it was through their erudition and scholarship that they aspired to realize the potential of Welsh as a vehicle for the word of God.[31] In addition to all the ways in which notions of outsider and insider have been rehearsed, and rehearsed again in the study of them, I have here made the terms asymmetrical. The spoken and the ineffable, the comparable and the non-comparable: the alternation is one that Enlightenment systems of knowledge inevitably stumble over, as though the latter were beyond their ken. Importance need have no truck with description, with canons of quality, with reference points beyond itself.

In sum, if trying to understand from, and to talk of a perspective from, the inside is already to take an outsider's view, what lies within being the outsider's inside, it mobilizes a relation to a wider world. The alternative to this perspective, the view that sees no boundary, where everything is part of what is in existence, lies on an 'inside' that summons no relation between inside and outside. There is indeed nothing particularly Welsh about such an oscillation. But in grasping a fragment of anthropological study in Wales with this in mind, I have suggested that as far as the aims and scope of study are concerned, anthropologists in general may find kindred scholars in Welsh ventures beyond their own time and ambitions.

Acknowledgements

This chapter was presented to the Learned Society of Wales, as a prelude to the symposium, under the title 'The language of relationship: anthropology's commitment to comparison'. My gratitude to John Morgan, among others, and to Peter Lord for his kind comments. I am very much a learner in things Welsh; that said, I should record thanks to my brother Julian Evans for keeping me abreast of family matters concerning Thomas Charles and others.

References

Bell, C. and Newby, H. 1971. *Community Studies: An Introduction to the Sociology of the Local Community*. London: Allen and Unwin.

Benedict, R. 1935. *Patterns of Culture*. London: Routledge and Kegan Paul.

---

31 White notes the persistent seventeenth-century reasoning on the survival of Welsh, namely that 'God had preordained the Welsh people to communicate with Him in the Welsh language' (White 1997a:236).

Bowie, F. 1993. 'Wales from within: conflicting interpretations of Welsh identity'. In S. Macdonald (ed.), *Inside European Identities: Ethnography in Western Europe*, pp. 167–93. Oxford: Berg.

Candea, M. 2019. *Comparison in Anthropology: The Impossible Method*. Cambridge: Cambridge University Press.

Clarke, J. n.d. 'Coleg y Bala: past and present, 1837–1988'. Pamphlet. Bala: Coleg y Bala Youth Centre.

Davies, E. and Rees, A. (eds). 1960. *Welsh Rural Communities*. Cardiff: University of Wales Press.

Day, G. 1998. 'A community of communities? Similarity and difference in Welsh rural community studies'. *Economic and Social Review* 29(3):233–57.

Degnen, C. and Tyler, K. (eds). 2017. 'Reconfiguring the anthropology of Britain: ethnographic, theoretical, and interdisciplinary perspectives'. *Sociological Review Monographs* 65(S1), special issue.

Emmett, I. 1964. *A North Wales Village: A Social Anthropological Study*. London: Routledge and Kegan Paul.

——— 1982a. 'Fe godwn ni eto: Stasis and change in a Welsh industrial town'. In A. Cohen (ed.), *Belonging: Identity and Social Organization in British Rural Cultures*, pp. 165–97. Manchester: Manchester University Press.

——— 1982b. 'Place, community and bilingualism in Blaenau Ffestiniog'. In A. Cohen (ed.), *Belonging: Identity and Social Organization in British Rural Cultures*, pp. 202–21. Manchester: Manchester University Press.

Evans, T.L. 1959. 'Edwards, Lewis'. In J.E. Lloyd and R.T. Jenkins (eds), *Dictionary of Welsh Biography to 1940*, p. 191. London: Society of Cymmrodorian.

Forde, C.D. 1934. *Habitat, Economy and Society*. London: Methuen.

Frankenberg, R. 1957. *Village on the Border: A Social Study of Religion, Politics and Football in a North Wales Community*. London: Cohen and West.

——— 1982. 'A social anthropology for Britain'. In R. Frankenberg (ed.), *Custom and Conflict in British Society*, pp. 1–35. Manchester: Manchester University Press.

——— 1994 [1969]. *Communities in Britain: Social Life in Town and Country*. Aldershot: Ashgate.

Frazer, J.G. 1918. *Folklore in the Old Testament*. London: Macmillan.

Gagné, R., Goldhill, S. and Lloyd, G.E.R. (eds). 2019. *Regimes of Comparatism: Frameworks of Comparison in History, Religion and Anthropology*. Leiden: Brill.

Jenkins, D.E. 1910. *The Life of Revd. Thomas Charles, BA, of Bala*, 2nd edn, 3 vols. Denbigh: Llewelyn Jenkins.

Jenkins, D. 1971. *The Agricultural Community in South-West Wales at the Turn of the Twentieth Century*. Cardiff: University of Wales Press.

Jenkins, G., Suggett, R. and White, E. 1997. 'The Welsh language in early modern Wales'. In G. Jenkins (ed.), *The Welsh Language before the Industrial Revolution*, pp. 45–122. Cardiff: University of Wales Press.

Lazar, S. 2012 'Disjunctive comparison: citizenship and trade unionism in Bolivia and Argentina'. *Journal of the Royal Anthropological Institute* 18(2):349–68.

Levitin, D. 2019 'What was the comparative history of religions in seventeenth-century Europe (and beyond)? Pagan monotheism/pagan animism from T'ien to Tylor'. In R. Gagné, S. Goldhill and G.E.R. Lloyd (eds), *Regimes of Comparatism: Frameworks of Comparison in History, Religion and Anthropology*, pp. 49–115. Leiden: Brill.

Lewis, I. 1973. 'Obituaries'. *Proceedings of the Royal Anthropological Institute for 1973*, pp. 56–8.

Lord, P. 1990. *Hugh Hughes, 1790–1863: Artisan Painter*. Aberystwyth: National Library of Wales.

——— 1996. 'The family of John Evans at breakfast: the concept of quality in painting'. *Planet: The Welsh Internationalist* 114:62–71.

——— 2016. *The Tradition: A New History of Welsh Art*. Cardigan: Parthian.

Mills, D. 2008. *Difficult Folk? A Political History of Social Anthropology*. Oxford: Berghahn Books.

Patterson, N.T. 1996a. 'The English just are, part 1'. *Planet: The Welsh Internationalist* 114:72–7.

——— 1996b. 'The English just are, part 2'. *Planet: The Welsh Internationalist* 115: 84–90.

Peake, H. and Fleure, H.J. 1927. *The Corridors of Time*, Vol. 1: *Apes and Men*. Oxford: Clarendon Press.

Rapport, N. (ed.). 2002. *British Subjects: An Anthropology of Britain*. Oxford: Berg.

Rees, A.D. 1950. *Life in a Welsh Countryside: A Social Study of Llanfihangel yng Ngwynfa*. Cardiff: University of Wales Press.

Rees, A. 2015. 'Fleure and the prehistory of European civilization'. *Wales Online*, 19 October: www.walesonline.co.uk/lifestyle/nostalgia/welsh-history-month-fleure-prehistory-10275494 (accessed 24 September 2020).

——— 2019. 'Doing "deep big history": race, landscape, and the humanity of H.J. Fleure (1977–1969)'. *History of the Human Sciences* 32(1):99–120.

Sheehan, J. 2019. 'Comparison and Christianity: sacrifice in the age of the encyclopaedia'. In R. Gagné, S. Goldhill and G.E.R. Lloyd (eds), *Regimes of Comparatism: Frameworks of Comparison in History, Religion and Anthropology*, pp. 177–209. Leiden: Brill.

Strathern. M. 2020. *Relations: An Anthropological Account*. Durham, NC: Duke University Press.

Stroumsa, G. 2019. 'History of religions: The comparative moment'. In R. Gagné, S. Goldhill and G.E.R. Lloyd (eds), *Regimes of Comparatism: Frameworks of Comparison in History, Religion and Anthropology*, pp. 318–42. Leiden: Brill.

Werbner, P. 2017. 'Barefoot in Britain – yet again: on multiple identities, intersection(ality) and marginality'. *Sociological Review* 65(S1):4–12.

White, E. 1997a. 'The established church, dissent and the Welsh language, c. 1660–1811'. In G. Jenkins (ed.), *The Welsh Language before the Industrial Revolution*, pp. 235–87. Cardiff: University of Wales Press.

——— 1997b. 'Popular schooling and the Welsh language, 1650–1800'. In G. Jenkins (ed.), *The Welsh Language before the Industrial Revolution*, pp. 317–41. Cardiff: University of Wales Press.

——— 2013. 'Welsh dissent and the Bible, c. 1750–1850'. In S. Mandelbrote and M. Ledger-Lomas (eds), *Dissent and the Bible in Britain, c. 1650–1950*, pp. 113–32. Oxford: Oxford University Press.

2

Gerald of Wales

Medieval ethnographer of the Welsh

HUW PRYCE

Introduction

The writings of Gerald of Wales (or Giraldus Cambrensis, *c*.1146–*c*.1223) address the two main concerns at the heart of this volume: anthropology and the Welsh. Not only did he write the first books specifically about Wales and the Welsh but one of those was also the first substantial work of ethnography composed in medieval Latin Christendom. This was the *Descriptio Kambriae* ('Description of Wales'), originally completed in *c*.1194, and a companion piece to Gerald's earlier *Itinerarium Kambriae* ('Journey round Wales') of 1191, an account of a preaching tour in 1188 to recruit Welsh troops for the Third Crusade (Bartlett 1982:216–17; Dimock 1868:ix–xxxix; Jones 1949).[1] Nineteenth- and early-twentieth-century historians of Wales including John Edward Lloyd relied heavily on Gerald's testimony, often in conjunction with the Welsh law books, in their attempts to reconstruct medieval Welsh society (cf. Pryce 2011b:136–45). Indeed, Lloyd went as far as to say that '[a] complete picture of Wales at the end of the twelfth century is given by Giraldus Cambrensis in his *Descriptio*' (Lloyd 1911:604). Subsequent historians have adopted a more nuanced approach. Rees Davies, who provided the first major synthesis of medieval Welsh history since Lloyd's magnum opus of

---

1 Unless otherwise indicated, translations from the *Itinerarium Kambriae* and *Descriptio Kambriae* are mine. As well as referring to the standard edition of the Latin texts (Gerald 1868) I have also usually given references to the most commonly used, but sometimes inaccurate, modern English translation (Gerald of Wales 1978b).

1911, acknowledged that Gerald remained a source of great importance for understanding Welsh society, declaring that his two books on Wales were '[f]ar and away the most important' of the 'contemporary descriptions of, and anecdotes about, Wales and the Welsh' surviving from the period 1063–1415 (Davies 1987:112). Moreover, both Gerald and his contemporary Walter Map (d.1209/10) 'in different ways presented a rounded and convincing picture of contemporary Wales' (ibid.:112).[2] However, Davies then immediately sounded a note of caution:

> Yet the very success of their picture is its own danger. It was a portrait drawn by worldly wise and widely travelled men anxious for literary fame; theirs is as much a work of art, particularly in Gerald's attachment to rhetorical conventions, as of observation. Their image of the Welsh is often as revealing of the values and assumptions of the Anglo-Norman ecclesiastical and aristocratic world as of the society they set out to portray.
>
> (ibid.:112–13)

A further aspect of the greater readiness of scholars in recent decades to assess Gerald's 'Description of Wales' critically, by taking account of the author's background, purpose and literary style, is the recognition of its significance as a pioneering work of medieval ethnography. This is due above all to the illuminating analysis by Robert Bartlett in what remains the single most important book on Gerald, first published almost forty years ago (Bartlett 1982). Subsequent studies of medieval ethnography have largely accepted and built on Bartlett's interpretation. For example, Shirin Khanmohamadi includes Gerald's writings on Wales as the earliest case study in her recent book on medieval European ethnography (Khanmohamadi 2014), while Patrick Fazioli has cited the 'Description of Wales' to support his argument that the Middle Ages deserve attention in histories of anthropology (Fazioli 2017:189–93; see also Fernandez-Armesto 1982; Rubiés 2009:esp. xxviii–xxix).

Gerald's 'Description of Wales' as a social anthropology of the Welsh

My aim in what follows is to assess the significance of the 'Description of Wales' as the earliest sustained attempt to provide what we might term a social anthropology of the Welsh, with respect both to the wider context of medieval ethnographic writing and to the particular historical context in which Gerald wrote. First, though, let me provide basic orientation by briefly introducing Gerald and his 'Description'.

---

2   On Map, see Smith 2017.

A learned churchman of mixed Norman and Welsh ancestry, Gerald wrote about Wales and the Welsh as both insider and outsider (Bartlett 1982; Davies 1946; Pryce 1998; Richter 1973; Roberts 1982). Born around 1146 in Manorbier, Pembrokeshire, the son of a local Marcher lord, Gerald de Barri, and his Cambro-Norman wife Angharad, Gerald was a product of Norman conquest, settlement, and intermarriage in south Wales. His perspective was strongly coloured, therefore, by his membership of a minor Marcher family with a big territorial stake in Wales but lacking substantial estates in England. As the youngest son, he was destined for a career in the Church, and was provided with the best education available at the time, culminating in two periods at the schools of Paris, soon to become a university.

In 1175 Gerald was appointed archdeacon of Brecon and sought to promote the principles of ecclesiastical reform he had imbibed in Paris, notably by campaigning for clerical celibacy. However, like many other educated clerics of his day, he was also employed as a royal servant, from 1184 until at least 1191, undertaking duties that took him to Ireland, Wales and France as well as England (Bartlett 2018:xv–xvi; Davies 1946:100–2, 105). It was during his period of royal service that Gerald wrote his first major prose works, two on Ireland – *Topographia Hibernica* ('Topography of Ireland', completed by March 1188) and *Expugnatio Hibernica* ('Conquest of Ireland', completed in the summer of 1189) – followed by the 'Journey round Wales' and the first version of *De Principis Instructione* ('Instruction for a ruler'), part mirror of princes, part excoriating denunciation of his erstwhile patron King Henry II, whose full publication he unsurprisingly suppressed for another quarter of a century (Bartlett 2018:xiii–xix). Gerald was still receiving payments from the royal exchequer when he completed the 'Description of Wales' around 1194 (ibid.:xvi). By dedicating the Irish and Welsh works to leading figures in the kingdom of England, he hoped to improve his prospects of being appointed to a bishopric. However, this never happened, although he was twice nominated as bishop of St David's (in 1176 and 1198), and on the second occasion unsuccessfully campaigned (until 1203) for the church to be elevated to an archbishopric for Wales independent of Canterbury (Bartlett 1982:45–57). Instead, Gerald is remembered above all as a gifted and prolific Latin author of the twelfth-century renaissance.

The 'Description of Wales' exists in two versions, the first completed in about 1194, and a revised and expanded version datable to about 1215 (Dimock 1868:xxxix–xlii). The latter fills just over eighty pages in the standard edition (Gerald 1868:155–227; 1978b:211–74). Here, I will focus on the first version, which reflects Gerald's original intentions. In a preface dedicating the work to Hubert Walter, justiciar of England and archbishop of Canterbury (1193–1205), Gerald declared that his aim was to provide a 'description of our Wales and the nature of its people, truly foreign and distinct from other nations', whose history had hitherto been neglected (Bartlett 1982:181–2; Gerald 1868:155).

As with his two earlier books on Ireland and his *Itinerarium Kambriae* ('Journey round Wales'), Gerald thus stressed the novelty of his subject, no doubt hoping that this would help to make his name as a writer and enhance his prospects of patronage. The work is formally divided into two parts, the bulk of which respectively include descriptions of what Gerald termed the praiseworthy and unpraiseworthy characteristics of the Welsh.[3] However, those descriptions are preceded by the first seven chapters of Book I, which effectively form a separate section focused mainly on the topography of Wales. Indeed, Gerald concludes the last of these chapters by stating that, since he has now finished explaining the nature of the land, genealogy of the princes, sources of rivers and reasons for the names given to Wales, he will now turn to 'the character and peculiarities of the people' (Gerald 1868:179; 1978b:232–3).

The theme is continued in Part II, but with a focus on the deficiencies of the Welsh. This leads on, moreover, to four concluding chapters that stress the continuing sinfulness of the Welsh and offer advice on how they can be conquered and governed, as well as, finally, on how they can resist. In the first edition the chapter on conquest went as far as recommending the expulsion of the Welsh from Wales and colonizing it with other people; Gerald added that some even thought it should be made into a forest inhabited entirely by wild beasts (Gerald 1868:225,n.4; 1978b:51–2; cf. Dimock 1868:xxx–xxxi). The 'Description of Wales' is, then, a carefully structured text by a highly educated author. Its juxtaposition of virtues and vices was indebted to the standard mode of argument – namely dialectic, used in the schools where Gerald had studied – while its writing style reflects his command of Latin prose and familiarity with biblical and classical learning (Bartlett 2013:4; Holmes 1970:229; Roberts 1982:87–8).

The 'Description of Wales' as ethnography

Bearing these introductory points in mind, let us turn to consider the significance of the 'Description of Wales' as a pioneering work of ethnography. A few comparisons serve to confirm that Gerald was justified in emphasizing its novelty. Bartlett and others have rightly stressed that Gerald effectively reinvented the ethnographic monograph over a thousand years after the ethnographic writing of classical antiquity, an achievement all the more remarkable as the most important examples of that writing – notably

---

3   The second part appears to have offended the Protestant churchman and scholar Dr David Powel of Ruabon (1549×1552–1598), since he omitted it from the earliest printed edition of Gerald's Welsh works (Dimock 1868:lvii)!

Herodotus' *Histories* and Tacitus' *Germania* – were accessible only in fragmentary form to medieval authors (Bartlett 1982:179–81; Khanmohamadi 2014:38). It is true that other western European writers of the eleventh and twelfth centuries had included observations on different peoples in historical works (Bartlett 1982:158–77). Indeed, Gerald had done something similar in his first major prose work, the 'Topography of Ireland', whose third part inserts descriptions of the Irish in a historically structured account indebted to medieval Irish learning (Gerald of Wales 1982:92–125; see also Boivin 1993:91–106).

One striking feature of the 'Description of Wales', however, is that the focus has shifted decisively towards portraying the people, with no attempt to provide a historical narrative: yes, as we shall see, Gerald still adopted a historical perspective, but this largely serves to provide explanations for particular characteristics of the 'ethnographic present' depicted in the bulk of 'the text. Indeed, the description of the Welsh is fuller than that of any people in any previous medieval Latin text, though several Muslim writers composed detailed topographical and ethnographic accounts of other peoples in Arabic from the mid ninth century onwards (Bartlett 2013:5–7).

About 80 per cent of the 'Description of Wales' consists of ethnographic description (Gerald 1868:179–213; 1978b:233–64). In line with the aim Gerald set out in his preface, this distils – or, as one scholar has put it, 'freezes' – the key characteristics of one ethnic group, the Welsh (Khanmohamadi 2014:50). It is generally accepted that the emphasis on the distinctiveness of the Welsh oversimplifies the nature of their society. For one thing, it focuses on those Welsh who enjoyed free status, ignoring the substantial numbers of the unfree (Davies 1987:112–13; Pryce 1987; cf. Jones 1961). This tacit elision explains how Gerald could declare that 'not only the nobles, but the whole people are trained in arms', the ploughman as much as the courtier (Bartlett 1982:196; Gerald 1868:179; cf. Gerald 1978b:233).

The point here was that warfare was not restricted to a knightly elite as in the Anglo-French world; but in pointing up that contrast Gerald overlooked class divisions within Welsh society itself. He likewise presented a misleadingly uniform picture in asserting that the Welsh did not live in towns or castles, but rather preferred to inhabit wattle huts in woods, despite some of them in fact having taken over Anglo-Norman towns and castles in south Wales by the later twelfth century (Gerald 1868:200–1; 1978b:251–2; see also Pryce 1987:269). Thanks to his own family background and career, Gerald was of course aware that things were more complicated than the 'Description' suggested. Indeed, his earlier 'Journey round Wales' reveals a multi-ethnic world in which, for example, the English and Welsh stood apart to hear the crusade preached at Llandaff and one of the daughters of the southern Welsh ruler Rhys ap Gruffudd (the Lord Rhys, d.1197) was married to William fitz Martin, the Anglo-Norman lord of Cemais in northern Pembrokeshire (Gerald 1868:67, 111; 1978b:126, 170). The work also gives a concise description of the Flemings originally settled by King Henry I (reigned 1100–35) in Dyfed – the part of Wales Gerald knew best – whose industrial and mercantile enterprise implicitly stand in contrast to the supposedly pastoral economy of the Welsh:

> A strong and powerful people, who show the strongest enmity to the Welsh in continuous military conflicts; a people, I say, highly experienced in wool-working and in trade; a people very capable in seeking profit by any effort or danger on land and sea; a people very ready to turn their hands alternately now to the plough, now to arms, according to the place and time.
>
> (Gerald 1868:83; 1978b:141–2; see also Toorians 1990)

We read also how the Flemings practised divination using rams' shoulder blades, illustrated by a story of how this led to the disclosure that a woman was pregnant by her husband's nephew (Gerald of Wales 1868:87; 1978b:145–6). The 'Journey round Wales' also reports that the preaching party was given lodging in the town of Cardigan by the Lord Rhys (Gerald 1868:112; 1978b:171). It should be noted, moreover, that Gerald briefly acknowledges Welsh interaction with the wider world towards the end of the 'Description' itself. In attempting to explain the territorial expansion achieved by some Welsh rulers in the late twelfth century at the expense of their conquerors, he observed that under the first three Norman kings (who reigned from 1066 to 1135), the Welsh 'increased greatly in numbers and gradually became familiar with and skilled in both weapons and horses through the Normans and English, with whom they had frequent contact by following the court and giving hostages'. As a result of this, and the distraction of the following three kings of England (who reigned from 1135 to 1199) by affairs in France, the Welsh, 'raising their necks and occupying lands, utterly refused to bear their old yoke' (Gerald of Wales 1868:218; 1978b:267).

The portrayal of the Welsh

The portrayal of the Welsh as occupying a hermetically sealed and timeless space in the ethnographic chapters of the 'Description' was, then, a deliberate choice, a heuristic device that allowed Gerald to distil what he considered to be the Welsh people's essential distinguishing characteristics. Gerald nowhere says how he obtained the information about the Welsh portrayed in the 'Description'. The work is clearly intended to apply to Wales as a whole and the Welsh in general, rather than to offer a depiction of a specific Welsh community. True, Gerald delineates the main topographical and political divisions of Wales in the opening chapters, including the numbers of *cantrefs* (the main territorial subdivisions) in each of the three principal kingdoms of Gwynedd, Powys and Deheubarth (Gerald 1868:165–76; 1978b:220–30). But the sense of place that permeates the topographically structured 'Journey round Wales' is lacking. Presumably the observations on the Welsh are based on an amalgam of experiences, including the preaching tour of 1188 that extended Gerald's knowledge of Wales by taking him into areas of the country, especially the north, with which he had previously been unfamiliar (cf. Jones 1949:126).

Scholars have largely, and I think correctly, concluded that the 'Description of Wales' contains substantial amounts of detailed description that can plausibly be seen as deriving from Gerald's first-hand observation – for example, the use by the Welsh of hazel twigs to clean their teeth; their eating of food on broad, flat pizza-like pieces of bread; the design of their coracles and agricultural implements; their part-singing and their hospitality, including the entertainment of guests by young female harpists (Gerald 1868:183–4, 185, 189–90, 201–2; 1978b:236–7, 238, 242, 252; see also Bartlett 1982:192–200; cf. Gransden 1972). Moreover, there is an attempt to explain how Welsh society worked by showing how different aspects of it – such as a preoccupation with warfare, devotion to liberty and concepts of honour – related to each other: to quote Robert Bartlett, '[t]he society Gerald presented in the *Descriptio Kambriae* strikes us as a coherent and plausible social world' (Bartlett 1982:194; cf. Nash 2018:212–13).

A general presumption in favour of Gerald's accuracy in the 'Description', based on first-hand observation, is further supported by its offering not only a fuller but also a more sympathetic picture of the Welsh than the 'Topography of Ireland' does of the Irish, who are condemned by Gerald as barbarians and barely Christian. True, there is an element of the noble savage here: as infants, 'they are for the most part abandoned to nature', which 'according to her own judgement arranges and disposes without the help of any art the limbs that she has produced ... until she finally forms and finishes them in their full strength with beautiful upright bodies and handsome and well-complexioned faces'. Yet Gerald hastens to add that such appearances are deceptive: 'But although they are fully endowed with natural gifts, their external characteristics of beard and dress, and internal cultivation of the mind, are so barbarous that they cannot be said to have any culture ... The people is [*sic*], then, a barbarous people, literally barbarous'. This was a result of their isolation:

> Since conventions are formed from living together in society, and since they are so removed in these distant parts from the ordinary world of men, as if they were in another world altogether and consequently cut off from well-

behaved and law-abiding people, they know only the barbarous habits in
which they were born and brought up ... their natural qualities are excellent.
But almost everything else is deplorable.

(Gerald of Wales 1982:100–3)

Earlier writers had described the Welsh in similar terms. By the end of
the twelfth century, Latin ecclesiastical writers had applied the concept of
the barbarian to peoples on the peripheries of powerful polities, including
the Irish, Welsh, Bretons, Scandinavians, Hungarians and Poles (Bartlett
1982:158–77; Gillingham 2000:26–31, 36–7, 44–8, 101–5; Jones 1971). Half a
century before Gerald wrote the 'Description', an English account of the reign
of King Stephen, the *Gesta Stephani* ('Deeds of Stephen'), offered the following
observations:

Now Wales is a country of woodland and pasture, immediately bordering
on England, stretching far along the coast on one side of it, abounding in
deer and fish, milk and herds; but it breeds men of an animal type, naturally
swift-footed, accustomed to war, volatile always in breaking their word as
in changing their abodes. When war came and the Normans conquered the
English [in 1066], this land also they added to their dominion and fortified
with numberless castles; they perseveringly civilized it after they had
vigorously subdued its inhabitants; to encourage peace they imposed law
and statutes on them; and they made the land so productive and abounding
in all kinds of resources that you would have reckoned it in no wise inferior
to the most fertile part of Britain.

(Anon. 1976:14–15)

The idyll was shattered, however, after the Welsh revolted against their
conquerors following the death of Henry I in December 1135. What needs to
be stressed here, however, is the contrast with Gerald's approach. While he
was familiar with the negative depictions of peoples living on the fringes of
powerful polities, as shown by his views on the Irish, Gerald almost entirely
avoided the language of barbarism in writing about the Welsh.[4] This is not
to say that Gerald was strongly sympathetic towards the Welsh. After all,
Book II of the 'Description' echoes criticisms made by the author of the
'Deeds of Stephen' and has parallels with Gerald's portrayal of the Irish. The
'Description of Wales' condemned the Welsh for a host of failings, including
perjury, inconstancy, love of plunder, weakness in battle, fratricide ('they
love their brothers more when they are dead than when they are alive') and

---

4   For rare exceptions, see Gerald (1868:201, 223); cf. Gerald (1978b:252, 271).

incest (Gerald 1868:212; 1978b:261). But rather than falling back on well-worn stereotypes of the barbarian, Gerald interpreted these failings as evidence of sin – an interpretation grounded in his understanding of the history of the Welsh, to which I shall return shortly.

Gerald's attitude to the Welsh

What was Gerald's attitude to the Welsh he described, and what does this imply about his motives for writing the 'Description'? As has often been remarked, the 'Description of Wales' is deeply, and no doubt deliberately, ambiguous, and thus open to different readings (Bartlett 1982:182–7; Khanmohamadi 2014:54–6; Fazioli 2017:193; Roberts 1982:86–7). That Gerald was more knowledgeable about and sympathetic to the Welsh than to the Irish is of course not surprising given his upbringing and career in Wales, and his hybrid identity as a member of a Marcher family nevertheless proud of his Welsh descent through his maternal grandmother Nest, daughter of Rhys ap Tewdwr, the king of south-west Wales killed by the Normans in 1093 (Pryce 2016). He wrote at less of a remove from his subject than English commentators on the Welsh such as the author of the account of King Stephen's reign mentioned earlier, medieval German historians writing about the Baltic peoples or Slavs, or friars such as William of Rubruck who composed accounts of their missions to the Mongols (cf. Bartlett 1982:158–9; Khanmohamadi 2014:57–87).

Indeed, Gerald presented himself as an insider with privileged knowledge of the exotic society he described. But he wrote at a remove, nevertheless. The 'Description of Wales' is not a precocious instance of a classical modern anthropological study based on participant observation by someone who had tried to live among his subjects and learn their language. It is true that Gerald knew some Welsh. For example, he quoted examples of alliteration in it as well as noting that Anglesey was called in Welsh *Mamkembre* (modern Welsh: *Mam Cymru*), that is, 'the mother of Wales', on account of its growing sufficient grain to feed the whole of Wales (Gerald 1868:177, 188; 1978b:230, 240). He also offered observations on the language, noting, for example, its close relationship to Cornish and Breton as well as its similarities with Greek and Latin, and declaring that the Welsh of north Wales was believed to be 'finer, more embellished and more praiseworthy to the same extent as that land is more free of foreigners' (Gerald 1868:177, 194; 1978b:231, 246; cf. Bartlett 1982:208–10). However, there is nothing to suggest that he was a fluent speaker of the language. When he preached the Third Crusade in Wales in 1188, the Welsh archdeacon of Bangor was employed to translate his and the archbishop of Canterbury's sermons into Welsh (Gerald 1868:55, 77, 126, 177, 193–4; 1978b:114, 135–6, 185–6, 231, 246; see also Richter 1979:61–2, 95). Moreover, while he called Wales his 'fatherland' (*patria*), this identification was two edged, and arguably signalled the ambition of Marcher families such as his to conquer Wales and make it their own, an ambition legitimized by intermarriage with Welsh royalty (Gerald 1868:157; 1978b:213).

It is pertinent to note in this context Bartlett's observation that the 'Description of Wales' 'has clear affinities with the "applied anthropology" of ethnographers working for political and military purposes' (Bartlett 1982:186; cf. Faletra 2014:156–60). More recently, Shirin Khanmohamadi has offered a different colonial analogy by drawing on the work of Jacob Gruber to characterize the 'Description of Wales' as an example of 'salvage anthropology', a concept originally applied to nineteenth-century efforts to record the characteristics of indigenous peoples whose distinctive lifeways were threatened with extinction by colonialism (Khanmohamadi 2014:39, 46; Gruber 1970). She has also emphasized how Gerald's depiction of the Welsh was informed by classical ideas regarding human progress from a primitive to a civilized state, as expressed by Lucretius and transmitted via Cicero to medieval writers like Gerald (Khanmohamadi 2014:14–20, 41–3; cf. Nash 2018:213). Gerald's familiarity with these ideas is shown by a passage in the 'Topography of Ireland', which, as ever, pulls no punches in its criticisms of the Irish.

> While man usually progresses from the woods to the fields, and from the fields to settlements and communities of citizens, this people despises work on the land, has little use for the money-making of towns, contemns [sic] the rights and privileges of citizenship, and desires neither to abandon, nor lose respect for, the life which it has been accustomed to lead in the woods and countryside.
>
> (Gerald of Wales 1982:101–2)

Although the 'Description of Wales' lacks any explicit statement of these successive stages of civilization, the scheme is surely implicit in its observations on some of the supposedly praiseworthy characteristics of the Welsh in Book I of the 'Description' – such as their pastoral economy, lack of towns and wattle dwellings on the edges of woods – and thus serves to complicate these by associating them with the backward and primitive.

There are strong grounds, then, for maintaining that the work shows 'several striking similarities with modern colonial anthropology' (Fazioli 2017:190). These are reinforced by its final chapters on how to conquer the Welsh, which partly adapt passages from Gerald's earlier account of the conquest of Ireland, in which his kinsmen had played a prominent role since the late 1160s (Gerald of Wales 1978a:244–53). The last chapter giving advice on how the Welsh can resist, while of a piece with the work's overall ambiguity and dialectical approach (and lacking any parallel in the works on Ireland), does not seriously undermine Gerald's overall argument: such advice was arguably at least as useful to potential conquerors, to whom the work was addressed, as to their victims.

Above all, Gerald adopted a moral approach informed by his understanding of history. Though not a narrative history, the 'Description of Wales' is categorized as historical writing by Gerald and has a strong historical dimension (Bartlett 1982:182–3; Pryce 2018:20–2). Crucially, it accepts the Welsh origin legend elaborated and popularized by Geoffrey of Monmouth in his *De Gestis Britonum* or *Historia Regum Britanniae*, completed over half a century earlier in *c.*1138, that derived the Britons, and thus their Welsh descendants, from Brutus of Troy and his son Kamber, after whom Wales was called *Kambria* (Geoffrey of Monmouth 2007; Gerald 1868:178, 193–4; 1978b:231–2, 245–6; see also Crick 1999). This helps to explain why Gerald made comparisons with accounts of the ancient Britons by Caesar and Lucan and why the preface to Book II refers to the inhabitants of Wales as the 'British people' (Gerald 1868:185–6, 205, 207; 1978b:238, 255, 257; see also Bartlett 1982:206). The continuity between the Britons and their Welsh descendants also informs Gerald's use of the sixth-century British churchman Gildas. Gerald declared that Gildas was the only British writer worth imitating, since 'committing to writing what he saw and himself knew and deploring rather than describing the ruin of his people, he composed a true rather than ornamental history' (Gerald 1868:158; cf. Gerald 1978b:214).

In his *De Excidio Britanniae* ('Ruin of Britain', *c.*540), Gildas adopted the mantle of an Old Testament prophet to his people as he related the history of Roman and post-Roman Britain and declared that the Britons' eventual loss of most of the island to the Anglo-Saxons was divine punishment for their sins (Charles-Edwards 2013:202–19). As I have argued elsewhere, the influence of Gildas is probably greater than has been generally appreciated, as Gerald used Book II of the 'Description' to highlight the vices of the Welsh, to argue that they had still not expiated the sins of their British ancestors, and to insist that therefore they were still doomed to defeat and loss (Pryce 2011a). Gerald wrote at a time of Welsh resurgence in south Wales, under the Lord Rhys and his sons, in the years following the death of King Henry II of England in 1189. One aim of his 'Description' was to puncture the new-found confidence that accompanied military victories against the Marcher lords and the English crown, a confidence given voice in a long-established tradition of political prophecy that foretold the Britons' recovery of their sovereignty over Britain (Williams 1979:71–86).

Conclusion

It would, of course, be rash to propose a monocausal explanation for such a complex and deliberately ambiguous work as the 'Description'. After all, Gerald's overriding concern was to make his mark as a writer to secure patronage from the powerful in the kingdom of England. The 'Description of Wales' cannot be reduced to a mere blueprint for colonial conquest: its detailed and in parts sympathetic portrait of the Welsh was also designed to demonstrate Gerald's status as a privileged observer bringing a hitherto unfamiliar society to his readers' attention in a new kind of literary work. Nevertheless, it seems safe to say that its pioneering depiction of the Welsh cannot be comprehended without attending to the context of conflict and conquest in which it was written. It was precisely this that gave salience to what may be termed the 'salvage' aspects of the work. The conclusion to the 'Description' reflects that context and encapsulates the challenge posed by the work's deep ambiguity; it therefore provides an appropriate place to draw this discussion to a close. There, Gerald quotes words allegedly addressed to Henry II, king of England, by an old Welsh soldier at Pencader, now in Carmarthenshire, who took the king's side against his compatriots, presumably in 1163.

> This people may be oppressed and in large part destroyed and weakened by your strength, O king, and that of others, now as in the past and many times again, as demanded by its merits. However, it will not be destroyed by the anger of man unless the anger of God concurs with it. And, in my opinion, no other people than this Welsh one, nor any other language, whatever may happen to the larger remnant of it, will answer for this corner of the earth before the Supreme Judge on the severe Day of Judgement.
>
> (Gerald 1868:227; 1978b:274)

In other words, the best the Welsh could hope for was to hang on to Wales, in whole or in part.[5] Moreover, the quotation concludes the work, and Gerald passes no comment on the old man's words. It may be, then, that the passage was intended to illustrate the point he had made immediately before it – namely that the memory of their Trojan ancestry and former dominion over Britain still inspired the Welsh to bravery and resistance. However, in referring to God's anger, Gerald also left open the possibility that the Welsh might be destroyed totally, and he studiously avoided saying whether the old man's hopes for their attenuated survival were justified.

---

5   For a different interpretation, see Cohen (2006:94–5).

References

Anon. 1976. *Gesta Stephani*, trans. K.R. Potter. Oxford: Clarendon Press.

Bartlett, R. 1982. *Gerald of Wales 1146–1223*. Oxford: Clarendon Press.

——— 2013. *Gerald of Wales and the Ethnographic Imagination*. Cambridge: Department of Anglo-Saxon, Norse and Celtic, University of Cambridge.

——— 2018. 'Introduction'. In Gerald of Wales, *Instruction for a Ruler (De Principis Instructione)*, ed. and trans. R. Bartlett, pp. xi–lxx. Oxford: Clarendon Press.

Boivin, J.-M. 1993. *L'Irlande au moyen âge: Giraud de Barri et la Topographia Hibernica*. Paris: Librairie Honoré Champion.

Charles-Edwards, T.M. 2013. *Wales and the Britons, 350–1064*. Oxford: Oxford University Press.

Cohen, J.J. 2006. *Hybridity, Identity and Monstrosity in Medieval Britain: On Difficult Middles*. Houndmills: Palgrave Macmillan.

Crick, J.C. 1999. 'The British past and the Welsh future: Gerald of Wales, Geoffrey of Monmouth and Arthur of Britain'. *Celtica* 23:60–75.

Davies, J.C. 1946. 'Giraldus Cambrensis, 1146–1946'. *Archaeologia Cambrensis* 96:85–108, 256–80.

Davies, R.R. 1987. *Conquest, Coexistence, and Change: Wales 1063–1415*. Oxford: Clarendon Press.

Dimock, J.F. 1868. 'Preface'. In Gerald of Wales, *Itinerarium Kambriae et Descriptio Kambriae*, pp. ix–lxxi. London: Longmans, Green, Reader and Dyer.

Faletra, M.A. 2014. *Wales and the Medieval Colonial Imagination: The Matters of Britain in the Twelfth Century*. New York: Palgrave Macmillan.

Fazioli, K.P. 2017. *The Mirror of the Medieval: An Anthropology of the Western Historical Imagination*. Oxford: Berghahn Books.

Fernandez-Armesto, F. 1982. 'Medieval ethnography'. *Journal of the Anthropological Society of Oxford* 13(3):275–86.

Geoffrey of Monmouth. 2007. *The History of the Kings of Britain*, trans. N. Wright and ed. M.D. Reeve. Woodbridge: Boydell.

Gerald of Wales. 1868. *Itinerarium Kambriae et Descriptio Kambriae*, ed. J.F. Dimock. London: Longmans, Green, Reader and Dyer.

——— 1978a. *Expugnatio Hibernica: The Conquest of Ireland*, ed. and trans. A.B. Scott and F.X. Martin. Dublin: Royal Irish Academy.

——— 1978b. *The Journey through Wales, and The Description of Wales*, trans. L. Thorpe. London: Penguin.

——— 1982. *The History and Topography of Ireland*, trans. J.J. O'Meara, rev. edn. Harmondsworth: Penguin.

Gillingham, J. 2000. *The English in the Twelfth Century: Imperialism, National Identity and Political Values*. Woodbridge: Boydell.

Gransden, A. 1972. 'Realistic observation in twelfth-century England'. *Speculum* 47:29–51.

Gruber, J.W. 1970. 'Ethnographic salvage and the shaping of anthropology'. *American Anthropologist* 72:1289–99.

Holmes, U.T. 1970. 'The *Kambriae Descriptio* of Gerald the Welshman'. *Medievalia et Humanistica* 1:217–31.

Jones, G.R.J. 1961. 'The tribal system in Wales: a re-assessment in the light of settlement studies'. *Welsh History Review* 1(2):111–32.

Jones, T. 1949. 'Gerald the Welshman's "Itinerary through Wales" and "Description of Wales": an appreciation and analysis'. *National Library of Wales Journal* 6:117–48, 197–222.

Jones, W.R. 1971. 'The image of the barbarian in medieval Europe'. *Comparative Studies in Society and History* 13:376–407.

Khanmohamadi, S. 2014. *In Light of Another's Word: European Ethnography in the Middle Ages*. Philadelphia: University of Pennsylvania Press.

Lloyd, J.E. 1911. *A History of Wales from the Earliest Times to the Edwardian Conquest*, vol. 2. London: Longmans, Green and Co.

Nash, O. 2018. 'Elements of identity: Gerald, the humours and national characteristics'. In G. Henley and A.J. McMullen (eds), *Gerald of Wales: New Perspectives on a Medieval Writer and Critic*, pp. 203–19. Cardiff: University of Wales Press.

Pryce, H. 1987. 'In search of a medieval society: Deheubarth in the writings of Gerald of Wales'. *Welsh History Review* 13(3):265–81.

——— 1998. 'A cross-border career: Giraldus Cambrensis between Wales and England'. In R. Schneider (ed.), *Grenzgänger*, pp. 45–60. Saarbrücken: Kommissionsverlag.

——— 2011a. 'Gerald of Wales, Gildas, and the *Descriptio Kambriae*'. In F. Edmonds and P. Russell (eds), *Tome: Studies in Medieval Celtic History and Law in Honour of Thomas Charles-Edwards*, pp. 115–24. Woodbridge: Boydell Press.

——— 2011b. *J.E. Lloyd and the Creation of Welsh History: Renewing a Nation's Past*. Cardiff: University of Wales Press.

——— 2016, 'Giraldus and the Geraldines'. In P. Crooks and S. Duffy (eds), *The Geraldines and Medieval Ireland: The Making of a Myth*, pp. 53–68. Dublin: Four Courts Press.

——— 2018. 'Gerald of Wales and the Welsh past'. In G. Henley and A. J. McMullen (eds), *Gerald of Wales: New Perspectives on a Medieval Writer and Critic*, pp. 19–45. Cardiff: University of Wales Press.

Richter, M. 1973. 'Gerald of Wales'. *Traditio* 29:379–90.

——— 1979. *Sprache und Gesellschaft im Mittelalter: Untersuchungen zur mündlichen Kommunikation in England von der Mitte des elften bis zum Beginn des vierzehnten Jahrhunderts*. Stuttgart: Hiersemann.

Roberts, B.F. 1982. *Gerald of Wales*. Cardiff: University of Wales Press.

Rubiés, J.-P. 2009. 'Introduction'. In J.-P. Rubiés (ed.), *Medieval Ethnographies: European Perceptions of the World Beyond*, pp. xiii–xxxviii. Farnham: Ashgate.

Smith, J.B. 2017. *Walter Map and the Matter of Britain.* Philadelphia: University of Pennsylvania Press.

Toorians, L. 1990. 'Wizo Flandrensis and the Flemish settlement in Pembrokeshire'. *Cambridge Medieval Celtic Studies* 20:99–118.

Williams, G. 1979. *Religion, Language and Nationality in Wales.* Cardiff: University of Wales Press.

3

Sir William Jones

Welsh Orientalist and comparative musicologist

JOHN O'CONNELL

Introduction

Is there anything more to be said about Sir William Jones (1746–1794)?
Libraries give pride of place to his works (e.g. Shore 1807) and letters (e.g.
Cannon 1970). Of course, there are hagiographic biographies of the 'Oriental'
Jones and the 'Orientalist' Jones completed respectively by Cannon (1990) and
Michael Franklin (2011), among others.[1] These publications do not include the
influential translations of the scholar's writings to be found in German and
French sources, among others. The range of Jones's scholarship is immense.
It covers subjects that include biology, physiology, mythology and theology.
There are treatises on medical matters and essays on legal issues. He also
collated dictionaries and grammars, and he wrote histories and chronologies.
He is particularly renowned for his literary collections, poems and dramas,
which are often translations and reworkings of Middle Eastern and South
Asian masterworks. As an early exponent of cultural relativism, Jones
exceptionally employed comparative methods to position 'Oriental' literature
alongside 'Occidental' classics on an equal basis.[2]

---

1   Since the biography of Sir William Jones has been minutely scrutinized and
     extensively covered by scholars in the past – such as Shore (1807) and more
     recently Cannon (1970, 1990) and Franklin (1995, 2011) – I have not attempted to
     reconstruct here a new biography of the outstanding Welsh polymath, Sir William
     Jones.
2   For the sake of consistency, the transliteration of musical terms in Sanskrit follows
     the conventions detailed in Arnold 2000:xviii–xx.

*Figure 1   Engraving of Sir William Jones by Sir Joshua Reynolds (1811), © Alamy
2020. Reproduced with permission.*

In this chapter, I focus on one aspect of Jones's output, namely music.
With specific reference to a musical treatise on Indian music entitled 'On the
musical modes of the Hindus', I show how Jones (1792) not only developed a
comparative approach to musicology but how he also initiated an empirical
method in anthropology by conducting ethnographic research with Indian
musicians (see also Zon 2007:48–79). Here, Jones's visit to Benares (Varanasi)
in 1784 to stay with the Fowke family was critical in his successful realization
of an early ethnomusicological experiment. That is, Margaret Fowke (1758–
1836) had already begun to collate and transcribe Indian melodies and, her

brother, Francis Fowke (1754-1820) had already started to collect and analyse Indian instruments. I also consider Jones as a Welsh Orientalist. I argue that Jones's interest in genealogy (inspired by his own Welsh pedigree) informed his concern for kinship relations in music and language. Further, I draw upon Marilyn Strathern's consideration of comparison in anthropology to examine Jones's status as an outsider in Wales and as an insider in India.

Anthropology by comparison

In her contribution to this volume, Strathern explores the place of community studies in Wales for advancing a comparative approach in anthropology.[3] In particular, she juxtaposes two works by the same artist to examine two types of comparison, one that concerns aesthetic value and one that concerns social status. For her, issues that concern artistic quality can be compared since they are bounded, and questions that concern societal importance cannot be compared since they are unbounded. Further, Strathern juxtaposes two religious works to interrogate the paradoxical status of education for Nonconformist enlightenment. By contrasting a liturgical text (the Bible) with a para-liturgical commentary (Thomas Charles's scriptural dictionary) she explores multiple levels of signification for comparative effect. Finally, Strathern investigates the dialogic interplay between macrocosm and microcosm. With reference to anthropology in Wales, she sees Wales both as an unbounded macrocosm and as a bounded microcosm either unsuited or suited to comparative analysis. Here, Strathern presents a nuanced reading of the insider/outsider dichotomy in Welsh ethnography.

I find Strathern's study of comparison in anthropology directly relevant to my study of comparison in musicology. Cultural traits like musical traits can be identified and compared. In both fields, similarity and dissimilarity can be contrasted across contexts. In the past, as comparative musicology, music provided an ideal locus for establishing scientifically sameness and difference. Musical pitches can be quantified as frequencies. Scales can be identified by number. Melodies can be codified according to their contour (and so forth). With mathematical precision musical traits can be compared across contexts. For example, a five-note scale in Mongolia might be compared with a five-note scale in Hungary. However, musicology like anthropology was not immune to the formulation of 'grand theory'. Scale types might be compared to show cultural diffusion and cultural evolution. Béla Bartók (1881–1945) was a principal advocate of this method. At its most controversial, comparative musicology was implicated in the statistical quagmire of the 'holocultural'

---

3   For a relevant collection that concerns comparative studies in anthropology, see the contributions to Fox and Gingrich 2002b, including that of Strathern 2002.

approach. Here, Alan Lomax (1976) attempted to formulate mathematical correlations between music and culture on a global scale.

Of course, the comparative approach in anthropology and (ethno) musicology has received critical attention. As Fox and Gingrich (2002a:1) remark, scholars have long regarded comparison as an outmoded methodology. The argument in anthropology is as follows. Seemingly isomorphic units of comparison are hard to identify, especially in postcolonial and proto-capitalist contexts. Discrete borders and boundaries are difficult to ascertain especially where regional variation exists. Again, comparison assumes that units of comparison are static and not dynamic. Further, units may be selected for comparison to satisfy the Eurocentric 'gaze' or to underscore scholarly prejudice. Like anthropology, (ethno)musicology has grappled with these issues. Seemingly commensurate traits such as tuning systems and scale structures may be difficult to isolate. Boundaries and borders are equally problematic. One musical tradition may involve distinctive tonalities and different modes. Here, regional variation is a common issue. Indeed, the choice of traits used for comparison may reveal a 'Western' preoccupation with acoustic principles which can be measured and analysed. In musicology as in anthropology, comparison had indeed become odious.

During the 1950s, the comparative approach to musicology was abandoned in favour of an anthropological approach to music.[4] As an anthropology of music, ethnomusicology advocated the study of 'music' in its cultural context using ethnographic methods. Although comparison would be retained (in the form of comparative music studies) as a branch of ethnomusicology, the comparative approach in musicology was widely discredited as ethnocentric and evolutionist. Is there a case to be made for a return to a musicology using comparison? If anthropology is to be followed, the answer is 'yes'. As Strathern argues, all ethnographic research involves comparison in the guise of translation. An insider as representative might become an outsider through representation. Indeed, with the new concern for reflexivity, an outsider as a scholar might become an insider as a musician. This is especially important in ethnomusicology (see Rice 1994). In this chapter, I examine the role of the Welsh polymath, Sir William Jones, as a comparative musicologist both from the perspective of his outsider status in Wales and his insider status in India.

Insider and outsider

Jones was not born in Wales, but his father was. Also called William Jones (1675–1749), Jones senior was raised in Anglesey in humble circumstances, a

---

4   For an overview of the transformation of ethnomusicology from comparative musicology to an anthropology of music, see Bohlman and Nettl 1988.

Welsh speaker who was proud of his Welsh heritage. To escape poverty, Jones senior moved to London with the promise of employment in a mercantile establishment. After a colonial escapade in the West Indies sponsored by his employers, the elder Jones enlisted in the navy as an instructor, thereby setting in motion his lifelong reputation in the fields of navigation (he was known as by the sobriquet 'Longitude Jones') and mathematics (he was especially famed for his work on differential calculus). As Cannon (1990:1–3) shows, Jones senior counted Isaac Newton (1642–1727) and Edmond Halley (1656–1742) as close associates, and he was elected a fellow of the Royal Society in 1713. Cleverly, Jones senior cultivated a network of aristocratic patrons for whom he worked as a tutor. One patron, Thomas Parker, Lord Macclesfield (1666–1732), would secure Jones's social advancement and sponsor Jones's second marriage to Mary Nix in 1731.

William Jones junior was the progeny of this union. Born in London in 1746, the younger Jones was brought up in an anglophone world that was quite different from his ancestral patrimony. With the death of Jones senior in 1749, Jones junior, then aged three, did not benefit directly from the didactic imprint of his father's intellect. However, Jones junior clearly inherited his father's facility with languages. Language instruction came in three stages. First, as a schoolboy, Jones acquired a thorough grounding in the classics at Harrow, where the boy became an expert in composing verse in imitation of Ovid and Sophocles, among others. Second, as a student, he taught himself to read and write the principal languages of the Middle East at Oxford University, translating manuscripts (available in the Bodleian Library) from Arabic, Persian and Turkish sources into English, French and Latin. Third, as an adult, by now Sir William Jones, from necessity learned Indian languages (including Sanskrit) when he was employed as a judge by the East India Company in Calcutta (Kolkata).

Jones once remarked that he knew almost every language but his own.[5] Although said in jest, Jones may indeed have underrepresented his own knowledge of the Welsh language. Employed as a barrister in the Carmarthen circuit between 1775 and 1783, Jones gained a working knowledge of Welsh. There was a practical reason for this. With English being the language of law and Welsh being the language of the people, Jones made every effort to represent the interests of his Welsh-speaking clients. There was also a social reason. Jones experienced first-hand the exploitation by English landlords of Welsh tenants, the courts being used as the principal vehicle by which to enforce foreign oppression. Further, there was a romantic reason. Jones clearly

---

5   See Franklin 2011:96, for an interesting explanation of this claim, which was apparently jokingly made by Jones to Louis XVI while in France.

relished his nostalgic engagement with 'the Celtic sublime'. His letters and his compositions at the time revel in the life and lore of Wales. Aware of his own lineage and not shy to hide it, Jones founded a drinking society called the Druids of Carmarthen. He was accorded the title 'chief bard' (*penncerdd*) in recognition of his principal standing as a Welsh legislator.

It is noteworthy that Jones did not learn Welsh fluently. Of the twenty-eight languages with which he was familiar, Jones would later admit that Welsh was one of 'twelve least studied [by him] but attainable' (Franklin 2011:96). This is a surprising remark for an outstanding linguist who had spent eight years on the Carmarthen circuit. It is also surprising for a comparative linguist who considered Irish and Welsh to be sister dialects in the Indo-European family of languages. Franklin (ibid.) suggests that Jones may have been ambivalent about his Welsh heritage. When visiting North Wales (1775) upon the invitation of the Whig MP Sir Roger Mostyn (1734–1796), Jones was especially enthusiastic in letter and verse about seeing his native land for the first time. However, when going on an excursion to Anglesey, Jones was happy to maintain the illusion of his princely lineage by visiting Thomas James, Lord Bulkeley of Baron Hill (1752–1822), and by not visiting his uncle in Llanbabo (a settlement nearby). Franklin (ibid.:60–1) maintains that Jones was reticent about introducing his new friends to relatives of low standing.

Similarity and difference

Here, it is worth comparing again father and son. It could be argued that Jones senior was an 'insider outside' while living in England, but Jones junior was an 'outsider inside' while working in Wales. Geography apart, there were similarities between the two men. Both had a professional interest in legal matters: Jones senior as a justice of the peace and Jones junior as a barrister. Both men were engaged as tutors by aristocratic patrons: Jones senior residing with the Macclesfields at Shirburn Castle and Jones junior living with the Spencer family at Althorp. This patronage ensured the social elevation of the two men. Both men expressed radical views on matters related to society and morality, religion and politics. Indeed, Jones junior was denied promotion for his association with and support for contemporary intellectuals such as Edmund Burke (1729–1797) and Benjamin Franklin (1705–1790). Where Jones senior was an active member of the Welsh community in London (he was a relative of the renowned Welsh antiquarians, the Morris brothers), Jones junior was an activist member of the political establishment (he was a member of the dining club called 'the Turk's Head', among other political associations).

Above all, there was one issue that united father and son. This was genealogy. Both men were explicitly aware of a Welsh pedigree that situated their family in direct descent from the princes of Gwynedd. Here, the Welsh bard, Lewis Morris (1701–1765) played a key role. As was customary, Morris, who also lived on Anglesey, visited the Jones household on New Year's Day to claim kinship. As part of the ritual, Morris presented the family with a pedigree confirming his and their royal descent.[6] While Jones junior may have been embarrassed by the lowly status of his Welsh relations, he was always proud of the elevated standing accorded to his Welsh ancestors. It is interesting that genealogy would subsequently feature prominently in Jones's comparative consideration of music and language, the notion of family and kinship being used to classify musical relations and linguistic connections. In imitation of a botanical precedent, Jones employed the notion of a family tree to explain connections (as branches) and origins (as roots) in other areas, including mythology and theology.

Jones junior may be indebted to Morris in another area. This was versification. Morris was famed for his revival of older forms of Welsh verse. In particular, he composed poetry in the style of *penillion*, an improvised mode of declamation that was intimately associated with the harping tradition (*cerdd dant*). Indeed, Lewis Morris helped compile a collection of Welsh songs. Entitled *Antient British Music* (1742), he provides information on the history and practice of harping. Like Morris, Jones composed verse in strict prosody. Instead of using the Welsh poetic convention known as *cynghanedd*, he employed quantitative and qualitative syllabic meters when composing poems in 'Classical' and 'Oriental' styles. Like Morris, Jones also aimed to translate texts faithfully, Morris from English to Welsh (see Jones 2000) and Jones from many languages to English. Both authors were aware of their audience, sometimes adopting a popular manner to secure readership. Like Morris, Jones collated or revised dictionaries and grammars. Both scholars were eager to compare Welsh epic cycles (such a *Y Gododdin*) with a Classical canon (such as the *Aeneid*).

Early on, Jones (1807a) composed one such epic. Entitled *Britain Discovered* (originally composed in 1770), Jones aimed explicitly to create a national epic on a par with the *Iliad*. Although unfinished, Jones hoped to write twelve books that concerned the colonization of Britain. Wishing to avoid another Arthurian cycle, he recreated the mythical voyage of the Phoenicians to the British Isles. Led by the heroic prince of Tyre, Britanus, a company of Tyrians take a circuitous route to Albion through the eastern Mediterranean. They only reach their destination in the last book after a major

---

6   Although believed to be lost by Cannon and Franklin (2005:50), Owen (1951:114) reproduced a copy of Jones's pedigree linking the Morrises and the Joneses, and showing the joint descent of both families from Hwfa ap Cynddelw, Lord of Llys Lifon (1085–1165).

struggle against the French (represented here as evil deities) in Gaul. Later, in 1788 Jones revisited *Britain Discovered* (1870b). The revised narrative is more convoluted, with a voyage that oscillates between Gaul and Iberia, Tyre and Carthage. In contrast to the first version, India rather than Greece controls the spirit world, Hindu divinities now worried that their sacred religion will not be honoured in Albion. They block the passage to the Atlantic at Gibraltar. Passage through the Straits of Gibraltar is secured by way of druidic ritual. The piece ends with the marriage of Britanus to Albione.

Wales to India

The two versions of *Britain Discovered* clearly show Jones's transformation from a Classicist to an Indianist. Not only does the later version demonstrate Jones's knowledge of Hinduism but it also alludes implicitly to a magical connection between Brahmin and druid – that is, between Wales and India. There are satirical references to contemporary events. For example, a druid predicts the Revolutionary War in America (1775 to 1783) and the siege of Gibraltar (1779 to 1783). In the second version there is an allegorical resonance where 'the nuptials Britanus and Albione [represent] royalty and liberty in the constitution of England' (Jones 1807b:451), a political position demonstrating Jones's liberal inclinations. In the same section, Jones as a druid 'recommends the government of the Indians by their own laws' (ibid.:452). This will be achieved when Britanus and Albione 'apply themselves to the regulation of their domain and the happiness of their subjects' (ibid.). Again, Jones advances a pluralistic vision where Indians are not subject to colonial rules. Such an aspiration would inform Jones's professional interest in Hindu as well as Muslim legal practice.

The transition from Classicist by way of Islamicist to Indianist occurred when Jones was appointed judge to the supreme court of judicature at Fort William, Bengal, in 1783. This appointment was a long time in coming. As early as 1778 Jones had applied for it (Franklin 2011:2), but due to his republican inclinations he was repeatedly turned down. Even as William Petty, Lord Shelburne (1737–1805), the then prime minister, approached the king, George III, to secure the post in question, a radical pamphlet by Jones entitled *The Principles of Government* (1782) was the subject of court action (ibid.:3). The relevant indictment deemed the publication to be 'false, wicked, malicious, seditious and scandalous libel' (Towers 1784:43). As was appropriate to his new station, Jones was knighted and awarded an impressive annuity (£6,000 a year). Newly married to Anna Shipley (1748–1829), who was a cousin of the Whig patron Georgina Cavendish, Duchess of Devonshire (1757–1806), Jones achieved the rare distinctions of financial independence and social standing while maintaining a certain degree of ideological integrity.

For Jones, Calcutta offered an opportunity for extending his intellectual boundaries. At the time of his arrival in the then capital of British India, Calcutta had already attracted senior scholars with an Indian specialism under the enlightened governorship of Warren Hastings, who served as governor between 1774 and 1785, and again in 1787. Within four months of his arrival, Jones set about forming the Asiatick Society, a learned society that was intentionally modelled on the Royal Society. Membership of this society included the Persian scholar Francis Gladwin (1744–1812) and the Sanskrit specialist Charles Wilkins (1749–1836). Jones was nominated president. The first meeting was convened in the courthouse at Fort William on 15 January 1784. The transactions of the society were published subsequently in the first volume of its journal, *Asiatick Researches* under the following heading: 'A discourse on the institution of a society'. Delivered by Jones, the discourse charted out the remit of the society as 'inquiring into the history and antiquities, the natural productions, arts, sciences and literature of Asia' (Jones 1788a:ix-xvi).

It is noteworthy that research would be limited to the 'geographical limits of Asia' with 'Hindustan' as its centre. Aware of the degenerate state of social intercourse in colonial India, Jones hoped that the society would 'afford entertainment' and 'convey knowledge' in equal measure (ibid.:x). Later, Jones itemized the broad spectrum of research activities to be undertaken, to include the arts and sciences, the manners and customs, and the geographies and histories of Asia (ibid.:xiii). Of significance here is the inclusion of mathematics and astronomy, manufacturing and agriculture, chirurgery [surgery] and medicine, grammar and rhetoric. The contents of the first volume of *Asiatick Researches* are representative.[7] There are articles on archaeology and architecture, botany and biology, and mining and minerals. There are also two extended essays by Jones. One is a comparative study of orthography in Asiatic languages (Jones 1788b) and the other is a comparative examination of deities in Eurasian religions (Jones 1788c). Further, Jones embellishes the volume with insightful commentaries and visionary discourses.

Theory in practice

In the first volume of *Asiatick Researches* there is one important article on Indian music. Entitled 'On the vina or Indian lyre' and published in the form of a letter extract (undated) to Jones by the music enthusiast Francis Fowke, the piece provides detailed information on the material construction of this instrument. The instrument in question, a *rudra vīṇā* or *bīn*, is more than

---

7   Twenty volumes of *Asiatick Researches* are available online at the Biodiversity Heritage Library (www.biodiversitylibrary.org).

3 feet in length. It has seven metal strings (made of steel and brass) that rest upon nineteen elevated frets. The instrument includes two large gourd resonators at each end, one of which is placed over the musician's left shoulder. Fowke provides information on string tuning and fret placement, and he uses the harpsichord to confirm the exact measurement of pitch. He represents the resulting gamut as semitones using the Indian version of solfa (called *sargam*). Although such a comparative move served inevitably to confirm the European character of Indian tonality, Fowke made important observations with respect to performance practice. He talks specifically about hand positioning and the fingering adopted, strings employed and plectra worn.[8]

Fowke illustrates the *vīṇā* with a drawing. Unable to find an artist who could draft 'two attendant musicians in the same drawing' (Jones 1788d:295), Fowke represents only one musician performing on the instrument in a traditional setting. Separately he provides a more detailed representation of the instrument itself. Apparently, the original drawing was not the one reproduced in *Asiatick Researches* as Jones wrote to Fowke in a letter dated 4 August 1787: 'Your drawing of the vina and the player on it will be engraved by the best artist here' (quoted in Woodfield 2000:178). As represented in Figure 2, a different version of the same instrument and instrumentalist (apparently engraved in 1805) was republished in the *Cyclopaedia* by Rees (1819:175). The drawing and the description are attributed to Sir William Jones, though it is not clear who the principal musician in the engraving is. According to Fowke (cited in Jones 1788d:295–6), the artist could be 'Jeewun' (Jiwan) Shah or his equally talented brother 'Pear Cawn' (Pir Khan). However, Fowke admits that it was 'Pear Cawn' who supplied the technical information for his treatise.

Soon after their arrival in India, in November 1784 Jones and his wife Anna visited Fowke in Benares (Franklin 2011:25), where the latter held the position of 'resident' in the city. Fowke was an amateur harpsichordist of some ability, and it was Jones who interested him in the study of Indian instruments (Woodfield 2000:12). However, it was Fowke's sister, Margaret, with whom Jones developed a productive relationship. Margaret Fowke had already collected 'Hindoostanee' airs. As was the fashion among her Anglo-Indian contemporaries (ibid.:149–80), Margaret transcribed by ear and arranged for

---

8   On the *rudra vīṇā* or *bīn* in North India, see the website Rudra Vina (rudravina. com). There it is claimed that the instrument has not significantly changed since the late-eighteenth century. The *vīṇā* that is performed today in the Carnatic tradition of South India is a good deal larger (being around five feet in length). It is also played using a different posture. For a visual portrayal of the musical instruments of North India, see Hardgrave and Slawek (1997).

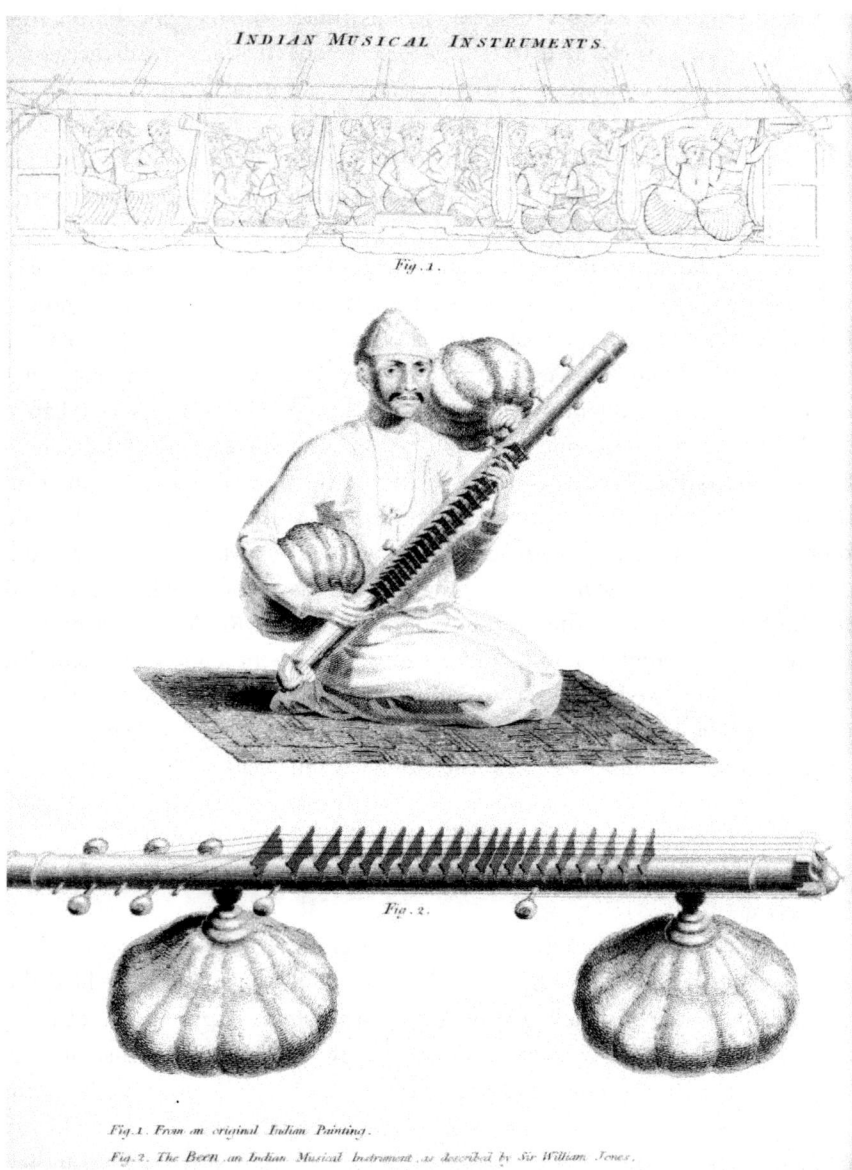

INDIAN MUSICAL INSTRUMENTS.

Fig. 1.

Fig. 2.

Fig. 1. From an original Indian Painting.
Fig. 2. The Been, an Indian Musical Instrument, as described by Sir William Jones.

Figure 2   A musician playing the vīṇā as portrayed by Rees (1819:175)..

pianoforte music played by local musicians. Like her friend Sophia Plowden (b. 1751), Margaret often performed these airs at musical soirées. Margaret even organized sessions where Indian instruments were tuned to her harpsichord to facilitate bi-musical interaction (Franklin 2011:30). For the translation of songs, Margaret solicited the services of Jones, who with the assistance of a resident scholar or *munshi* (whom Jones calls 'moonshee'), translated relevant texts from the local dialect of Hindi into English by way of Persian (Woodfield 2000:169).

Woodfield (ibid.:169) suggests that Jones was already interested in Indian music when he came to Benares. In his 'Preliminary discourse', published in *Asiatick Researches*, Jones mentions music as one of the pleasurable subjects, worthy of scholarly inquiry, the others being architecture, painting and poetry (Jones 1788a:xiv). Here, he does not classify music as one of the 'inferior' arts. Shortly after his return to Calcutta, Jones addressed the same subject in an address to the Asiatick Society. In it, Jones claimed that 'the Hindu system of music has ... been formed on truer principles than our own' (Jones 1788e:410). He asserted that 'the skill of the native composers is directed ... to the natural expression of strong passions' (ibid.). In this process, he believed that the development of melody in Indian music has been sacrificed, 'though some of their tunes are pleasing even to a European ear' (ibid.). He concludes by comparing Indian music with the Arabian and Persian systems, both from the perspective of aesthetic appreciation and theoretical sophistication.

Kith and kin

Franklin (2011:31) claims that Jones was also interested in a musical treatise on Indian music while in Benares. Unable yet to read Sanskrit, Jones was studying a theoretical discourse on Indian music entitled *Rāgavibodha* (dated 1609) by Somanātha in Persian translation. He also had access to relevant treatises in Persian, such as *Tuḥfat al-Hind* (dated 1675) by Mirza Khan and *Saṅgītadarpaṇa* by Damodara (dated *c.*1625). As a result of this research, Jones wrote an important dissertation on Indian music entitled 'On the musical modes of the Hindus', which, in revised and extended form, appeared in the third volume of *Asiatick Researches* (Jones 1792). From the outset, Jones argued that Indian music, like all music, is a science that is subject to natural laws. He invoked acoustic principles to generate a standard set of seven pitches (*svaras*) that constituted the tonal material of an Indian scale (see Table 1). In similar fashion to the Western concept of solfa, he showed how these notes could be represented as a standard set of syllables (*sargam*).

Solfa	Ut [Do]	Re	Mi	Fa	Sol	La	Si	Ut [Do]
Sargam	Sa	Ri	Ga	Ma	Pa	Dha	Ni	Sa

Table 1   A comparative representation of Solfa and Sargam.

So far, Jones (ibid.:63) showed that the theoretical basis of Indian music is no different from other musical traditions in Europe and Asia in general, and India and Persia in particular. By contrast, he then examined microtonal intervals called *śrutis* to understand the distinctive character of Indian scales (see Table 2). In contrast to Western music, where the relationship between intervals is equal, Jones (ibid.:69) found that the intervallic structure of Indian music was unequal, where a whole tone was represented by four *śruti*s, a third tone by three *śruti*s and a semitone by two *śruti*s. Following a scientific precedent set by Francis Fowke (see above), Jones then reconstructed the standard scale of the Indian gamut with reference to an exact reproduction to scale of a *vīṇā* with its nineteen frets, noting that the intervals between the first and the second, the fourth and the fifth were whole steps, each composed of four *śruti*s. The intervals between the second and the third, the sixth and the seventh were third tones, each composed of three *śruti*s.

Fret #	7	9	10	12	14	14	17	18
Note	Sa	Ri	Ga	Ma	Pa	Dha	Ni	Sa
Interval	First	Second	Third	Fourth	Fifth	Sixth	Seventh	Octave
Śruti #	4ś	3ś	2ś	4ś	4ś	3ś	2ś	

Table 2   The intervallic structure of Indian music in śrutis.

Jones (ibid.:76) classified Indian *rāga*s in terms of celestial families. There are six principal modes called *rāga*s. These male modes are also classified according to the six seasonal divisions of the Indian year. Each male *rāga* is married to five secondary modes called *rāgiṇī*s. These female modes are classified according to the five temporal divisions of the Indian day. In sum, six families formed out of the union of one male *raga* and five female *rāgiṇī*s produce six modes per family or thirty-six modes in total. These families can be represented visually (as paintings or *rāgamāla*s) or aesthetically (as tastes or *rāsa*s). Jones then provided a table of the musical composition of these families by reproducing the tonal arrangement using the *sargam* of each mode according to its kinship relationship to the principal mode. Jones does not go further. If he had he would have included the tonal arrangement of subordinate modes called *putra*s, eight sons considered to be the offspring of each family. That makes forty-eight children in total.

Jones (ibid.:63) calculated that there were eighty-four possible modes in Indian music. He showed how these modes could be represented as families, with thirty-six parent modes and forty-eight infant modes. That is, eighty-four musical deities in total. Jones also demonstrated how the classification of Indian modes was related to seasonal time and diurnal variation, showing the importance of time theory in the performance of Indian music. Elsewhere, Jones (ibid.:70) personified music theory following a similar principle. When considering microtonal inflections in performance practice, he showed how the twenty-two intervals or *śruti*s in the Indian gamut were conceptualized as nymphs. When distinguishing between a major and a minor scale he states:

> The two scales are made to coincide by taking a *sruti* from [the fifth note]
> *pa* and by adding it to [the sixth note] *dha* or, in the language of Indian
> artists by raising [the nymph called] Sevaretna to the class of [the nymph
> called] Santa and her sisters.
>
> (ibid.:70)

In this way, Jones demonstrated how even theoretical principles could be
understood in terms of sibling relations.

Musicology by comparison

Jones explicitly adopts a comparative approach in his scholarly study of Indian
music. Recalling Strathern's consideration of comparison in anthropology,
Jones's method comprises comparative moves that involve juxtaposition
and translation in addition to a more standard search for similarity and
difference. Predictably, Jones finds similarities between Indian music and
other musical traditions. He considers the influence of musical affect upon
animals and humans in India with reference to China, Greece and Persia. He
finds similarities in the music theories of India and Persia, and he notes the
widespread significance of the numbers seven, twelve and eighty-four in the
classification of modal systems throughout Asia and Europe. However, he
shows differences in the conceptualization of these systems, since the Persians
explain modal taxonomy with reference to locality and Indians interpret
modal classes with reference to deity. In his personification of Indian modes
and in his explication of Indian music, Jones (ibid.:68) speculatively compares
the Indian god of purification, Pavan, with the Greek god Pan, and the Indian
god of destruction, Ishvara, with the Egyptian god Osiris.

Perhaps the most important aspect of Jones's comparative method
was ethnographic. Jones admits that he was unable to examine the second
chapter of Somanātha's treatise, which contains descriptions of musical
composition and instrumental practice, without the 'assistance in the practical
part from a European professor and a native player on the vina' (ibid.:67).
This is a significant flaw in Jones's dissertation, and has been highlighted
by Zon (2006:200). However, when trying to determine whether there was
'any difference in practice between the Indian scale and that of our own, I
requested a German professor of music [perhaps a Mr Oehme] to accompany
with his violin a Hindu lutenist [probably Shah], who sung by note some
popular airs' (Jones 1792:70). The German professor assured Jones that the
scales were indeed the same. To support his thesis, Jones cites his friend, John
Shore (1751–1834), who assured him that 'when the voice of a native singer
was in tune with his harpsichord, he found the Hindu series of seven notes
to ascend, like ours with a sharp third' (ibid.:70). This was hardly surprising.

Although this musical experiment was not very scientific, Jones's method also involved juxtaposition: the juxtaposition of a German instrumentalist and an Indian musician. There were other instances of juxtaposition. When investigating the evolution of scale types in Indian music, Jones noted that 'the native musicians' have a diatonic and a chromatic scale, but they also have an 'enharmonick genus' (ibid.:69). Later he connects this finding to the apparent 'invention of an enharmonick melody' by the Greek philosopher Aristoxenus (*c.*300 BC), Jones provocatively arguing that the Indians had invented the enharmonic genus before the Greeks (ibid.:75). Jones also juxtaposed scale types to show spatial connections. When analysing five note or pentatonic scales in Indian music, he noted the similarity between this type and 'the Chinese scale'. Citing a 'Scotch gentleman skilled in musick', he concludes that 'the wild, but charming melodies of the ancient highlanders were formed by a similar mutilation of the natural scale' (ibid.:83). Although this juxtaposition was not quite appropriate, Jones was employing a methodology that would later be developed in comparative musicology.

When considering the question of comparison by translation, the issue of quality is significant. Indeed, Jones had taken care to provide different translations of an original, a transliteration, a translation and an interpretation. Although Jones first accessed musical treatises on Indian music in Persian, he bemoaned that the Persian-speaking 'Moghols have no idea of accurate translation and give that name to a mixture of gloss and text with a flimsy paraphrase of them both' (ibid.:65). He was especially critical of the Moghul pretence of 'writ[ing] Sanskrit words in Arabic letters' in their attempt to provide an authentic representation of an original (ibid.). Perhaps tellingly, Jones adds, 'a man, who knows the Hindus only from Persian books, does not know the Hindus' (ibid.). This is exactly what Jones had attempted to do in Benares. Concerning contemporary scholars on South Asia, Jones was especially contemptuous: 'That a European who follows the ruddy rivulets of "Muselman" writers on India, instead of drinking from the pure fountain of Hindu learning, will be in perpetual danger of misleading himself and others' (ibid.).

The lineage of language

As Strathern argues with respect to aesthetic judgement, Jones compares the quality of two languages (Sanskrit and Persian) and the value of two religions (Hinduism and Islam). As Schofield (2010) argues, Jones initiated a bifurcated discourse in colonial scholarship.[9] By separating the Hindu and the

---

9   Schofield is not alone in criticizing Jones. Of concern, Jones represents Indian music as a homogeneous category, not recognizing important regional variation

Muslim historically into discreet temporal categories, Jones was able to lament the demise of a golden age in which Sanskrit was superseded by Persian following the conquest of North India by the Moghuls during the sixteenth century. This explains Jones's negative attitude towards Persian translations of Sanskrit treatises. Recalling Strathern again, Jones contends that Sanskrit was widely revered to be 'the language of the gods' (Jones 1792:65; see also Schofield 2010:492). It was a macrocosm as it is universal (*márga*) and unbounded, and thereby not appropriate for comparison. By contrast, regional (*deśī*) dialects of Sanskrit were not so divinely inspired. They were vernacular variations of a 'classical' *Ursprache* that could be compared to assess their musical relevance. For example, Jones compared explicitly the regional languages of Mathura (Braj) and the Punjab (Punjabi).

Schofield makes an important observation about music in terms of language. She argues that some styles of Indian music were believed to be universal and unbounded (*márga*) and others to be regional (*deśī*) and bounded. In contrast to Jones, she contends that Moghuls participated actively in the 'classicization' of an Indian musical canon. This is interesting in that Jones had previously compared Persian music favourably with a Western musical canon. What is significant is this: Jones wrote his dissertation in two parts, the first under the influence of a Middle Eastern musical bias by way of Persian, and second under the influence of a South Asian musical bias by way of Sanskrit. It is in the latter stage that Jones acknowledged the divine lineage of Indian modes, a marital union between Bhramā and Saraswatī to produce a son, Nārada, who was the mythological creator of the sacred *vīṇā*. Of importance, Jones recognized this familial connection in his comparative essay on Indian deities (Jones 1788c), portraying Nārada with his *vīṇā* in a representative *rāgamāla* (ibid.:262).

But what of the lineage of language? Jones learned Sanskrit out of professional necessity as a judge, not for academic reasons as a musicologist. As Franklin (2011:34) explains, Jones was concerned about the accurate translation of court transactions produced by local interpreters or pandits. Also, he wished to create a digest of Hindu law to be used in Indian courts.

---

throughout the subcontinent. In his comparative study of three relevant scholars, Bor (2000) admonishes Jones for his reliance upon recent treatises (all written during the seventeenth century) and for his denigration of Persian sources on musical matters. Accordingly, Bor considers Jones's dissertation on Indian music to be 'of little relevance today' (ibid.:6). Although Jones would not have claimed to be a music specialist (he had no systematic training in the subject), his reliance upon one treatise by Somanātha is significant. As Simms (2000:48) argues, the *Rāgavibodha* (1609) represents an important consideration of performance practice in North and South India during a major period of musical change.

Although he found it difficult to find an instructor to teach him 'the language of the gods', through royal intervention he eventually succeeded, Jones and his wife spending time in autumn 1785 at Nadi[y]a University, Bengal, a known centre for Sanskrit studies. At first, Jones began to study a legal treatise, the *Mānavadharmaśāstra* ('Laws of Manu'). Like Thomas Charles's dictionary, discussed by Strathern, this ancient treatise (dating from *c.*300 BC) was a complex para-liturgical text explaining the Indian Vedas. As a microcosm juxtaposed alongside a macrocosm, Jones had a privileged insight into rules governing social status and sacred ritual in ancient India. Within a year, Jones was able to arbitrate with authority on contentious issues related to Indian law.

However, Jones would address the lineage of languages even earlier. In his third anniversary discourse delivered to the Asiatick Society (2 February, 1786), Jones claimed, 'The Sanskrit language, whatever be its antiquity, is of a wonderful structure' (Jones 1788f:422–3). For Jones, it is 'more perfect than the Greek, more copious than the Latin, and more exquisitely refined than either' (ibid.:422). By way of comparison, Jones claimed that Greek and Latin bore a strong affinity with Sanskrit, 'both in the roots of verbs and the forms of grammar, than could possibly have been produced by accident' (ibid.:423). Looking at the shared lineage of Greek, Latin and Sanskrit, Jones argued 'that no philologer could examine them all three, without believing them to have sprung from some common source, which, perhaps, no longer exists' (ibid.). Looking at the origin of languages nearer to his home, Jones concluded:

> There is a similar reason, though not quite so forcible, for supposing that both the Gothic and the Celtic, though blended with a very different idiom, had the same origin with the Sanskrit; and the old Persian might be added to the same family.
>
> (ibid.)

The language of music
The 'Third anniversary discourse' was published (1788) after the first version (1784) but before the revised version (1792) of Jones's dissertation on Indian modes appeared. The question remains: To what extent did Jones's comparative study of Indian music inform his comparative approach to Indian languages? To invoke Strathern again, Jones isolated units of comparison to establish affinity in music (by way of scale and genus) and language (by way of root and structure). Jones compared the quality of music (Persian versus Hindu) and language (Latin versus Sanskrit). Further, Jones juxtaposed the notion of classicism in Asia and Europe to establish chronology in music (in the realm of theory) and language (in the realm of orthography). In contrast

to language, Jones does not search for a common lineage in music, an ur-form from which all musics evolved. However, Jones does allude to a universal theory of music and language in which the Chinese and the Tartars among others are not excluded. Indeed, Jones proposed a global search for an ethnic heartland in which humans evolved and from where humans diffused (Jones 1788f:430).

The central connection between his essays on music and language is the notion of family. Jones references family explicitly when considering the relationship between languages, while he references family implicitly when considering the conceptualization of music in terms of genealogy and kinship. Of course, the issue of the origin and evolution of the human species would receive critical attention during the nineteenth century when the whole concept of a biblical chronology would be contested. While Jones (ibid.:425) still subscribed to a timeline provided by the Old Testament in his innovative interrogation of language and ethnicity, he employed (somewhat unsystematically) the language of evolution in his choice of classes and his construction of taxonomies. Although used by him elsewhere to classify botanical types using Sanskrit terms with reference to a Linnaean typology (Franklin 2011:246), Jones employed the term 'genus' to signify a musical phenomenon (the enharmonic genus) and the term 'species' to connote a linguistic fact (the dialect species). In this way, Jones adapted a biological system of classification to music and language to show a hierarchical system of classes that had evolved and diffused.

Perhaps Cannon and Franklin (2005:69) overstate the intermediate position held by Jones between Carl Linnaeus (1707–1778) and Charles Darwin (1809–1882) in the established chronology of evolutionary theory. However, there is evidence that Jones was thinking about the origins of musical species before delivering his address on language in 1786. The evidence is in the form of a letter to the Sanskritist Charles Wilkins, dated 24 April 1784 (see Cannon 1970, ii:646).[10] In it, Jones confirms that his 'present pursuit is the Indian system of musick'. Although slightly different from 'our major mode', Jones is amazed to find that the 'Hindu scale ... consists of two tetrachords exactly equal'. He finds that 'the Indians have not only semitones, but even an *enharmonick* kind, or thirds and quarter of notes'. It is noteworthy that Jones italicizes the term 'enharmonic' in the original. However, he does not qualify here 'enharmonic' with reference to the Linnaean class 'genus'. The discussion is framed by another finding, the discovery of a reference to platonic metaphysics and morality in a 'Hindu work of high antiquity and authority'.

---

10   All subsequent quotes in this paragraph are from Jones's letter to Wilkins.

As in his dissertation on Indian modes, Jones implies that developments in Indian music (as in Indian philosophy) predated those in Greek music (and Greek philosophy). Further, Jones suggests that theoretical principles in Indian music informed the articulation of similar principles in Greek treatises. In this way, Jones disrupted the contemporary representation of musical evolution in European civilization by placing India rather than Greece as its cradle. It is interesting that Jones delivered his preliminary findings on Indian music to the Asiatick Society in March 1784 not as 'On the musical modes of the Hindus' but as a 'Treatise on the musical modes of the Persians' (ibid.:647). This is significant since Jones was already complaining to Wilkins that 'Persian translations from the Sanskrit are so defective' (ibid.:646). Not yet conversant in Sanskrit, Jones confided to his friend that: 'All my hopes ... of being acquainted with the poetry, philosophy and arts of the Hindus are grounded on the expectation of living to see the fruits of your learned labours' (ibid.). This was not to be, as Wilkins left India in 1786.

Borders and boundaries

In sum, Jones was primarily interested in the lineage of Indian music before he delivered his address on the matter in 1786. However, Jones became interested in the genealogy of Indian music only after his analysis of musical sources in Sanskrit in 1785. That would still have allowed Jones to talk about a family of musics in the same way he talked about a family of languages. But he did not. Rather, he emphasized the social construction of modal taxonomies in Indian music, a phenomenon he believed to be unique to musical treatises in Sanskrit. This explains his comparative classification of Persian music in terms of locality and Indian music in terms of deity. However, Jones's approach to a musicology by comparison led him to construct a 'grand theory' of musical association; that is, between China, India and Scotland. As is clear in his preliminary discourse (Jones 1788a), a similar comparative approach to language led Jones to a 'grand theory' of ethnic origin and cultural diffusion. Is there anything to be learned today from Jones's approach to comparison?

Returning to Strathern, Jones challenged the contemporary construction of borders and boundaries in language and music. In terms of language, Jones contested the primary position accorded to Hebrew in Genesis, where it is the first language, given to Adam by God (Franklin 2011:38). By arguing that Sanskrit was the 'language of the gods', Jones upset the standard chronology of biblical exegesis. By linking Sanskrit to other Asian and European languages, Jones proposed the equality of Asian and European tongues. In this way, Jones traduced the borderline between Britain and India and disrupted the boundary between the colonizer and the colonized. In terms of music, Jones argued for the similarity of Indian and Greek music (in theory) and sameness of the 'their' music and 'our' music (in practice). He even attempted to demonstrate this similitude by comparing a European instrumentalist with an Indian vocalist using a harpsichord as a reference point. However unscientific this experiment might have been, Jones demonstrated a degree of cultural relativism that was extremely rare among his English contemporaries in the East India Company.

Jones's dissertation on Indian music has its own chronology. It quickly diffused across the borderlands of continents and the boundaries of nations. Two 'disjunctive' contexts are worthy of comparison: Austria and Ireland. Translated into German (Jones 1802) and dedicated to Joseph Haydn (1732–1809), Jones's dissertation made its own impact on Western 'classical' music through the compositions of Franz Schubert (1897–1828) and Ludwig van Beethoven (1770–1827), among others. As Solomon (1982) argues, composers were seduced by a contemporary fashion for all things Indian, be they mythological or folkloric. And Jones's research into Indian music fitted the bill. If Tolley (1992) is to be believed, even Haydn was entranced by the musical tract. However, the reception of this work must be understood in the context of the reception of Jones's other work, namely on language. Jones's systematic approach to comparative linguistics was widely emulated by German scholars like Jacob Grimm (1785–1863) and Friedrich Rückert (1788–1866). Significantly, another German linguist, Franz Bopp (1791–1867), would use his profound knowledge of Sanskrit to publish a comparative study of Celtic languages (Bopp 1838).

In Ireland, Jones's dissertation on Indian music had a different impact. That scion of Irish Orientalism, Thomas Moore (1779–1852), was profoundly influenced by the literary and scholarly output of Jones. There were two strands to this influence. First, Moore emulated the poetic *topoi* of Jones in his Orientalist fantasy, *Lalla Rookh* (Moore 1817). There is a direct connection between the poem entitled 'Hafiz' (composed in 1771) by Jones (1807c) and the character Hafed in Moore's work. Second, Moore invokes the dissertation on Indian music by Jones in his poems and his memoirs, sometimes without proper attribution. For example, in the song 'Bendemeer's stream', Moore (1817:29) reiterates the Persianate tropes of the rose (Persian, *gol*) and the nightingale (Persian, *bol bol*) made fashionable in 'Oriental' prose by Jones. The musical influence of Jones is also to be found there. When referencing the 'pathetic mode of Isfahan', Moore adds in a footnote: 'The Persians, like the ancient Greeks, call their musical modes or *perdas* by the names of different countries or cities' (ibid.:29). As in other instances, Moore fails to acknowledge Jones.

Occident as Orient

There is a difference between the two contexts. In Austria by way of German, Jones was invoked to construct an exotic representation of the 'Oriental' other.[11] In Ireland by way of English, Jones was invoked to deconstruct an exoticized representation of the 'Occidental' self. In the two contexts, different stratagems were employed. In German-language scholarship, Jones provided a comparative model for undertaking 'grand theories' of Orientalist research. For this, Edward Said (1978:79) famously chastised the Welsh Orientalist. In English-language literature, Jones offered a comparable medium for completing allegorical representations of 'Occidental' alterity. As I show elsewhere by way of a reflexive turn (see O'Connell 2017:76), Moore famously employed allegory to criticize the English in Ireland. Like Vallancey before him,[12] Moore alluded to a contemporary discourse in Ireland that traced the chronology of Irish history back to the Phoenicians and beyond. In this sense, the Irish were the 'Orientals' of the West. As part of this narrative, the Irish traced their lineage back to Moses, thereby confirming their own connection to the Chosen People (ibid.:xix, 89).

Recently, the subject of Irish Orientalism has received attention in literature and music. Here, the themes of 'Occidentalism' and 'Orientalism' are juxtaposed (see Lennon 2008), the Irish occupying an 'Oriental' alterity in the English imagination. Such Western 'otherness' is visibly marked and audibly inscribed, so much so that some Irish writers and Irish musicians have actively engaged in self-exoticization – such masters as William Butler Yates (1865–1939) and Seán O Riada (1931–1971) come to mind. Should we not be speaking about a Welsh Orientalism? Franklin (2011:58–61) alludes to this possibility in his outstanding biography of Sir William Jones. He suggests that the innate concern for the correct realization of poetic meters and the native fascination with genealogical provenance informed the romantic and enlightened approach by Jones to all things 'Oriental'. In Strathern's (1988) words, Jones as an individual was 'dividual', since he was both insider and outsider, 'Occidental' and 'Oriental'. Further, Jones strategically transcended the borderland between the colonizer (in India) and the colonized (in Wales), and, of course, he uniquely negotiated the boundaries between the academic and the artist, the scientist and the sage.

---

11   For a discussion of the impact of Jones in the German-speaking world, see Lehmann 1995.
12   Elsewhere, Jones was very scathing of Vallancey's comparative study of Irish and Sanskrit (Vallancey 1772). See Cannon and Franklin 2005:64.

References

Arnold, A. (ed.). 2000. *The Garland Encyclopedia of World Music: South Asia, the Indian Subcontinent*. New York: Garland Publishing.

Bohlman, P.V. and Nettl, B. (eds). 1988. *Comparative Musicology and Anthropology of Music*. Chicago: University of Chicago Press.

Bopp, F. 1838. 'Über die celtischen Sprachen vom Gesichtspunkte der vergleichenden Sprachforschung'. *Abhandlungen der Königlichen Akademie der Wissenschaften zu Berlin* 1838:187–272.

Bor, J. 2000. 'Three important essays on Hindustani music'. *Journal of the Indian Musicological Society* 36/37:5–16.

Cannon, G. 1990. *The Life and Mind of Oriental Jones*. New York: Cambridge University Press.

——— (ed.). 1970. *The Letters of Sir William Jones*, 2 vols. Oxford: Clarendon Press.

Cannon, G. and Franklin, M.J. 2005. 'A Cymmrodor claims kin in Calcutta: an assessment of Sir William Jones as philologer, polymath, and pluralist'. *Transactions of the Honourable Society of Cymmrodirion* 11:50–67.

Fox, R.G. and Gingrich, A. (eds). 2002a. 'Introduction'. In R.G. Fox and A. Gingrich (eds), *Anthropology, by Comparison*, pp. 1–24. London: Routledge.

——— (eds). 2002b. *Anthropology, by Comparison*. London: Routledge.

Franklin, M.J. 2011. *Orientalist Jones: Sir William Jones, Poet, Lawyer, and Linguist, 1746–1794*. Oxford: Oxford University Press.

——— (ed.). 1995. *Sir William Jones: Selected Poetical and Prose Works*. Cardiff: University of Wales Press.

Hardgrave, R. and Slawek, S. 1997. *Musical Instruments of North India: Eighteenth Century Portraits by Baltazar Solvyns*. Delhi: Manohar Publishers.

Jones, A.R. 2000. '"Put It in a Welsh Dress"': Poetical Translations by Lewis Morris'. *National Library of Wales Journal* 31(4):345–56.

Jones, W. 1788a [1784]. 'A discourse on the institution of a society'. *Asiatick Researches* 1:ix–xvi.

——— 1788b. 'A Dissertation on the orthography of Asiatick words in Roman letters'. *Asiatick Researches* 1:1–56.

——— 1788c [1784]. 'On the gods of Greece, Italy and India'. *Asiatick Researches* 1:221–75.

——— 1788d. 'An extract of a letter from Francis Fowke esq'. *Asiatick Researches* 1:295–9.

——— 1788e [1785]. 'The second anniversary discourse'. *Asiatick Researches* 1:405–14.

——— 1788f [1786]. 'The third anniversary discourse'. *Asiatick Researches* 1:415–31.

——— 1792 [1784]. 'On the musical modes of the Hindus'. *Asiatick Researches* 3:55–87.

——— 1802. *Über die Musik der Indier: Eine Abhandlung des Sir William Jones*, trans. F. von Dalberg. Erfurt: Beyer und Maring.

—— 1807a [1770]. 'Britain discovered'. In J. Shore (ed.), *The Works of Sir William Jones*, vol. 1 pp. 475–82. London: J. Stockdale.

—— 1807b [1788]. 'Britain discovered', rev. edn. In J. Shore (ed.), *The Works of Sir William Jones*, vol. 1, pp. 483–90. London: J. Stockdale.

—— 1807c [1771]. 'A Persian song of Hafiz'. In J. Shore (ed.), *The Works of Sir William Jones*, vol. 10, p. 251. London: J. Stockdale.

Lehmann, W.P. 1995. 'The impact of Jones in German-speaking areas'. In G. Cannon and K.R. Brine (eds), *Objects of Enquiry: The Life, Contributions, and Influences of Sir William Jones (1746–1794)*, pp. 131–40. New York: New York University Press.

Lennon, J. 2008. *Irish Orientalism: A Literary and Intellectual History*. Syracuse, NY: Syracuse University Press.

Lomax, A. 1976. *Cantometrics: An Approach to the Anthropology of Music*. Berkeley: Extension Media Center, University of California.

Moore, T. 1817. *Lalla Rookh: An Oriental Romance*. London: Longman.

Morris, L. 1742. 'Historical account of the rise and progress of music among the antient Britons'. In J. Parry and E. Williams (eds), *Antient British Music*, pt. 1. London: Mickleborough.

O'Connell, J.M. 2017. *Commemorating Gallipoli through Music: Remembering and Forgetting*. Lanham, MD: Lexington Books.

Owen, H. 1951. *The Life and Works of Lewis Morris (1701–1765)*. Caernarvon: Anglesey Antiquarian Society and Field Club.

Rees, A. 1819. *The Cyclopaedia: Universal Dictionary of Arts, Sciences and Literature, vol. 3*. London: Longman.

Rice, T. 1994. *May It Fill Your Soul: Experiencing Bulgarian Music*. Chicago: University of Chicago Press.

Said, E.W. 1978. *Orientalism*. New York: Pantheon.

Schofield, K.B. 2010. 'Reviving the Golden Age again: "classicization", Hindustani music and the Mughals'. *Ethnomusicology* 54(3):484–517.

Shore, J (ed.). 1807. *The Works of Sir William Jones*, 13 vols. London: J. Stockdale.

Simms, R. 2000. 'Introduction to the music of South Asia: scholarship since 1300'. In A. Arnold (ed.), *The Garland Encyclopedia of World Music: South Asia, the Indian Subcontinent*, pp. 42–60. New York: Garland Publishing

Solomon, M. 1982. 'Beethoven's Tagebuch of 1812–1818'. In A. Tyson (ed.), *Beethoven Studies 3*, pp. 193–285. Cambridge: Cambridge University Press

Strathern, M. 1988. *The Gender of the Gift: Problems with Women and Problems with Society in Melanesia*. Berkeley: University of California Press.

—— 2002. 'Foreword'. In R.G. Fox and A. Gingrich (eds), *Anthropology, by Comparison*, pp. xiii–xvii. London: Routledge.

Tolley, T. 1992. 'Music in the circle of Sir William Jones: a contribution to the history of Haydn's early reputation'. *Music and Letters* 73(4):525–50.

Towers, J. 1784. *Observations on the Rights and Duty of Juries in Trials for Libels*. London: Debrett.

Vallancey, C. 1772. *An Essay on the Antiquity of the Irish Language: Being a Collation of the Irish with the Punic Language*. Dublin: S. Powell.

Woodfield, I. 2000. *Music of the Raj: A Social and Economic History of Music in Late Eighteenth Century Anglo-Indian Society*. Cambridge: Cambridge University Press.

Zon, B. 2006. "'From very acute and plausible" to "curiously misinterpreted": Sir William Jones's "On the musical modes of the Hindus" (1792) and its reception in later musical treatises'. In M.J. Franklin (ed.), *Romantic Representations of British India*, pp. 197–219. London: Routledge.

——— 2007. *Representing Non-Western Music in Nineteenth Century Britain*. Rochester, NY: University of Rochester Press.

4

Wales in miniature

Iorwerth C. Peate and the Welsh Folk Museum

Elen Phillips

Introduction

St Fagans National Museum of History, on the outskirts of Cardiff, is a unique resource. Home to Wales's national collections of history and archaeology, the museum holds in one place an indoor gallery and learning complex, over forty relocated historic buildings, archaeological constructs and a collections centre – all enclosed within 100 acres of formal gardens and parkland. With over 600,000 visitors a year and a free-entry policy, St Fagans is Wales's most popular heritage attraction and its largest provider of learning outside the classroom. It is also the second most visited open-air museum in Europe (Thomas and Williams 2015).

In 2012, the museum embarked on a transformational £30 million redevelopment. Billed as the Making History project, this led to a complete redesign of its galleries, resulting in new exhibition spaces and improved learning facilities (Amgueddfa Cymru 2013). Participation became the underlying principle of the project; a desire to work collaboratively to create history with rather than for the people of Wales. In the planning and delivery phase, over 200 external organizations informed and co-created gallery content. Completed in late 2018, the project embodied more than bricks and mortar; it propelled the museum on a journey towards becoming an active and activist organization, one with greater community agency at the core of its work (Hughes and Phillips 2019). For this, it received the Art Fund Museum of the Year award in 2019 (Brown 2019).

Revisiting founding principles

The creation of St Fagans in 1948 as Britain's first national open-air museum was viewed as a symbolic achievement in the post-war reconstruction of Wales. The museum's current shift towards an activist agenda is traceable back to this period, and the values and vision of its first curator, Iorwerth Cyfeiliog Peate (1901–1982). An outspoken political and social commentator, lifelong pacifist and poet, Peate was a member of staff at the National Museum of Wales from 1927 until his retirement in 1971. Under his direction, the Welsh Folk Museum (as St Fagans was then known) took its inspiration from Skansen open-air museum in Sweden and embraced folk culture, and its intersections with anthropology, as the dominant disciplinary lens through which communities were to be studied and represented in its collection.

This chapter examines Peate's curatorial legacy through the collecting and recording activities he practised and implemented during his lengthy career at the National Museum of Wales. It will consider how his academic and political interest in folk culture assumed a leading role in shaping his museological practice and ultimately the representational displays of Welsh life constructed at St Fagans under his tenure. Museums, as commentators have observed, are rarely as neutral and objective as their rhetoric might suggest (Janes and Sandell 2019). The ideological outlook and biases of curators, consciously or otherwise, are central to the construction of knowledge in the museum context. In the case of Peate, along with other prominent Welsh nationalists of the interwar years, he advocated 'the fashioning of rural, agricultural Wales as the cornerstone of the nation' (Bohata 2004:81). He promoted the concept of an inclusive *gwerin* or 'folk' (Peate 1941) and considered folk museums to have restorative, identity-affirming abilities. Influenced by the Scandinavian model, Peate imagined St Fagans, therefore, as a museum capable of preserving and invigorating a culture he perceived to be under threat:

> Politics, religion, music, drama, dances, crafts, art, architecture, agriculture, dress, furniture – all these are found in the Scandinavian folk museums. This is an attempt to bring the museum to the core of all life, banishing completely the old idea that it is merely a repository for the dry bones of a dead culture ... As a picture of the past and a mirror of the present, it [the Welsh Folk Museum] will be an inspiration for our country's future: from it will radiate energy to vitalize Welsh life.
>
> (Peate 1948:35, 57)

Formative years

Iorwerth Cyfeiliog Peate was born and raised in Llanbryn-Mair, Montgomeryshire – an area once celebrated for its radical nineteenth-century Nonconformist traditions of pacifism and independent thought. The 'Llanbryn-Mair tradition' was often cited by Peate in his writings as being at the core of his world view (Peate 1976), a sentiment retold by those who knew and collaborated with him. Trefor M. Owen (1926–2015), his predecessor at St Fagans, said of the community: 'This is the rock whence he was hewn. This is the tradition which created him' (quoted in WFM 1979:13). Peate's father and grandfather were village carpenters and wheelwrights – a heritage which impacted greatly on his ideology, but a career path which he, despite an apparent sense of guilt, did not aspire to follow (Owen 2009).

In 1918, he entered the University College of Wales, Aberystwyth, and graduated three years later in colonial history, geography and anthropology. Throughout his years at Aberystwyth, Peate was influenced by Herbert John Fleure (1877–1969), who in 1917 was endowed the Gregynog chair of geography and anthropology. A native of Guernsey, since 1905 Fleure had dedicated himself to the exploration of racial types in Wales, based on cranial measurements and physical characteristics (Fleure and Davies 1958). No doubt encouraged by his mentor, Peate subsequently conducted a study exploring the links between dialect and racial types in the Dyfi valley, for which he was awarded an master's degree (Peate 1924). Although Fleure's geographical and anthropological perspectives would continue to influence Peate's thinking until the early 1930s, his interest in folklife and its associated material culture was cultivated during his postgraduate years, thanks in part to summers spent in the company of the Norwegian linguist Alf Sommerfelt, who in the early 1920s studied the dialect of Peate's home district of Cyfeiliog.

The National Museum of Wales

Peate's forty-four-year career at the National Museum of Wales began in April 1927 on his appointment as a qualified assistant in the Department of Archaeology. His first task was to catalogue and classify the Welsh Bygones collection – an assortment of around two thousand specimens which had been transferred to the National Museum from the Cardiff Municipal Museum in 1912. The bulk of this collection had been amassed by prominent Welsh folklorists and antiquarians of the late nineteenth and early twentieth century, with donations from the likes of Glamorgan historian Thomas Christopher Evans (1846–1918) and the artist Thomas Henry Thomas (1839–1915). A companion guide to the collection was subsequently published, entitled the *Guide to the Collection of Welsh Bygones* (Peate 1929), the first museological volume of its kind to be published in Britain. While it was Peate who authored the catalogue and commentary, the book's introduction was written by Dr (later Sir) Cyril Fox (1882–1967), the director of the National Museum of Wales. Peate would later comment in his autobiography that it was Fox who coined the subtitle 'a descriptive account of old-fashioned life in Wales' – much to his annoyance (Peate 1976:106). In a paper published on his retirement, he recalled:

> In carrying out this task, it became obvious to me that the small collection
> (approximately two thousand objects) should be expanded into a truly
> national folk collection representing every possible aspect of Welsh culture
> and tradition.
>
> (Peate 1971:161)

Peate began the work of expanding and developing the Bygones collection in 1928/9, encouraged at directorate level by Cyril Fox. Formerly the museum's keeper of archaeology, the temptation exists to present Fox and Peate as opposites – the British/English archaeologist versus the unwavering Welsh-speaking nationalist. However, as Alexandra Ward argues, 'In practice their individual and combined approach to folk material culture was more complex and engaged in a continual process of convergence and divergence as differing ideologies, politics and values were expressed' (Ward 2008:211).

In the *Guide to the Collection of Welsh Bygones*, both Fox's and Peate's contributions reveal their anxieties about the future of Welsh crafts and the impact of increasing levels of mechanization and materialism on rural communities. Fox wrote:

> It may be hoped that the growing appreciation among Welsh people of
> the native social organization may help to maintain these and other crafts
> … the existence of which in the future must, having regard to present-day
> tendencies, be regarded as precarious.
>
> (Fox 1929:xvi)

Echoing the sentiments of Fox, Peate argued:

> Anyone who knows the real Wales well can estimate the importance of
> these craftsmen in the life of their communities, and with the decline of the
> demand for their services comes the disintegration of small societies of folk
> which are of real value in a civilised state … The mass-production resulting
> from the Industrial Revolution in squeezing the rural craftsman out of

existence has also, it is more than probable, impoverished the spiritual life of
the people.

(Peate 1929:1, 2)

For Peate, as indicated by the language of this passage, the rural craftsman
represented the 'true' and 'authentic' spirit of a nation – an ideology that was
central to his image of the *gwerin* and would underpin his curatorial practice
throughout his career.

Peate's quest to transform the Bygones collection into a 'national folk
collection' gathered momentum during the 1930s – a decade which saw a
series of management and governance decisions pave the way to transforming
the collection into a self-contained folk museum. In 1932, the Sub-Department
of Folk Culture and Industries was established within the existing Department
of Archaeology, with Peate assuming the role of assistant keeper in charge.
Two years later, following a benchmarking visit to eighteen folk museums in
Scandinavia at the turn of the decade, Cyril Fox announced that a national
open-air museum in Wales was 'educationally, culturally and historically a
vital and urgent need' (cited in Ward 2008:242). In 1936, Peate became keeper
of an independent department, the Department of Folk Culture – a move he
would later describe as 'an essential preliminary' to the establishment of a folk
museum for Wales (NMW 1946:7).

This rise in his curatorial standing afforded Peate the opportunity to be
in contact with European colleagues who were also undertaking pioneering
research in the fields of folklore and folklife studies (Peate 1971). They included
Seamus O'Duilearga (director of the Irish Folklore Commission) and the
Swedish folklorists Carl von Sydow (University of Lund) and Åke Campbell
(University of Uppsala). During this period, Peate also met with Francis
Arthur Bather of the Natural History Museum, London. Bather was among
a group of academics and curators who had attempted to create a British
Folk Museum in the Crystal Palace in 1912 (Bassett 1982). Peate became
increasingly interested in his notion of the 'past in the present', as made explicit
in his bilingual booklet, *Amgueddfeydd Gwerin/Folk Museums*, in which he
quotes extensively from Bather's writings:

It is not enough … to show and preserve the things that have been; it is
necessary to trace their organic continuity with the things that are and the
things that shall be. An object that has once been used, and formed indeed
a necessary part of the domestic economy of some human household,
when placed behind the glass on the shelf of a museum, becomes a mere
curio … It is time for us to get rid of the idea that a museum is a place
for the preservation only of that which is dead. It may be well to preserve

objects because they represent the past that has utterly vanished – objects that may gratify a more or less intelligent curiosity but can never be of any practical use to human beings. But it is of more importance that a museum should preserve objects capable of yielding some lesson of use for our own time. And still more important is the preservation of arts, industries, and customs, which from their truly national character, afford the firmest foundation for the national life of the future.

(Bather, quoted in Peate 1948:11–12)

The independent status of a newly established Department of Folk Culture gave Peate the opportunity to experiment with contemporary collecting methodologies, in addition to exercising increasing creative control over the values and interpretations ascribed to the material in his care. In December 1937, he published a questionnaire on folk culture which, following a public appeal, was sent to 493 respondents across Wales (NMW 1937). The questionnaire was divided into four sections, each containing sub-themes for participants to provide information about their district. The sections followed the classification system he had devised while cataloguing the Bygones collection:

- domestic life – house types; cooking customs; furniture; tableware; ornaments; lighting; dairying; laundering; dress;
- corporate life – civil development; ecclesiastical material; fighting services; transport;
- cultural life – education; entertainment, sports and games; folklore and customs; institutions;
- crafts and industries – agriculture; corn-milling; smithing; crafts in general.

Once again, the questionnaire's introduction was written by Cyril Fox:

This questionnaire has been prepared in the hope that persons in each parish in Wales will study the life of that parish on the lines indicated therein and will import information to the Department of Folk Culture in the National Museum of Wales. The pamphlet indicates the direction in which the Welsh public can help in the work of this Department and its National Museum … Photographs and drawings will be gladly received … It is hoped, moreover, that correspondents, once they have established contact, will keep in constant touch with the Museum so that the Department is kept well-informed of any developments (e.g., the demolition of old houses, the sale of furniture, implements etc.) which are relevant to its work.

(ibid.:1)

Such an approach to collecting indicates that Peate was an early advocate of a dialogical museum model – one which placed community knowledge at the heart of its practice. In preparing the questionnaire, Peate was effectively asking those taking part to become regular informants, to use their community intelligence to assist the museum in its objectives. Although the number of returns accessioned into the collection failed to constitute a substantial body of work, the initiative did spur on similar, more successful, collecting drives during the second half of the century (Lloyd Hughes 1979:159–60). Questionnaires and answer books on various topics, initiated by the museum, as well as external organizations – such as the Committee of Welsh Calendar Customs (1946), Anglesey Rural Council (1957) and the Agricultural Section of the Guild of Graduates of the University of Wales (late 1930s) – today form a significant part of the museum's manuscript archive.

The Welsh Folk Museum

The formation of the Department of Folk Culture in 1936 was undoubtedly a significant milestone in Peate's career and served to boost the museological status of folk culture within the National Museum of Wales. However, having received the kudos of leading a full department, it was not until after the Second World War that the long-awaited campaign to establish a folk museum for Wales was realized. In March 1946, the Earl of Plymouth donated St Fagans Castle with 20 acres of land (later increasing to 98 acres) to the National Museum for this purpose. In September of that year, Peate spent a month in Scandinavia as part of a delegation invited by the Museum Association of Sweden. During the trip, which he described as the most memorable of his career, he was able to see first-hand the theories of Bather and others in practice. He recalled visiting Skansen, Maihaugen in Lillehammer and Bygødy, near Oslo, in his customary, over-expressive prose:

> I felt that I had consciously conquered Time and had returned to a distant
> past to find revealed to me the spirit of far-off ages whose mystery I had
> never expected to penetrate ... The living past of Norway took shape before
> me and I felt that I had understood its traditions and the very foundations of
> its society.
>
> (Peate 1948:28–9)

On his retirement, he described the Scandinavian visit in far more pragmatic terms: 'I was able to study the content, the lay-out and the administration of national, regional and local folk museums, to admire virtues and assess weaknesses' (Peate 1971:163).

The Welsh Folk Museum opened its gates on 1 July 1948, with Peate as its keeper (later curator) in charge. Accounts of the museum's history invariably (mistakenly) refer to Peate as its founder, regardless of others, including Cyril Fox, who had been equally instrumental in its creation. However, it was Peate who ultimately turned the vision into action. As Thomas and Burrow put it, 'While the museum had opened the door, it was Peate who stepped through it' (Thomas and Burrow 2014:242). He set out his blueprint for St Fagans in a series of brochures, pamphlets and public lectures leading up to the opening in 1948:

> The aim will be to form in the Folk Museum as complete a picture of the
> Welsh past as it is possible, to create 'Wales in miniature' where the visitor
> can wander … and see not only the Welsh way of life but the variations in
> and the continuity of our culture.
>
> (NMW 1946:11)

Peate conceived of the new museum in three parts, each with a different function. The castle area and its formal gardens was to illustrate the life of the Welsh gentry; a main museum block with galleries, a lecture room and library was to be a national centre for the study of Welsh folklife; and an open-air section was to be for re-erected buildings. Each of these elements was integral to his vision; through them he imagined a museum at the heart of the national discourse in Wales – a 'social centre for national movements and conferences of all kinds' (Peate 1948:57).

The subject and audience of the Welsh Folk Museum was clearly stated in its name. As for who constituted the 'folk' or *gwerin* – as previously mentioned – Peate promoted the concept of inclusivity:

> Folk culture … as a museum subject – and this needs repeated emphasis –
> is concerned not with the life of a class or stratum but with the life of the
> complete society, rural and urban, high and low degree, master and man.
> It is a study of the mental, spiritual, and material struggle of the whole
> community: none is excluded. To equate 'folk' with a 'lower class' is a
> fundamental misconception.
>
> (Peate 1941:46)

Peate was unwavering in his 'defence' of folk culture throughout his career, both in definition and theory, and stubbornly refused to embrace new research ideas found in adjacent academic disciplines. He strongly disliked the term 'ethnology' favoured in Scandinavia. Praising the work of A.T. Lucas, director of the National Museum of Ireland, he exalted: 'not for him the grandiose terminology of those ethnologists who lose sight of people in the fogs of the Academian grove' (quoted in Owen 1998:xii). He was equally critical of sociology ('that pseudo-science') and of the community studies conducted by Alwyn D. Rees, E.G. Bowen and colleagues at Aberystwyth. Reviewing the study of Welsh rural communities written by four of Rees's former students (Jenkins *et al.* 1960), Peate declared that he 'doubted the value of such studies – in Timbuktu or Wales' (quoted in Rees 1961).

Elected president of Section H of the British Association for the Advancement of Science in 1958, Peate used his inaugural presidential address at Glasgow once again to uphold his trademark views on folk culture. In it, he dismissed the American anthropologist Robert Redfield's use of the term 'folk society' to denote a community small in scale, isolated and homogeneous in race and custom (Peate 1959:97; see also Owen 1971:19) and reiterated his holistic definition of folk culture, albeit with a caveat not explicitly mentioned in his earlier texts: 'The study of folk life, as I see it, is the study of life of communities and nations which are comparatively unaffected by a high degree of industrialization' (Peate 1959:100).

This shift in definition to exclude industrial communities became visibly obvious as the Welsh Folk Museum developed and expanded during the 1950s and 1960s. Peate's choice as to which buildings should be re-erected at St Fagans produced a vision of Wales which reflected his own ideological outlook and his formative years in rural Montgomeryshire. The first buildings to be moved to the museum were farmhouses, craft workshops, barns, mills and a rural chapel. The pioneering sentiment of the 'nation in miniature' was displaced by the belief that the museum's role was to defend and promote rural communities and their values. To paraphrase Rhiannon Mason, the museum became engaged in not what constituted Welsh life, but more in the representation of what had disappeared from it (Mason 2007:162–3).

Peate's campaign of preservation and revival took on a new urgency with the development of a sound archive at the museum. Echoing the Scandinavian museologists and linguists who had inspired his thinking, he had always stressed the need to collect oral traditions as well as material culture. As he stated in his autobiography, 'a plough is not enough without knowing all the dialectal names for its parts' (Peate 1976:152). In October 1957, following the appointment of a dialectologist to its staff, the museum embarked on the systematic recording of Welsh oral traditions and dialects. The creation of this post represented one of the first museum appointments in Britain to be solely concerned with the collecting of oral testimony (Kavanagh 2000:63). This ground-breaking fieldwork followed a radio appeal on the BBC Welsh Home Service by Griffith John Williams (1892–1963) for public donations to purchase £2,000 worth of audio equipment for the planned recording programme. The following passage is a transcription of part of that appeal:

> We have, in St Fagans, one of the half dozen best national collections in the world. This is a great achievement. But a folk museum must illustrate not only the material side of life and culture, but also activities of the mind and spirit. Therefore, another important task must be undertaken. Welsh oral traditions must be collected; tales and local legends; customs and beliefs; plant lore; animal lore; proverbial sayings ... This, of course, includes the Welsh language itself: the language as it is spoken in every part of Wales; the vocabulary of all the dialects; and the technical terms used by craftsmen, farmers, miners, quarrymen ... I know you will agree with me when I say that it is not only a matter of great importance but also of extreme urgency. In many parts of the eastern counties only very old people can speak Welsh. The death of the last Welsh speaker in the village (and I have known many of those) is like the loss of a valuable manuscript which contains material that cannot be found anywhere else ... This material must be collected now, and thousands of recordings must be made throughout Wales ... If we Welshmen do not give the Welsh Folk Museum this opportunity, we will be severely criticised by future generations.
>
> (Williams 1958)

The funds raised together with a grant from the Gulbenkian Foundation enabled the museum to purchase a Land Rover, a portable tape recorder and a device known as the 'vibroverter' to record informants in farmhouses without electricity (Thomas 2005). Most of the initial recordings were conducted by Vincent H. Phillips, a dialectologist previously based at University College of Wales, Cardiff. The museum's annual reports for the period 1957 to 1960 testify to the magnitude of the task:

> The national 'Survey of Oral Traditions', begun in late 1957, proves to be one of the most important projects undertaken by the Folk Museum, but the vastness of the work which ought to be completed within the next few years becomes daily more apparent. It is work of a desperate urgency since word-forms and intonations disappear far more quickly and completely than the more solid material evidence of culture. It is small wonder, therefore, that the great folk museums of Scandinavia, engaged in similar work, employ large staffs of research workers for this purpose. Mr Vincent H. Phillips ... has had, apart from the co-operation of several part-time voluntary

collectors whose assistance is gratefully acknowledged, to work alone in the field ... It is obvious that the staff is too small for the task before it.

(NMW 1960:38)

In 1963, the Department of Oral Traditions and Dialects was formed, a move which Peate described as the 'crowning glory' of the Welsh Folk Museum (Peate 1976:152). Graduate research assistants were employed to support Phillips in his work, resulting in the collection of a broader range of subject matter, beyond language and dialect. These included domestic life, folk tales and narratives, traditional music, sports and games, vernacular architecture, death and burial customs, love and marriage, traditional medicine and seasonal customs. A caravan was purchased to enable the museum's researchers to spend extended periods out in the field, but despite the holistic approach advocated by Peate, those engaged in recording oral testimony did not routinely collect its associated material culture, and vice versa. Beth Thomas, a sociolinguist who joined the department in 1977 and later became keeper of social history, suggests that St Fagans in the 1960s and 1970s existed as a combination of research institute and museum, and that the resulting disconnect between departments engaged in their own fields of research meant that the 'situation did not work as it might have done' (cited in Thomas 2005).

Conclusion: curatorial legacy

Iorwerth Peate retired as head of the Welsh Folk Museum in February 1971, having lived 'above the shop' in a converted flat in St Fagans Castle since 1948. His ashes, along with those of his wife Nansi, are buried behind Penrhiw Chapel, the small whitewashed Unitarian chapel rebuilt in the museum's grounds in 1956. In the years since his death in 1982, Peate's methods of curatorship have come under intense scrutiny, particularly from within the labour history movement in Wales. For historians, such as Dai Smith and Hywel Francis, the museum presented a past devoid of politics and dissent, an 'atrophied and hackneyed' (Dicks 2003:156–8) version of history which privileged rural culture over urban and industrial development (Mason 2007:155–7). As recently as 2007, the museologist Gaynor Kavanagh delivered an institutional critique of the museum for its collective airbrushing of difficult histories. Using imagery that clearly referenced Peate's representational ideology, she argued:

The traditional Welsh kitchen was also home to traditional Welsh abuse, poverty, hunger, and illiteracy ... [It] can be argued that the traditional Welsh anything is in fact a fantasy of grand proportions. The term

'traditional' is a euphemism for denial ... [The National Museum of Wales]
clings to a singular narrative that fails to resonate, that deals in cliché rather
than experiences. It never becomes compelling because it gets no further
than a neat and anodyne fantasy. Better to stay silent and say nothing, than
to remember and speak in ways that depart from established practices, the
practices of tradition, the practices of denial; the things that hurt.

(Kavanagh, quoted in William 2007:213)

In response, Eurwyn Wiliam, then deputy-director general of Amgueddfa
Cymru/National Museum Wales, questioned the extent to which any other
national museum in Britain had fully grappled with these issues, but conceded
that the challenge Kavanagh had given the museum 'is a real one and one that
it must address' (quoted in William 2007:218–9).

Of course, such challenges are not unique to St Fagans and its folk
museum inheritance. As Rhiannon Mason suggests, museums that claim
to represent the 'nation in miniature' with 'universalizing statements' are
inevitably fraught with difficulties, because 'no museum can possibly capture
the entirety of a nation' (Mason 2007:82). However, as she argues, they can
function as both the subject of national debates on issues around identity,
culture and politics, as well as being the physical spaces in which these debates
can occur (ibid.:150).

Fifty years on from his retirement, Peate's imprint on St Fagans remains
considerable, and in many ways his vision of a community-centred, participatory
museum still provides a touchstone against which the ongoing developments
at the museum are measured (Thomas and Williams 2015). While criticism of
the folk museum model and Peate's curatorial legacy are undoubtedly valid,
the visual and ideological museum he conceived was far from being devoid
of politics. On the contrary, St Fagans was a political statement in itself, an
'artefact' that Peate cultivated and produced; a space to be contested and
debated; a 'place for feeling as well as thinking' (Amgueddfa Cymru 2013:3).

References

Amgueddfa Cymru/National Museum of Wales. 2013. 'Sain Ffagan Amgueddfa Werin
    Cymru Project Creu Hanes/St Fagans National History Museum Making
    History Project': issuu.com/amgueddfacymru/docs/st_fagans_brochure
    (accessed 29 November 2020).
Bassett, D. 1982. 'The making of a national museum'. *Transactions of the Honourable
    Society of Cymmrodorion* 1982:153–85.
Bohata, K. 2004. *Postcolonialism Revisited: Writing Wales in English*. Cardiff:
    University of Wales Press.

Brown, M. 2019. 'Revamped St Fagans in Wales is 2019 Art Fund museum of the year'. *Guardian*, 3 July: www.theguardian.com/culture/2019/jul/03/st-fagans-history-museum-wales-wins-art-fund-museum-of-the-year-2019 (accessed 30 October 2019).

Dicks, B. 2003. *Culture on Display: The Production of Contemporary Visuality.* Maidenhead: Open University Press.

Fleure, H.J. and Davies, E. 1958. 'Physical character among Welshmen', *Journal of the Royal Anthropological Institute* 88(1):45–95.

Fox, C. 1929. 'Introduction'. In I.C. Peate (ed.), *Guide to the Collection of Welsh Bygones: A Descriptive Account of Old-fashioned Life in Wales*, pp. xiv-xvi. Cardiff: National Museum of Wales.

Hughes, S. and Phillips, E. 2019. 'From vision to action: the journey towards activism at St Fagans National Museum of History'. In R.R. Janes and R. Sandell (eds), *Museum Activism*, pp. 245–55. London: Routledge.

Janes, R.R. and Sandell, R. 2019. 'Posterity has arrived: the necessary emergence of museum activism'. R.R. Janes and R. Sandell (eds), *Museum Activism*, pp. 1–21. London: Routledge.

Jenkins, D., Jones, E., Hughes, T.J. and Owen, T.M. 1960. *Welsh Rural Communities.* Cardiff: University of Wales Press.

Kavanagh, G. 2000. *Dream Spaces: Memory and the Museum.* London: Leicester University Press.

Lloyd Hughes, A. 1979. 'Llawysgrifau Amgueddfa Werin Cymru'. *Y Traethodydd* 134(572):159–61.

Mason, R. 2007. *Museums, Nations, Identities: Wales and its National Museums.* Cardiff: University of Wales Press.

NMW (National Museum of Wales). 1937. 'Questionnaire on Welsh folk culture/ Holwyddoreg ar ddiwylliant gwerin Cymru'. Cardiff: National Museum of Wales.

——— 1946. 'St Fagans Castle: A Folk Museum for the Nation'. Cardiff: National Museum of Wales.

——— 1960. 'Annual report, National Museum of Wales 1959–60'. Cardiff: National Museum of Wales.

Owen, T.M. 1971. 'Folk life studies to-day'. *Amgueddfa: Bulletin of the National Museum of Wales* 8:19–26.

——— 1998. 'Rhagymadrodd'. In I.C. Peate, *Diwylliant Gwerin Cymru,* 3rd edn, pp. xi–xvi. Denbigh: Gwasg Gee.

——— 2009. 'Peate, Iorwerth Cyfeiliog (1901–1982), curator of the Welsh Folk Museum, 1948–1971, scholar and poet'. *Dictionary of Welsh Biography*: biography.wales/article/s6-PEAT-CYF-1901# (accessed 30 October 2019).

Peate, I.C. 1924. 'The Dyfi basin: its people, antiquities, dialects, folklore and
place-names, studied in correlation to one another, with a special
aim of ascertaining what degree of correlation there may be between
physical anthropology, archaeology, and dialect distribution'. MA thesis.
Aberystwyth: University College of Wales.

——— 1929. *Guide to the Collection of Welsh Bygones: A Descriptive Account of Old-
fashioned Life in Wales*. Cardiff: National Museum of Wales.

——— 1933. *Y Crefftwr yng Nghymru: Rhagymadrodd i Hanes Crefft*. Aberystwyth:
Gwasg Aberystwyth.

——— 1941. 'The place of folk culture in the museum'. *Museums Journal* 41(3):45–50.

——— 1945. *Welsh Crafts and Industries*. Cardiff: National Museum of Wales.

——— 1948. *Amgueddfeydd Gwerin/Folk Museums*. Cardiff: University of Wales
Press.

——— 1959. 'The study of folk life: and its part in the defence of civilisation'. *Gwerin*
2(3):97–109.

——— 1971. 'The Welsh Folk Museum'. In S. Williams (ed.), *Glamorgan Historian*, vol.
7, pp. 161–72. Cowbridge: D. Brown and Sons.

——— 1976. *Rhwng Dau Fyd: Darn o hunangofiant*. Denbigh: Gwasg Gee.

Rees, A.D. 1961. 'Ysgolheigion a gwerthoedd'. *Baner ac Amserau Cymru*, 23 February.

Thomas, B. 2005. 'A special responsibility: folk life archives at the Museum of Welsh
Life'. Paper presented at the conference 'Dialect and folk life studies in
Britain: the Leeds Archive of Vernacular Culture in its context', University
of Leeds, 19 March.

Thomas, B. and Burrow, S. 2014. 'Changing St Fagans: what would Iorwerth Peate
say?' In N. Kristović (ed.), *Founding Fathers: International Yearbook*, pp.
229–50. Belgrade: Sirogojno Open-Air Museum.

Thomas, B. and Williams, N. 2015. 'Moving towards cultural democracy:
redeveloping St Fagans'. *Transactions of the Honourable Society of
Cymmrodorion* 21:140–45.

Ward, A. 2008. 'Archaeology, heritage, and identity: the creation and development of
a national museum in Wales'. PhD thesis. Cardiff: Cardiff University.

WFM (Welsh Folk Museum). 1979. 'Presentation of the Cymmrodorion Medal:
Iorwerth Cyfeiliog Peate'. Cardiff: National Museum of Wales.

William, E. 2007. 'To teach the world about Wales and the Welsh people about their
fatherland: 100 years of the National Museum of Wales'. *Transactions of the
Honourable Society of Cymmrodorion* 14:213–27.

Williams, G.J. 1958. 'The week's good cause radio appeal'. BBC Welsh Home Service,
2 March. St Fagans National Museum of History, Sound Archive recording
71/1.

5

Anthropological perspectives on religion in Wales

FIONA BOWIE

Introduction: representations

The poem 'A Welsh testament' by one of Wales's most famous and famously taciturn poets, R.S. Thomas (1913–2000), offers a glimpse of themes that run through the anthropology of religion in Wales. As highlighted in the Introduction to this volume, the complexity of Welsh identity and the importance of place provide an intertwined thread linking a range of studies and approaches to the social anthropologies of the Welsh. In this chapter I provide chronological examples of the ways in which these two themes have been reprised, using R.S. Thomas's poem as a prelude, and the poet as a proxy anthropologist.

Thomas begins his poem (Thomas 1993) with a depiction of the landscape, the weather, the Welsh language and Welsh history. We hear the voice of a Welsh hill farmer. This man did not choose the Welsh tongue, the cold wet weather or the restricted and monotonous life of a shepherd. English tourists see him as the 'exotic other' representing an imagined simplicity and authenticity. There is an 'us' and 'them', the non-Welsh speaker with a different word for 'heaven', a necessary counterpoint to the narrator.

All right, I was Welsh. Does it matter?
I spoke a tongue that was passed on
To me in the place I happened to be,
A place huddled between grey walls
Of cloud for at least half the year.

Visitors to Wales value his situatedness in the landscape, a landscape that includes a Christian inheritance in which the language of the chapel, with its black bound Bible and black clad preachers, play a leading role. But God, in whatever language, is 'too big to be nailed to the wall of a stone chapel'.

> Even God had a Welsh name:
> He spoke to him in the old language;
> He was to have a peculiar care
> For the Welsh people. History showed us
> He was too big to be nailed to the wall
> Of a stone chapel, yet still we crammed him
> Between the boards of a black book.

The farmer is self-aware and aware of the gaze of the tourists, of their differently situated perspectives, of the projected images that he represents and of the rather more mundane realities of his life.

> I saw them stand
> By the thorn hedges, watching me string
> The far flocks on a shrill whistle.
> And always there was their eyes; strong
> Pressure on me: You are Welsh, they said;
> Speak to us so; keep your fields free
> Of the smell of petrol, the loud roar
> Of hot tractors; we must have peace
> And quietness.

The poem plays with notions of looking and seeing, landscape and expectation. Writing on visualism and landscape in Normandy, northern France, Judith Okely (2001) makes reference to Johannes Fabian's (1983) critique of the priority given to the visual in anthropological knowledge at the expense of other dimensions of experience. While acknowledging this bias, Okely argues that there are ways of understanding the visual that incorporate other senses and avoid abstraction. The English tourist in Thomas's poem may look at the landscape, or even see it, but in a detached and often romanticized manner, through the lens of mythic literature, clichés and landscape artists. Both the Normandy peasant farmer and Welsh shepherd, on the other hand, see the land in a way that 'embraces the whole body, neither vision alone nor the disparate senses. The whole body is the means to understand and resonate with the world' (Okely 2001:104).

Okely argues that 'To look at the landscape as detached outsider risks not seeing it as lived, worked, and sensed by its inhabitants' (ibid.:104). In R.S. Thomas's poem, the watching outsiders' gaze places the farmer as part of the visual landscape; they want to preserve the vision, to hear the Welsh language, as part of a rural tableaux. The harshness of the work, the exposure to the weather and the working necessity of noisy, smelly tractors, are understood by the poet as part of the total lived aesthetic, the landscape as experienced by the often nameless individuals who live in and shape it through their physical engagement with it. In 'A Welsh testament', the poet, like the anthropologist, places himself in a position of privileged knowing, able to both look at and see the landscape, to understand the difference between the detached gaze and experiential knowing.

R.S. Thomas mentions the physical characteristics of the farmer, 'My high cheek-bones, my length of skull, / Drew them as to a rare portrait, / By a dead master'. Thomas might be speaking of himself here, with his own pronounced high cheek bones and long head. The experience of the scene set out by the poet is coloured by knowledge of a Welsh artistic tradition of rugged mountain landscapes with scattered stone cottages, hardy quarry workers, lone shepherds and their dogs by the likes of Kyffin Williams and Stephen John Owen.

In the same way, both Judith Okely and the elderly French peasants among whom she conducted fieldwork could not but help but view the Normandy landscape through the eyes of French impressionist painters as well as their own. Perhaps R.S. Thomas also had in mind the early research of H.J. Fleure into the morphology of the Welsh, or Eric Sunderland measuring the heads of neighbours for his doctorate in anthropology in his hometown of Ammanford in South Wales in the 1950s.[1] No view of the landscape is innocent and unformed; we bring our experience and expectations, hopes and prejudices,

---

1   H.J. Fleure in Aberystwyth had a long-standing interest in physical anthropology, while avoiding crude racial stereotypes. His influential article on the geographical distribution of anthropological types in Wales (Fleure and James 1916) illustrated Fleure's insistence on seeing human evolution, landscape and culture as interrelated parts of the study of 'man'. The German/American anthropologist Franz Boas measured the skulls of New York immigrants in the 1930s, demonstrating that there is a fluid relationship between physical features and notions of 'race' (Boas 1940), but it remained a popular means of distinguishing peoples until advances in haematology enabled blood group analysis to largely replace craniology, - shift reflected in Sunderland's later work in biological anthropology (Roberts and Sunderland 1973). Even the name of the discipline changed from 'physical' to 'biological' in the 1970s/1980s.

familiarity and unfamiliarity to our knowing and sensing of the world around us.

Thomas was an Anglican clergyman as well as a poet, a first-language English-speaker who learnt Welsh in adulthood, becoming a passionate Welsh nationalist. He was a disappointed romantic who sought to preserve a Welsh-medium rural way of life in an unspoilt landscape, while being aware that many of his parishioners were keen to escape just such an existence. He abhorred machinery and 'gadgets', which for him symbolized 'English' commercialization, distracting people from communitarian and spiritual values. His austerity and exaggerated poverty would not have been out of place in a penitential medieval Celtic monastery. Born in the capital city of Cardiff in the south of Wales, Thomas spent most of his life in largely English-speaking areas of north-east Wales before moving further west to the Llyn Peninsula, where he could immerse himself in Welsh-medium culture. With his pacifism and staunch defence of Welsh language and culture, Thomas was a man of the margins and of paradox, but reflexively so.

An anthropological take on Thomas's poem 'A Welsh testament' might point to its 'recursive' structure. In mathematics and logic, recursion refers to a proposition from which a set of rules can be derived, which are then applied to other cases (the recursive step).[2] Within anthropology, recursion has been used in a slightly different but related manner, both to question the original assumptions on which categories are constructed and to allow new concepts of truth to emerge (Holbraad 2012). In presenting representational categories such as the rural Welsh-speaking native and the English-speaking incomer, Thomas also undermines them. The farmer steps out of the landscape and his assigned role. Thomas allows us to experience his unhappiness with the weather, with his drab and repetitive work, his frustration with the smallness of chapel Christianity with its attempts to confine Christ to a book. Thomas's farmer has been assigned a role that he no longer wishes to play; he represents a concept of race or tribe that holds little meaning. Questions of authenticity and representation are thrown into confusion by the encounter between the farmer and the tourist, something new occurs – a conceptual door is opened through which either may choose to step.[3]

---

2   Classic examples include the Fibonacci sequence or fractals. A series of Russian dolls or the Droste effect – an image in which an image of the original appears to be repeated on a smaller and smaller scale – also exhibit recursion.

3   For a concise description of recursive anthropology in the wider context of the 'ontological turn', see Heywood (2017).

I never wanted the drab role
Life assigned me, an actor playing
To the past's audience upon a stage
Of earth and stone; the absurd label
Of birth, of race hanging askew
About my shoulders. I was in prison
Until you came; your voice was a key
Turning in the enormous lock
Of hopelessness. Did the door open
To let me out or yourselves in?

The irony of the quintessential Welsh-speaking farmer, the *cymro cymraeg*, depicted through the medium of English may be a further recursive step, questioning the categories of Welsh versus English, Welsh-speaker, English-speaker and English-speaking Welsh, insider and outsider. It is the English, or English-speaking, tourists who are essentialized, assigned assumed attitudes and opinions. We do not hear their voices, but they exist as a cypher for the shepherd (or poet) to question his own identity and situatedness in a place. It is not clear what new truths emerge, other than to warn the reader that easy assumptions concerning race, identity, place, language and religion are easily undermined and can dissolve like the mist as you approach them. There are many scholarly accounts of the origins of the Welsh (see e.g. Watkin 1994), but they fail to capture the interplay of place, language, genes, culture, identity, exclusion and belonging that go to make up any people, the Welsh included. R.S. Thomas in a few terse verses initiates a conversation concerning birth and place, religion, language, personhood and what it might mean to be Welsh.

Stepping back in time we find one of the earliest representations of the Welsh, their customs and beliefs, in the *Annals* of the Roman historian and senator Tacitus (56 CE–120 CE). In his dramatic account of the meeting between the Roman forces and Druids in around the year 57 CE, Tacitus viewed these early Britons with the eye of an outsider; these natives, driven to their last retreat on the island of Anglesey (Ynys Môn), were most certainly 'other' to the 'civilized' Roman:

In the style of Furies, in robes of deathly black and with dishevelled hair, they brandished their torches; while a circle of Druids, lifting their hands to heaven and showering imprecations, struck the troops with such an awe at the extraordinary spectacle that, as though their limbs were paralysed, they exposed their bodies to wounds without an attempt at movement. (Tacitus, Annals 14:30)

While there were armed warriors among the defending British forces, it was the druid priests with their uplifted arms, shouting curses at the invaders, and the wild-haired women in their black robes bearing torches that struck fear and awe into the Romans. The soldiers had to be reminded that their adversaries were only barbarians, men with inferior weapons and crazy women. Once they had gained their composure, the Romans massacred men, women and children and threw them onto the funeral pyres lit by their own torches. To complete the victory, they sought to extinguish the spiritual force of the Britons by destroying the druids' sacred oak groves, smashing their temples and killing indiscriminately the remaining inhabitants and refugees on the island. The only two religions the Romans attempted to destroy were Christianity and the religion of the druids. What happened in time, however, was the emergence of a Romano-British culture, and the merging of Christianity with elements of the pre-Christian druidic religion in ways that have continued to resonate down the centuries.

Transformations

The Lives of the medieval Welsh saints are replete with stories that illustrate the imaginative transformation of the druidic priest into a Christian hero. St Beuno, for example, was a seventh-century abbot, said to have been born in Berriew in Powys in the late sixth century. After his ordination into the priesthood at the monastery at Bangor in Gwynedd, Beuno became a Christian missionary in what were still largely pagan areas of east and north-west Wales. He died in Clynnog Fawr on the north coast of the Llyn Peninsula in 640 CE.[4] The Middle Welsh fourteenth-century account of the life of Beuno is said to be based on a lost Latin original (Sims-Williams 2018). It gives us insights into political relations between the Welsh and English and between various Welsh princedoms. It also presents the saint as having druidic qualities. St Beuno made generous use of curses when he wanted something or when crossed by his enemies. He could foretell the future and read the auguries of birds. Most impressive of all, Beuno had the power to restore the dead to life, most notably his niece, St Gwenfrewi (Winifred), who had been beheaded by Caradog, a scorned suitor. The blood from her severed head sanctified the ground, giving rise to a healing well, St Winifred's Well in Holywell, where the revivified Winifred went on to found a convent. St Beuno called on heaven to curse

---

4   Possibly two individuals have been conflated, one associated with Holywell in north-east Wales and one with Clynnog Fawr in the north-west. The historical accuracy or inaccuracy of the accounts is not under discussion here, but rather their ability to represent a transition and melding of pre-Christian druid tropes with Christian themes. See Wolcott (n.d.).

Caradog and according to legend he fell dead on the spot and was swallowed up by the ground. Beuno was associated with the oak tree, which was sacred to druids. An oak tree planted over his father's grave in Powys had a branch that grew into an arch touching the ground. It was said that any Englishman (Sais) passing under the arch would die immediately, whereas a Welshman could pass unharmed.[5]

St Winifred also combines in her person and legends different traditions. There are several versions of her life, including one said to be by a contemporary, a British monk called Elerius, a later one compiled in the twelfth century by Robert Pennant, prior of Shrewsbury Abbey, and a fifteenth century version in Caxton's 1483 edition of *The Golden Legend*.[6] Winifred neither fits neatly into the virgin/martyr category of Welsh hagiography, as she was reputedly killed but then restored to life by her uncle Beuno, nor into the nun and abbess genre of Anglo-Saxon hagiography. The medieval iconography of Winifred depicts her as both abbess and martyr. A statue of St Winifred in the Lady chapel endowed by Henry VII in Westminster Abbey depicts her as both a learned figure holding a book and as a martyr, with her decapitated head beside her. The visual iconography ties in more closely with the tradition of women as educated leaders than does the literary tradition. A seal of St Winifred in Holywell, where she founded an abbey, depicts her with crozier and book (Gray 2000). The earlier traditions had Winifred travelling to Rome on pilgrimage, where she was impressed by the Benedictine form of communal monasticism. The Celtic tradition was for communities of hermits to live rather separate lives, which could include family units (the *clas* system). Winifred is said to have organized a synod of bishops on her return to Britain

---

5   Madeleine Gray (2000) cautions that in practice we know little of the pre-Roman druidic religion, and the assimilation of Christianity would have been gradual. A theological discourse of orthodoxy and authenticity versus inauthentic/syncretic and possibly heretical forms of religion is one element in the meeting and mixing of beliefs and practices. In the case of early medieval accounts of saints' lives, often written in the twelfth century to make contemporary points about relations between the Normans, Welsh and English, we have a mix of oral and written hagiographical traditions that both conform to and show some differences from those elsewhere in Europe (Guimarães 2010).

6   For an edition of the life of St Winifred, see Gregory (2015), which contains a useful summary of the various sources and versions of St Winifred's *vita* or life, and a broader discussion of Welsh hagiography. Henken (1991) shows how Welsh hagiography tends to depict male saints in a heroic mould, their birth marked by miraculous omens, whereas female saints are cast in a more domestic mould, their sanctity resting on a confrontation with male sexuality. Winifred is something of an exception to this rule, bridging the more powerful Anglo-Saxon women abbess tradition and Welsh virgin-martyr trope.

to promote the new monasticism based on the Rule of St Benedict. Her twelfth century biographer, Robert Pennant, played down this image of Winifred as an influential institutional figure in the Church, but was responsible for having her bones moved from the small community at Gwytherin, where she lived and died after Beuno's death, to Shrewsbury Abbey, thereby encouraging her cult in both Wales and England.

St Winifred draws together two countries, generally antagonistic towards one another, as well as two monastic, literary and iconographic traditions. She has elements of women from the Mabinogion with miraculous powers and, like saints Dwynwen and Melangell, had miraculous help to reject male advances and went onto found a religious community. The element of martyrdom and of the supernatural power of the severed head and its blood are suggestive of earlier Celtic head cults (Mac Cana 2020). Here, textual, archaeological and iconographic evidence converge. For the Celts, as for both Neolithic and Mesolithic peoples in Europe, the severed head was not just a symbol of victory or power, but a religious symbol with apotropaic qualities (the ability to ward off evil), and wider associations, as in Winifred's case, with holy wells and healing.

One could simply regard Welsh Christianity as syncretic, but that raises questions concerning the nature of power and who decides what is a proper, authentic or pure form of religion (Shaw and Stewart 1994). Descriptions of St Beuno and St Winifred remind us that miraculous personal powers and a relationship with natural and supernatural worlds are commonplace for Welsh holy men and women in the Middle Ages. One might think of the land rising under St David when he preached in Llandewi Brefi, as well as St Beuno's famous oak tree with its power over life and death. We find in the lives of the Celtic saints not just a melding of different iconographic, textual and cultural traditions, but a palimpsest of religious energy centred on specific locations. Luciana Guimarães (2010:71) makes the point that the Welsh hagiographers make use of long-established rules that conform to hagiographical trends elsewhere in Europe, but with a greater emphasis on control over natural phenomena. In accounts of both Welsh and Irish saints' lives we have a high proportion of incidents that evoke awe through demonstrating the saint's miraculous ability to affect nature, as well as incidents that occur in secular stories, by way of explaining natural features of the landscape in local and regional sites (ibid.:67–8). This place-based, nature-based religion presumably resonated with medieval audiences.[7]

---

7   Madeleine Gray (2011) notes that medieval accounts of the Marian shrine and holy well at Penrhys in South Wales are replete with descriptions of the natural setting, making favourable allusions to the parallels between the water, plants, birds and

Figure 1   Pennant Melangell Church. Photograph by Gerald Morgan (public domain).

A good example of the importance of place can be seen in the life of the Irish saint Melangell, who is thought to have lived in the late sixth or early seventh century. She was given the area around her hermit community of virgins at Pennant, in the Tanat Valley in Powys, by its landowner Prince Brychwel and his successors as a permanent sanctuary. It was said that he came across the saint sheltering a hare that had been pursued by his hounds. Legend has it that anyone who attempts to kill a hare or to pollute the sanctuary will come to a sticky end. This remote site has long been an important cultic centre. It incorporates a Bronze Age circle, an early medieval church and a twelfth-century church and shrine with St Melangell's relics. The twelfth-century church and shrine were restored in the 1980s and 1990s by the reverends Paul and Evelyn Davies as a centre of healing and pilgrimage. The website for the shrine draws attention to the ways in which time, place and tradition are contained in the current church, which is itself a Grade I listed building. This ancient church contains a fifteenth-century oak screen telling the story of Melangell and Prince Brochwel/Brychwel, two medieval effigies, one of which is thought to represent the saint, a Norman font, a Georgian pulpit, chandelier and commandment board, a series of contemporary stone

topographical features of the locale and the spiritual and theological beauty of the Virgin Mary and her shrine. Gray contrasts this generally favourable attitude to nature in medieval Welsh verse to a European literary pilgrimage tradition in which nature and landscape, if mentioned at all, are seen as hardships to be overcome, compared unfavourably to cultivated and built environments.

carvings of the hare and 'the giants rib' – a whale's rib of unknown origin.[8] To add further to the richness of the site, the sixteenth-century incumbent of Pennant Melangell was none other than William Morgan, first translator of the Bible into Welsh.

Pennant Melangell can be described as a 'dense place', one 'manufactured by the human imagination, dwelling as much in our interpretation of the place as in the place itself', as the theologian and geographer Beldon Lane (2002:239) put it when writing about the tension between place and placelessness in Christian spirituality. Lane does not dismiss the power of the physical landscape and a sense of presence, or the relationship between place and the human body and imagination. He is sympathetic to the 'embodied lifeworld' of David Abram and the 'flesh of the world' of Maurice Merleau-Ponty, described as 'an intertwined, and actively intertwining, lattice of mutually dependent phenomena, both sensorial and sentient, of which our own sensing bodies are a part' (Abram 1997:85). Lane, however, takes a more Durkheimian view of sacred places than Abram. For Lane, religious sites are not meaningful in and of themselves. It is the 'symbolic meanings (the stories) we attach to them [that] are the secrets that tell us most about who we are' (Lane 2002:240). R.S. Thomas, as well as those who composed the narrative lives of Welsh saints, also understood the vital role of storytelling in anchoring us within our lifeworlds.

Land and language

David Abram argues that language plays a role in the shift from what he sees as a participatory to a non-participatory understanding of the world, although it is not the only factor. The druids and Celtic saints, along with indigenous peoples past and present, are described as 'participant' with the speech of birds, wolves and the wind. We can see this, for example, in Swedish *kulning* or 'herd calling' and other vocal traditions that imitate or interact with the natural world. How is it, asks Abram, that non-human nature so often 'seems to stand mute and dumb, devoid of any meaning besides that which we [in the West] choose to give it?' (Abram 1997:91). The answer, he suggests, lies in the seeds of estrangement from the natural world sown jointly by Hebraic religion and Hellenistic philosophy.

Despite their differences, both these traditions shared an intellectual distance from the non-human environment and writing (ibid.:95). Writing, like language, may well have originated from observation of and participation in the 'more than human world': 'The swooping flight of birds is a kind of

---

8   See the Shrine Church and Centre of Saint Melangell website: stmelangell.org/the-shrine-church-of-saint-melangell (accessed 23 November 2020).

cursive script written on the wind; it is this script that was studied by the ancient "augurs", who could read therein the course of the future' (ibid.:95). Both druids and Celtic saints like Beuno were able to read the signs of birds in flight. Modern superstitions about meeting certain birds at particular times of day (often owls and crows) might be seen as remnants of these traditions, although one does not have to look very far to find individuals who still claim this affinity with non-human animals.[9]

This estrangement was a gradual process, never quite complete. Abram points to the interpenetration of human and non-human scripts evident in the Chinese word for writing, *wen*. According to J. Gernet, *wen* can refer to the simple written word and to literature, but also 'to veins in stones and wood, to constellations, represented by the strokes connecting the stars, to the tracks of birds and quadrupeds on the ground ... to tattoos and even ... to the designs that decorate the turtle's shell' (quoted in Abram 1997:96). The turtle shell is rich in symbolism in Chinese history and religion, a potent and magical object. As writing systems moved further from idiographic, pictographic and hieroglyphic systems to alphabetical ones, the links between the non-human world and writing weakened, even if it did not altogether disappear. For example, the Hebrew *alpha*, which became a capital 'A', is the word for ox, and depicted a horned ox's head – still visible in inverted form in the Latin alphabet.

This detour into language is intended to remind us that while a sequential history of religion in Wales might appear to be marked by events that abruptly alter the direction of travel (the Roman defeat of the druids on Anglesey in around 57 CE, the great period of Celtic church-building and the 'golden age' of saints in the sixth and seventh centuries, the Reformation and Henry VIII's suppression of the Welsh monasteries between 1536 and 1540, William Morgan's translation of the Bible into Welsh in 1588), there were many detours and intersections along the way. The Celtic Church in Wales amalgamated elements of druidic religion and pre-Christian ways of being in the world with membership of a universal Catholic Church.[10]

---

9   My maternal grandfather had an uncle who was a Church of Scotland minister in Ayrshire with a reputation both as a fiery hell-and-damnation preacher and as someone who could 'see the fairies and hear (i.e. interpret) the songs of the seals'. In Wales also, the links between the Protestant Bible-based preacher and seer were never completely severed, and in the various forms of nature religion now flourishing the interrelationship between people, place and the other-than-human world are once more coming into view.

10 The notion of a Celtic Church is somewhat controversial and the debates as to whether the term is meaningful often polarized. This is not the place to rehearse the various arguments (see Davies 1975; Davies 1996). In using the term 'Celtic

As mentioned above, the gradual shift from the Celtic *clas* system to Roman Catholic forms of monastic organization espoused by Benedictine and Augustinian foundations are attributed to St Winifred. At its height, the Cistercian order, following the Rule of St Benedict, had thirteen houses in Wales, and excelled at combining international networks and local power (Burton and Kerr 2011). Dedications to Welsh and non-Welsh saints were common, and the Virgin Mary and St Christopher featured in medieval wall paintings. While Mary could intercede for sinners as they faced judgement, St Christopher could protect the faithful from an evil death, as well as aiding travellers and pilgrims (Gray 2013). Universal saints were often domesticated and localized.

In parts of the Celtic world the family Bible with its family tree hand-drawn in the front traces genealogies to St Anne, the mother of Mary, or even to Adam, as a way of claiming kinship with these great characters of the Hebrew Bible, recasting the universal Christian narrative in the familiar idiom of kinship. In Wales there is also a tradition that St Mary and St Margaret of Antioch visited the country. If Mary did not actually journey to Wales during her earthly life, she descended from Heaven to travel the land, leaving imprints of her presence on the landscape. Noting the very localized nature of cultic centres in Wales, Gray records that Mary is 'reputed to have visited Cydweli, Aberdaron, Rhiw and Lanfair, on the coast south of Harlech' (ibid.:250). From Llanfair her journey continued to Hafod-y-llyn, 'and where she knelt to prey the prints of her knees could be seen in the rock and a holy well sprang up' (ibid.:251). At Aberdaron there is a holy well from which pilgrims drank on their way to Bardsey Island, which is said to display a handprint of the Virgin Mary (ibid. 251). These are not intellectual visions or even shared apparitions of the Virgin Mary, but an assertion of her interactions and sacred power visible in specific places in the landscape. Like the Aborigines' Songlines, these stories weave a mythic web linking people and places both horizontally with one another across Wales and beyond, and vertically, linking the faithful with both chthonic and heavenly realms. The iconoclasm of the sixteenth century, with its suppression of pilgrimage centres and shrines, such as that of Penrhys (restored in the twentieth century), destroyed much of this heritage, but failed to completely erase it.

Church' as a descriptive term for the early medieval Christian Church in Wales I am not assuming a bounded entity or Celtic exceptionalism. Contemporary debates around the nature of Celtic religion and spirituality need not prevent us from seeking to understand religion in Wales and other parts of the Celtic-speaking world both within a wider international context and in its specific local expressions.

In 1988, the Royal Mint at Llantrisant issued a set of commemorative stamps to celebrate 400 years since the publication of Bishop William Morgan's translation of the Bible into Welsh, certainly a pivotal moment in Welsh religious history. Morgan's Bible was the first official translation into any of the languages of the British Isles. It had a crucial impact on the survival of the Welsh language, its liturgy and prayers, giving the church and chapel a central role in Welsh life – as R.S. Thomas illustrates in 'A Welsh testament'. Hymns too played an important if less formal role. They were often composed, written out by hand and circulated within families, to be displayed in the competitive environment of the Christmas Plygain, a nocturnal carol service. The term Plygain is first recorded in the thirteenth-century Black Book of Carmarthen, and after the Reformation the service replaced the Latin Mass as a key Protestant element of Welsh liturgical worship. The tradition, which never completely died out, was revived in the late twentieth century, with churches, such as St Twrog's in Maentwrog, Gwynedd, attracting visitors from throughout Wales and beyond to their annual Plygain services. Despite the transition from Catholic to Protestant forms of Christianity, in medieval churches such as St Twrog's the Plygain carols continued to extol Mary and the saints in a very un-Protestant manner, and Mary retained her association with numerous churches, shrines, healing wells and features of the landscape.

The celebration of words and of the Word in Scripture also remain tied to the non-human or more-than-human landscape, revealing layers of association between human thought, faith and place. In Maentwrog there are legends associating the site of the church and the sixth-century St Twrog with what on a pan-European basis resembles elements of an ancient rock cult. Rock cults are often linked to fertility or to displays of power, fusing person and place. Maentwrog takes its name from the large stone, or *maen*, near the current church belfry door. St Twrog is said to have thrown the stone from the top of Moelwyn, a nearby mountain, crushing a pagan alter in the valley below. Legend has it that the saint's handprints can still be seen on the stone.

Although today's church was completed in 1896, the yew trees in its circular church yard, or *llan*, are thought to be over 1,300 years old, and the site was almost certainly a pre-Christian place of worship. The medieval church was dedicated to St Mary and was associated with a holy well and with the nearby Llyn Mair, Mary's lake. Another location in which saints are associated with rocks is Pumpsaint in Carmarthenshire. This hamlet on the site of a Roman fort near the Dolaucothi gold mines is named after five Celtic saints who are said to have rested there, leaving the imprint of their bodies on the large stone against which they slept. Archaeologists may tell us that the impressions are more likely the result of Roman anvils, but the legend of the resting saints persists, with the standing stone as a visible witness to their progress through the landscape.

This association between holy people who leave an impression on a rock, holy water (used for healing), pilgrimage and liturgy is found in many parts of the world where pre-Christian and Christian forms of worship have survived alongside and merged into one another. One is reminded, for example, of Robert Hertz's account of the cult of St Besse in Italy's Graian Alps (Hertz 1983). Hertz, a pupil of Émile Durkheim, spent the summer of 1916 in the nearby village of Cogne and participated in the annual August pilgrimage to the shrine. The cult of St Besse has the mixture of threat and favour that we find in the life of St Beuno. The saint can grant favours and offer protection to devotees but also harm those who fail to keep their promises. Hertz says of early twentieth-century Pyrenean devotions, 'the rocks are still the immediate and the avowed objects of devotion; or, if people feel the need to represent their power in concrete form, they do so in the guise of special spirits, half angels, half serpents, inhabiting the sacred rocks' (ibid.:82–3).

Pilgrims to the shrine to this day attempt to take small flakes of the holy and powerful rock back with them to be worn as protective amulets or to be added to water, thereby giving it healing properties. Medieval art historian James Bugslag (2004) has drawn attention to the ways in which natural elements such as the rock of St Besse are often physically incorporated into Christian churches and chapels. Where Marian shrines are linked to holy wells and springs, these chthonic elements are often particularly marked, such A in the nineteenth-century shrine of Lourdes in the French Pyrenees, which remains a popular centre of pilgrimage and healing. We can see elements of this association in the Marian shrine of Penrys, a place in which human and natural elements continue to infuse and inspire one another.

Pilgrimage and persons

Pilgrimages are the largest gatherings of human beings on earth.[11] In the Middle Ages, Christian pilgrims would travel throughout the year to

---

11   The Hindu *Kumbh Mela* at Allahabad is by far the largest. The last *Maha Kumbh* or great Kumbh, celebrated every twelve years, in 2013 was attended by an estimated 120 million pilgrims. Around 20 million Shia Muslims attend the annual Arba'een pilgrimage to Karbala in Iraq, and an estimated 2 to 3 million pilgrims take part in the Islamic annual Hajj to Mecca. Pope Francis's Roman Catholic mass in the Philippines in 2015 attracted a congregation of some 7 million people (see Nivedya 2018). With rapidly increasing international live participation in online worship, we can expect to see new data sets in coming years illustrating the continued power of religion to gather and to move people, both physically and spiritually. The role of place and of places remains important, if not a specific

Canterbury, Rome and Jerusalem. Others would walk the Camino de Santiago – a series of long-distance pilgrimage routes through France and Spain that have been used since at least the ninth century. The Camino has seen a steady resurgence of popularity in recent decades. The ideal timing for pilgrims to end the journey at the tomb of St James the Apostle is on his feast day, 25 July, in Compostela in north-west Spain. Medieval pilgrims to Rome, Jerusalem and Compostela could earn a plenary indulgence, an assurance from the pope that the slate of their sins would be wiped clean ensuring entry into heaven. This transactional element is common to pilgrimages, and in the Middle Ages three pilgrimages to Ynys Enlli (Bardsey Island), off the tip of the Llyn Peninsula in north Wales, was equivalent to one pilgrimage to Rome. In the case of this Welsh pilgrimage, it was not a saint, holy relic or impressive building that drew pilgrims but the place itself. Known as the island of 20,000 saints, many who made the journey to Ynys Enlli (Bardsey Island) hoped to die and be buried there.

The attraction of Ynys Enlli (Bardsey Island) as a place of pilgrimage may have something to do with the topography of this tiny island (some 440 acres or 179 hectares) which is separated from the Llyn Peninsula and Cardigan Bay to the east by Bardsey Mountain and by strong tidal currents, while looking west towards Ireland and the setting sun. St Cadfan built a monastery on the island in 516 CE, and it was already a major centre of pilgrimage by the early thirteenth century, with an abbey belonging to the Augustinian Canons Regular. Although the monastery was dissolved in 1537, services are still held in its ruins (see Figure 5.2), as well as in the Victorian chapel built by Lord Newborough for his tenants in 1875, and in the tiny oratory (Y Betws), a converted pig sty in the grounds of Carreg Fawr. Bardsey Island, now owned and managed by the Bardsey Island Trust, is a popular destination for bird lovers, pilgrims and those seeking peace, reflection and renewal.[12]

Ynys Enlli (Bardsey) is now the end point of the North Wales Pilgrim's Way, which describes itself as 'The Welsh Camino',[13] a new route that takes in older pilgrimage trails, running 140 miles from Caergybia (Holyhead) to Ynys

---

focus of these new virtual events. In live streaming a 'coronavirus' Easter service from his kitchen table in 2020, the Anglican Archbishop of Canterbury, Justin Welby, was not diminishing the role of churches as centres of worship so much as affirming the presence of the sacred everywhere, including a domestic space such as a kitchen during a period in which people were urged to 'stay home' in response to the Covid-19 pandemic.

12   For Bardsey's religious history, see Allchin (2002). A summary of the history of the trust's Spirituality Committee is given by Wilcox (2020).

13   The route is called 'the Welsh Camino' on the website of the North Wales Pilgrim's Way: pilgrims-way-north-wales.org (accessed 9 October 2020).

Figure 2   The ruined Augustinian abbey on Bardsey Island (Ynys Enlli) is the end
point of the North Wales Pilgrims Way. Copyright Fiona Bowie.

Enlli (Bardsey Island). The point of departure was for centuries the little village
of Aberdaron, where R.S. Thomas was vicar of St Hywyn's from 1967 to 1978,
and Ynys Enlli was part of his parish (although not a part he was keen to visit).
Pilgrimages, both organized and individual, have seen a resurgence in recent
decades, and new heritage footpaths and pilgrimage routes are increasingly
linking great abbeys and medieval churches with other historic sites, including
Palaeolithic standing stones and Bronze Age burial mounds, medieval castles,
nineteenth-century industrial ruins and sheep farms. While the landscape of
Wales remains a star attraction for visitors, the layers of human occupation
and history add considerably to a sense of dwelling in the landscape.[14]

14   Both Wales and Cumbria now have long distance footpaths known as 'the
     Cistercian Way' with accompanying websites that allow individuals and groups to
     plan their own pilgrimages. They incorporate archaeological sites from different
     periods along with Cistercian foundations and other places of religious interest.

It is tempting to see something fixed or inevitable about history, whether in the distant or recent past, but things happen because of individuals and the networks of people they inspire. Both Cadfan and Hywyn were drawn from their native Brittany to settle in a remote part of north-west Wales. As St Hywyn's Church website puts it, for both men their hermit cells and the little monastic communities (*clas*) around them were the places 'where they felt God had called them to live, to pray and to die'.[15] In the same way, two Anglican sisters from the Community of the Sisters of the Love of God from the Convent of the Incarnation at Fairacres in Oxford lived more recently as hermits on Bardsey and the Llyn Peninsula. It was a matter of regret for Sister Helen Mary that she was airlifted off Bardsey towards the end of her life and that she was not given the opportunity to die there as so many of her predecessors had also aspired to.

A key figure behind the revival of Welsh pilgrimage traditions was A.M. (Donald) Allchin, an Anglican priest, canon of Canterbury Cathedral, warden of the Anglican–Orthodox Centre of St Theosavia's at Oxford, theologian and author. Allchin was 'visitor' (spiritual advisor) to the Fairacres sisters, and would regularly visit those living as hermits, including Sister Helen Mary on Bardsey and Sister Verena on the Llyn Peninsula. Allchin was also a lover of small countries (Denmark, Romania and Wales), friend of Roman Catholic hermit and author Thomas Merton, and of R.S. Thomas. Allchin published translations of Welsh religious texts into English, including the work the eighteenth-century Methodist hymn writer and mystic Ann Griffiths (1735–1805). He inspired an ambitious and varied three days of activities to commemorate the bicentenary of Ann Griffiths's death in 2005. These activities took place in the chapels associated with Ann Griffiths in Meifod, Powys, culminating with a bilingual Eucharist at Llanfihangel-yng-Ngwynfa parish church and hymn singing in the nearby Ann Griffiths memorial chapel. Anthropologists are good at looking at communities, but communities also depend upon these individuals and networks (a key concept of the Manchester School of anthropology), which always extend beyond a single time and place, linking even the most rural and inward-looking community to a much wider web of influence and connections.

See: britishpilgrimage.org/portfolio/welsh-cistercian-way and britishpilgrimage. org/portfolio/cumbrian-cistercian-way (accessed 9 October 2020).

15   Quoted from the website of St Hywyn's Church, Aberdaron: www.st-hywyn.org. uk/st_hywyn.html (accessed 9 October 2020).

Communities and networks

In the 2011 census, the population of Llanfihangel-yng-Ngwynfa ward was just over 1,000, a similar size to that of the 1841 census.[16] The village itself is little more than a hamlet surrounded by scattered farms, but this quiet, rural spot is celebrated not only as the home of Ann Griffiths and Welsh Methodism, but also for its role in the anthropology of Wales. The influential Welsh community studies initiated by Alwyn Rees in the 1940s (see Rees 1996), together with colleagues and students at University College in Aberystwyth and continued by Ronald Frankenberg (1990) and others at Manchester University in the 1950s, give us valuable insights into religious life in rural Wales in the middle decades of the twentieth century. In an appraisal of Rees's study of Llanfihangel-yng-Ngwynfa, Frankenberg (1994) noted that the Independents, Baptists, Calvinist Methodists and Wesleyan Methodists lived in slightly different worlds. Their kinship and social networks varied, with families usually faithful to a single denomination. They also had distinct cultural and imaginal worlds. As Frankenberg observed: 'Even the child's view of world geography will differ. The Methodist will hear missionary descriptions of the Khasi Hills in Assam whereas the Independent will learn more of mission life in the South Sea islands' (ibid.:60). The heroes of one denomination were scarcely known in another. Just as Christians in medieval Wales were very much part of the wider Catholic world through pilgrimage, people, beliefs and practices, the wider world of empire reached into the hills and valleys, informed the rituals and stories, and were rehearsed in churches, chapels and school rooms of nineteenth- and twentieth-century Wales.

A detailed survey of the village of Llanddulas in north-east Wales (in the old county of Denbighshire) published in the 1980s (Jones and Rawcliffe 1985) still follows the structure of Rees's earlier work, although it is somewhat less ethnographic than the studies produced by anthropologists. The influence of the church and chapel is still apparent in Llanddulas, as can be seen in an 1850 parish survey, which listed religious affiliation by household. With a village population of little over 300 in total, 64 heads of households were registered as members of the Anglican Church, 46 as Wesleyan Methodists,

---

16   Figures from 'Llanfyllin and district, population graphs: census figures for Llanfihangel-yng-Ngwynfa parish', Powys Digital History Project: history.powys. org.uk/school1/llanfyllin/hangpop.shtml (accessed 9 October 2020). The word *gwynfa* refers to the countryside and can be translated as 'fair' or 'blessed' place and, like much of old rural county of Montgomeryshire, consists of low hills with sheep pasture and woodlands, fertile valleys and rivers. *Llanfihangel* is the 'church' or 'enclosure' (*llan*) of St Michael, the saint/angel to whom the parish church is dedicated. As Rees (1996:101) explains, the name refers to an area or territory (*cwmwyd* or commote), not to a nucleated settlement.

22 as Calvinistic Methodists, 14 as Independents, 21 as Baptists, 16 had a floating affiliation or attended house churches and only 15 heads of household seldom or never attended church or chapel (ibid.:210). The church or chapels were often larger than needed for the size of their congregation, but were nevertheless well attended, with up to three services and a Sunday school on Sunday, as well as meetings or 'sittings' during the week. As illustrated above, this diversification in religious affiliation enabled a network of links to other chapels and preachers belonging to the same denomination outside the village. Each one had their own ministerial training colleges, preachers and clergy, missionaries and publications, forming arterial links to the rest of Wales and the world beyond.

Criticisms have been made of Welsh community studies, some valid and some less so, but their fine-grained ethnographic detail opens a window onto a world that has all but vanished. A recent reappraisal of Welsh community studies was co-edited by Charlotte Aull Davies and Stephanie Jones (2003). One of my favourite articles in this collection is Sue Philpin's study of wool measuring (Philpin 2003). Wool measuring as a treatment for depression is mentioned in nineteenth-century literature, and probably has very much older roots. It was still being practised in rural mid Wales when Philpin did her research in the 1990s. Although this might not look at first sight like a religious practice, this is only the case if we define religion as an intellectual exercise formalized in institutional settings, as opposed to a cosmology and set of shared practices.

Wool measuring is informed by common notions concerning health and illness and a cosmology that diverges from mainstream biomedicine. Such 'animistic' and 'pagan' or 'folk' forms of practice persist throughout the British Isles, among those who consider themselves Christians as well those who define themselves as pagans. Apparent contradictions between relatively abstract doctrinal beliefs and practices and those used instrumentally in particular situations tend to concern religious elites (theologians, clergy) rather more than the general populace (Stringer 2008). In brief, a sufferer contacts the wool measurer, who uses a pre-determined length of wool that is attached to a solid object at one end. The therapist measures the wool from inner elbow to the tip of the middle finger over several days. The extent to which the wool departs from an ideal cubit in length determines the severity and course of the illness. The sufferer need not be present when the wool is measured, or even know that the measuring is taking place. The wool measurer needs only the name and date of birth of the patient.[17] Measuring

---

17   In this, the technique is like various forms of spiritual healing and spirit release therapy, where the real 'work' is taking place at an energetic level and not just on

the wool constitutes both the diagnosis and treatment. Philpin reflects that taking part in wool measuring helped her to feel part of the community and she suggests that a sense of community would also be of therapeutic benefit to the patient (despite the fact that they need not know that healing has been requested and is taking place). This latter observation is like Edith Turner's sense of inclusion when taking the part of a healer in the Ihamba tooth ritual in Central Africa (Turner 1992). In this case the opportunity for the community to come together to support the patient is central to the cure, but unlike Philpot, Turner gives equal weight to social/community and metaphysical dimensions of healing.

Experience and belief are closely related and are culturally informed, but culture does not necessarily account for the totality of the event. The survival of wool measuring as a therapeutic practice is presumably because at some level it works, and people get better because of it, which suggests that a purely constructivist explanation is insufficient. This brings us back to recent enactivist approaches to experience in which the human agent and the environment are seen as closely entwined,[18] and to an ontological anthropology that is open and curious as to how and why things might 'work' (Bowie 2020). Edith Turner 'saw' a spirit leave the sick woman at the centre of the healing ritual, to her own surprise. What she saw was culturally appropriate to the situation, but nevertheless it exceeded the notion of what is possible from a socially or scientifically reductive/constructivist Western scientific perspective, as well as exceeding her previous cultural experience and expectations.

One of the few ethnographic works to focus specifically on religion in Wales is Vieda Skultans's study of a Spiritualist church in Swansea (Skultans 2000). Most Spiritualist churches follow the style of worship of a Christian church or chapel, with hymn singing and prayers, with the addition of a platform medium and often a 'development circle' for those who wish to develop their mediumistic skills in a safe, controlled setting. Some Spiritualist congregations are explicitly Christian and others not, but the feel and often location is familiar to those with a church or chapel background. There are, however, representatives of other religions in Wales, and the days when almost everyone in a village or town was associated with a place of worship have

---

the 'physical plane', with minimal information, typically a name and location or date of birth, needed to form an energetic link between the patient or client (Bowie forthcoming).

18   See e.g. James Gibson's ecological approach to visual perception (Gibson 1986), Francisco Varela's 'embodied mind' perspective (Varela 2016) and David Abram's 'sensuous ecology' (Abram 1997).

passed. Figures from the 2011 census show that compared to England and Wales as a whole, a higher proportion of the Welsh population state that they have no religion, and between 2001 and 2011 the proportion of the population describing themselves as Christian dropped from just under 72 per cent to 57 per cent, while those with no religion rose over the same period from 18.5 per cent to 32 per cent. Although the number of Muslims doubled in this period, they still comprise only 1.5 per cent of the population, and all non-Christian religious groups are heavily concentrated in the larger cities of South Wales, particularly Newport, Cardiff and Swansea.

Figures for the different Christian denominations are hard to come by, but it appears that all denominations are experiencing a fall in membership, with the Church in Wales leading the way. These difficulties could be one factor in the improved relations between denominations, and a greater involvement of churches in inter-faith dialogue. In the face of secularization, any faith is seen as something believers have in common, and Cytun, Churches Together in Wales, succeeds in uniting denominations that until relatively recently had little contact with one another. Even the Roman Catholics now participate, something unimaginable a few decades ago when Wales was still regarded as mission territory by the Roman Catholic Church.

Spiritual and religious or increasingly secular?

The statistics of declining attendance at places of worship and of official membership of a religious body indicate that religious practices in Wales are changing, if not disappearing all together. The lack of anthropological research on religion in contemporary Wales is something I am seeking to address to understand what the nature of this change might be. It is possible that, as Grace Davie (1994, 2012, 2015) and Heelas and Woodhead (2005) have suggested, increasing numbers people are identifying as 'spiritual' rather than 'religious', and can speak of 'believing' without necessarily 'belonging'.

Alongside declining church and chapel attendance, the variety of faith groups and forms of religious expression has increased. General surveys and statistics can present us with a broad outline, but what is harder to determine in a changing religious landscape is the role of place and environment, relations with spiritual beings (such as angels, saints, the deceased, fairies and nature spirits) and of personal revelations and experience (whether spontaneous, ritualized or induced) within the contemporary religious landscape. To this end I am conducting a series of interviews with people who are willing to talk about their own beliefs, religious practice and spiritual journeys, and who are also able to contextualize these in relation to a religious community, or communities of practice, of some kind.

Many of those to whom I have spoken or approached would not appear in official statistics of religion. Of those who do, statistics present a very partial picture of their religious life. As Martin Stringer (2008:ix) pointed out, there may be continuity in an underlying religious sensibility that is coming into focus as Christianity retreats as a dominant religious expression in society. A common theme emerging from my interviews is the importance of place and of the sanctity of the natural world. The kind of contacts with other-than-human beings, visible and invisible, that appear in the lives of druids and the Celtic saints are also apparent in religious practices among those I have encountered. Making music together, dancing, walking (pilgrimage) and what might broadly be described as 'energy work' also feature. Despite superficial differences of religious adherence, place of origin, language and background, many of those I have talked to are actually very similar to one another in their values and outlook on life.[19] Whether they are more broadly representative of the population, or of those who profess religious beliefs, is still to be determined.

I asked each of my interviewees to select a place and an object that is of significance in their religious life and/or spiritual journey. This is partly a warm-up technique but also because religion is so often based around places and material objects. No one has had a problem finding items and places of significance, although selecting one can be a challenge. For Dan Frett, an American information technology executive and an ordained Anglican priest, the Wye Valley was his place of choice, not least as walking his dogs brought pleasure to both the dogs and to Dan, strengthening his sense of belonging to the place and to God. The fact that Dan was relatively new to the area did not appear to diminish his sense of connection with the beautiful and dramatic landscape of the Wye Valley in the borderlands of South Wales.

Tamzin Powell was born and raised in South Wales, with family connections to the Forest of Dean and Wye Valley. She is a teacher, amateur musician and songwriter, as well as an anthropologist. She conducted postgraduate research on the 'cunning folk' or Wiccans (which she spells with two 'c's to distinguish them from American Wicans) in the Wye Valley and

---

19 Their ideas are also in cases disquietingly like my own, despite my efforts to find individuals as diverse as possible to get a sense of the wide range of religious expression in contemporary Wales. This raises interesting methodological issues around the psychology of shared meanings and attention that we find in Peter Fonagy's work on mentalization, seen from the perspective of neuroscience and social cognition (see Fonagy *et al.* 2002). It reminds us that there is no neutral position from which to conduct social scientific research and that the interviewer is never a disinterested recorder, but co-creator in each encounter.

Forest of Dean (Powell 2017). Her way into the practice was through music, but she became an initiated priestess of a local coven. During the research she also discovered that generations of her family had links to various forms of esoteric practice, and she realized that a period living with her grandparents in childhood had been formative in her later development. She chose her grandfather's ashes together with a photo of one of the notes he used to leave around the house as her significant object, and his cottage as her place of inspiration. For Tamzin, the local area is also resonant with energy, both good and bad, that can be addressed and harnessed in ritual and magical practices. The local landscape had layers of meaning both through these perceived energies and as the location of various forms of ritual activity.

Like some of my other interviewees, Jane Pearl has moved from a 'fear-based' Christian church, the Church of Christ in Bowling Green, Kentucky, in the USA, to a much more accepting and open form of belief and practice. She lives in the Wye Valley near Monmouth where she is a singer-songwriter playing with local groups, and a felt-maker. As someone who has moved around for much of her life, Jane chose the shared space created by music, meditation and chanting has her special place – something ephemeral but powerful and portable. She also practices as a medium for those who come to her for help. Jane was aware of her mediumistic gifts from an early age, but it was many years before they were able to find expression. Jane, like others I spoke to in this area, seemed to think that there is something about living on or near a geographical border that facilitates exploration with alternative lifestyles and beliefs.

Jane put me in contact with a musician friend, Colin Duggan, a Welsh-speaking member of the Thai Buddhist congregation in South Wales. Through Colin I met Barry Taylor, a part-time primary-school teacher and Welsh-language tutor in the South Wales Valleys. Barry started life as a Pentecostal Christian and attended London Bible College, which led to him losing his faith, and instead of becoming a minister he became an atheist. Barry now describes himself as a Buddhist atheist, and he chose the room at the Tibetan Buddhist Centre in Brynmawr in South Wales, in which he was received into the faith, and his meditation beads as his place and object. This Tibetan Buddhist Meditation Centre located in the former Calvary Baptist Chapel on King Street, Brynmawr is itself a sensory feast and powerful cultural symbol of change and continuity. The grief that accompanies loss of the chapel and its congregation is somehow acknowledged and embraced by the extraordinary skill, effort and devotion that has gone into reconstructing this piece of Tibet in South Wales.

Figure 3   Barry Taylor at the Palpung Changchub Dargye Ling Tibetan Buddhist Centre in Brynmawr, South Wales. Copyright Fiona Bowie.

Endings and beginnings

For the druids of Anglesey who faced the Roman legionaries, for the Cistercians in Wales during the Reformation and for Nonconformist Christians witnessing the closure of their theological colleges and chapels, the end of an era may be experienced as a death and a loss. With hindsight we can see lines of continuity and adaptation, whether between Christian and druidic practices in the lives of the Welsh saints, or the importance of Mary in Welsh Protestantism. Pilgrimages are undergoing a revival, linking places in the landscape with historical figures and events, while creating new expressions of communitas (Turner 2012). It can be tempting to regard any religious group as a coherent and discrete entity, overlooking fluidity in membership and the wide range of opinions and practices among adherents. Martin Stringer (2008:38–9) expressed some surprise at the way in which Anglo-Catholic Christians in Manchester discussing death moved between orthodox views of the importance of saying a requiem to help the soul of the deceased get to Heaven, and belief in reincarnation. These seemingly contradictory views may be used in different circumstances, one more abstract and the other personal for example, but they could also express enduring, consistent personal experience, whether first- or second-hand. Believers might be able to reproduce church teachings in appropriate circumstances, while also developing a world view that relies on experiential encounters that are either at odds with, or are unrepresented by, formal religious doctrines and dogmas.

Reincarnation would be a case in point. Rather than being an abstract belief or simple wishful thinking, past-life memories raise questions and issues regarding church teachings on reincarnation that are not easily dismissed. Personal experiences of phenomena such as contact with the deceased, out-of-body and near-death experiences, telepathic contact with others, precognition, evidential dreams and unlikely synchronicities occur regularly and in similar forms whether sanctioned by orthodox religion and supported by cultural expectation or not. The extent to which these experiences become incorporated into formal belief systems or remain detached, and often private, varies across time and place, even if the phenomena themselves remain remarkably consistent.

From the four brief sketches presented above, the churches and chapels that dominated earlier ethnographic studies no longer represent all of religion in Wales today. They are part of the story and form a cultural background for many people, but there is much more going on, with a wide variety of belief and practice evident along with less visible spiritual pathways. There are networks and threads of connections among those I have interviewed, some direct, some indirect. Musical connections link a Wiccan and a medium on the Welsh Borders who play in folk bands with Welsh-speaking Buddhists in the South Wales Valleys. These Buddhists are in turn part of immigrant faith communities, both Thai and Tibetan, as they worship with those seeking to establish their lives thousands of miles from home. I talked with members of different churches as well as to people of various faiths, to shamans and druids, to spiritual healers and hermits. Some are born in Wales, others are incomers, both English- and Welsh-speaking. Each has a unique spiritual journey and a story to tell that I hope will provide a kaleidoscopic picture of religion in Wales today.

Conclusion

Further ethnographic research may help address the question of the extent to which contemporary notions of spirituality as an inner potential for self-realization and self-fulfilment are visible in Wales. Have loyalties to a specific community or tradition continued to play an important part in religious and spiritual life, or have they been displaced by a more individual, sometimes commercial, or universal notion of spirituality? How do New Age and alternative forms of spirituality anchor themselves to a place, and how stable are the communities that are develop around these forms of religion? Are immigrants more conservative in their religion than those 'at home', or do encounters with the local environment and local converts help indigenize Islam, Judaism, Buddhism and Hinduism in Wales, just as the Cistercians 'went native' in the Middle Ages? What, if anything, replaces the chapels and churches that have closed? Do those who built and supported them for generations now find themselves without a religious home and identity? For Iorwerth Peate (see Phillips, this volume), spiritual and religious life was very much part of the agenda when seeking to preserve oral histories, vocabularies and customs associated with Welsh life. One of the first buildings reconstructed in the grounds of the Welsh Folk Museum was a rural chapel. With the rapid decline in membership of Christian churches and chapels, such buildings are losing their influence and significance within their communities.

It is noteworthy that Clare Wenger's insightful report on employment in mid Wales talks about the importance of seeing questions of employment, rural poverty and well-being in the context of 'the total fabric of Mid-Wales society' without mentioning religion (Wenger 1980:193). Respondents to her survey valued the peaceful and beautiful environment, slower pace of life and sense of community of rural Mid Wales, but this can be both attractive and limiting, as R.S. Thomas's farmer articulated it in 'A Welsh testament'. Wenger suggests that a sense of failure or perceived failure can be harder to live with in a small community, leading to outward migration, which might suggest that religion continues to play a part in reinforcing and shaping community sentiment. Wenger deals at length with the role of local councils, language and identity in providing a social context, but churches, chapels and other religious groupings are surprisingly absent from her analysis.

The question as to where religion fits within the 'total fabric' of contemporary Welsh society has yet to be determined and is undergoing rapid change. The growth of ecologically based pagan and New Age forms of religious expression (while acknowledging the limitations of such labels) suggests that an emphasis on 'nature' and place will retain its centrality. Quite what links exist, if any, between the druids and medieval Christian saints with their knowledge of trees, birds, rocks and landscape and these newer nature spiritualities is as yet unclear, but one might expect to find some recurring themes as well as discontinuities. These are questions still to be addressed in future work on the anthropology of religion in Wales today.

References

Abram, D. 1997. *The Spell of the Sensuous: Perception and Language in a More-Than-Human World*. New York: Vintage Books.

Allchin, A.M. 2002. 'Bardsey: a place of pilgrimage', 2nd edn. Pwllheli: Bardsey Island Trust.

Boas, F. 1940. *Race, Language and Culture*. Chicago: Chicago University Press.

Bowie, F. 2020. 'Experience and ontology in the study of religion'. In N. Roubekas and T. Ryba (eds), *Interpreting, Explaining and Theorizing Religion and Myth*, pp. 196–216. Leiden: Brill.

——— 2021 forthcoming. 'Spirit possession and spirit release therapy: notions of self and afterlife as reflected in contemporary practices of healing'. In M. Muscari, E. Voss and M. Zilliger (eds), *Skill and Scale in Transnational Mediumship*. Springer.

Bugslag, J. 2004. 'Pilgrimages to Chartres: the visual evidence'. In S. Blick and R. Tekippe (eds), *Art and Architecture of Late Medieval Pilgrimage in Northern Europe and England*, pp. 135–83. Leiden: Brill.

Burton, J. and Kerr, J. 2011. *The Cistercians in the Middle Ages*. Woodbridge: Boydell and Brewer.

Davie, G. 1994. *Religion in Britain Since 1945: Believing without Belonging*. Oxford: Blackwell.

——— 2012. 'Spirituality and religion'. *Journal for the Study of Spirituality* 2(2):163–69.

——— 2015. *Religion in Britain: A Persistent Paradox*, 2nd edn. Chichester: Wiley.

Davies, C.A. and Jones, S. (eds). 2003. *Welsh Communities: New Ethnographic Perspectives*. Cardiff: University of Wales Press.

Davies, O. 1996. *Celtic Christianity in Early Medieval Wales*. Cardiff: University of Wales Press.

Davies, W. 1975. 'The Celtic Church'. *Journal of Religious History* 8(4):406–11.

Fabian, J. 1983. *Time and the Other: How Anthropology Makes Its Object*. New York: Columbia University Press.

Fleure, H.J. and James, T.C. 1916. 'Geographical distribution of anthropological types in Wales'. *Journal of the Royal Anthropological Institute* 46:35–153.

Fonagy, P., Gergely, G., Jurist, E.J. and Target, M. 2002. *Affect Regulation, Mentalization and the Development of the Self*. New York: Other Press.

Frankenberg, R. 1990 [1957]. *Village on the Border: A Social Study of Religion, Politics and Football in a North Wales Community*. Prospect Heights, IL: Waveland Press.

——— 1994 [1965]. *Communities in Britain: Social Life in Town and Country*. Aldershot: Gregg Revivals.

Gibson, J.J. 1986. *The Ecological Approach to Visual Perception*. Hillsdale, NJ: Lawrence Erlbaum Associates.

Gray, M. 2000. *Images of Piety: The Iconography of Traditional Religion in Late Medieval Wales*. Oxford: British Archaeological Reports.

——— 2011. 'Sacred space and the natural world: the holy well and shrine of the Virgin Mary at Penrhys'. *European Review of History* 18(2):243–60.

——— 2013. 'A new history of Wales: Dr Madeleine Gray asks: "Was Wales ever really a nation of chapelgoers?"' *Wales Online*, 28 March: www.walesonline. co.uk/news/wales-news/new-history-wales-dr-madeline-1899296 (accessed 8 October 2020).

Gregory, J.R. 2015. 'The life of St Winifred: the Vita S. Wenefrede form BL Lansdowne MS 436'. *Medieval Feminist Forum*, subsidia series 4:1–39.

Guimarães, L.M. 2010. 'Saints' encounters with secular rulers in the Welsh Saints' Lives in the Vespasian Legendary: miracles between belief and religious politics'. In M. Foster (ed.), *Spiritual Temporalities in Late-Medieval Europe*, pp. 57–76. Newcastle upon Tyne: Cambridge Scholars Publishing.

Heelas, P. and Woodhead, L. 2005. *The Spiritual Revolution: Why Religion Is Giving Way to Spirituality*. Oxford: Blackwell.

Henken, M. 1991. *The Welsh Saints: A Study in Patterned Lives*. Woodbridge: Brewer.

Hertz, R. 1983 [1913]. 'St Besse: a study of an Alpine cult'. In Stephen Wilson (ed.), *Saints and their Cults*, pp. 55–100. Cambridge: Cambridge University Press.

Heywood, P. 2017. 'The ontological turn'. *Cambridge Encyclopedia of Anthropology*: www.anthroencyclopedia.com/entry/ontological-turn (accessed 8 October 2020).

Holbraad, M. 2012. *Truth in Motion: The Recursive Anthropology of Cuban Divination*. Chicago: University of Chicago Press.

Jones, B. and Rawcliffe, M. 1985. *Llanddulas: Heritage of a Village*. Denbigh: Gee and Son.

Lane, B.C. 2002. *Landscapes of the Sacred: Geography and Narrative in American Spirituality*. Baltimore: Johns Hopkins University Press.

Mac Cana, P. 2020. 'Head: the Celtic head cult'. *Encyclopedia.com*: www.encyclopedia. com/environment/encyclopedias-almanacs-transcripts-and-maps/head-celtic-head-cult (accessed 9 October 2020).

Nivedya. 2018. '10 largest religious gatherings around the world'. *Owlcation*, 14 June: owlcation.com/humanities/10-Largest-Religious-Gatherings-In-Human-History (accessed 9 October 2020).

Okely, J. 2001. 'Visualism and landscape: looking and seeing in Normandy'. Ethnos 66(1):99–120.

Philpin, S. 2003. 'Wool measurement: community and healing in rural Wales'. In C.A.Davies and S. Jones (eds), *Welsh Communities: New Ethnographic Perspectives*, pp. 117–34. Cardiff: University of Wales Press.

Powell, T. 2017. *The Witches Ways in the Welsh Borders: Ethnography of Contemporary and Historical Customs of Cunning Folk Magic*. Scotts Valley, CA: CreateSpace Publishing.

Rees, A.D. 1996 [1950]. *Life in a Welsh Countryside: A Social Study of Llanfihangel yng Ngwnfa*. Cardiff: Cardiff University Press.

Roberts, D.F. and Sunderland, E. (eds). 1973. *Genetic Variation in Britain*. London: Taylor & Francis

Shaw, R. and Stewart, C. 1994. 'Introduction: problematizing syncretism'. In C. Stewart and R. Shaw (eds), *Syncretism/Anti-Syncretism: The Politics of Religious Synthesis*, pp. 1–26. London: Routledge.

Sims-Williams, P. 2018. *Buchedd Beuno: The Middle Welsh Life of St Beuno*. Dublin: Dublin Institute for Advanced Studies, School of Celtic Studies.

Skultans, V. 2000 [1974]. *Intimacy and Ritual: A Study of Spiritualism, Mediums and Groups*. Oxford: Routledge.

Stringer, M. 2008. *Contemporary Western Ethnography and the Definition of Religion*. London: Continuum.

Thomas, R.S. 1993. 'A Welsh testament' [1961]. In *Collected Poems 1945–1990*, pp. 117–18. London: Dent.

Turner, E. 2012. *Communitas: The Anthropology of Collective Joy*. New York: Palgrave Macmillan.

Turner, E., with Blodget, W., Kahona, S. and Benwa, F. 1992. *Experiencing Ritual: A New Interpretation of African Healing*. Philadelphia: University of Pennsylvania Press.

Varela, F.J., Thompson, E. and Rosch, E. (eds). 2016. *The Embodied Mind: Cognitive Science and Human Experience*, rev. edn. Cambridge, MA: MIT Press.

Watkin, M. 1994. 'Who are the Welsh?' *International Journal of Anthropology* 9(1):53–68.

Wenger, G.C. 1980. *Mid-Wales, Deprivation or Development: A Study of Patterns of Employment in Selected Communities*. Cardiff: University of Wales Press.

Wilcox, H. 2020. 'The spiritual life of Bardsey/Enlli: a brief history of the Trust's Spirituality Committee'. *Dros y Don/Across the Sound: Bardsey Island Trust Yearbook*, pp. 13–21.

Wolcott, D. n.d. 'Composite Lives of St Bueno'. *Ancient Wales Studies*: www.ancientwalesstudies.org/id23.html (accessed 9 October 2020).

6

The Welsh in diaspora

Patagonia

Iwan Wyn Rees

Introduction

Patagonia, and specifically the (perceived) survival of *Y Wladfa* (*Gymreig*) (literally 'the (Welsh) colony'), has long been the subject of fascination if not romanticization in Wales. Indeed, the stereotype of Welsh descendants surviving in this 'exotic outpost' in South America in spite of the barren desert or *paith* (steppe) that surrounds their communities, often embodied by a singing Welsh-speaking *gaucho* on horseback, is particularly dominant in Welsh media representations of the region. Similarly, popular tourist attractions such as the Welsh tea rooms (*casas de té galés*), which are particularly numerous in the small town of Gaiman, and the Nonconformist chapels established by the early Welsh settlers feature prominently in Welsh media productions.

As interesting as these stereotypical projections of Patagonian Welshness may be, they clearly do not suffice to give an accurate portrayal of the complex socio-political, cultural, religious and linguistic changes that the Welsh settlers and their descendants, or the 'Welsh ethnic community' as Williams (1991) puts it, have experienced in present-day Chubut Province, Argentina, since the establishment of *Y Wladfa* there over 150 years ago in 1865.

The empirical data presented below are of a linguistic nature and will thus be of particular interest to (socio)linguists. However, this chapter is written with multidisciplinary readers in mind and ought to be accessible to historians (of Wales and of diasporas generally), social anthropologists and sociologists, as well as Latin American scholars whose research also relates to linguistic matters.

The focus of the study lies in the social and cultural implications of various linguistic phenomena that I have identified in contemporary varieties of Patagonian Welsh following a field trip to Chubut Province in 2016.[1] The main findings explored in this chapter consist of two distinct strands. First, the relationship between the linguistic phenomenon of Hispanicization and recent changes to the type and density of social networks in which Welsh speakers in Chubut have participated; and second, the language standardization that has occurred in recent decades among specific types of speakers of Patagonian Welsh, which can be attributed mainly to a specific educational programme, namely the British Council's 'Welsh language project in Chubut' (see details below).

My analysis of the first element will also explore how national identities of various kinds (including strong Welsh identities) can be associated with types of social networks. The significance of some speakers' experiences (or perceptions) of a former distinctive 'Welsh circle' will therefore be probed. In a similar vein, my interpretation of the second phenomenon will also consider how the revitalization of Welsh in Chubut is intertwined with increased transnational contact, and more specifically with linguistic norms determined and promulgated predominantly by institutions in Wales. Consequently, the findings presented below will raise important broad questions about the way in which the instruction of heritage languages is undertaken in postcolonial contexts.

Differing interpretations of *Y Wladfa*

The history of the Welsh colony in Patagonia is most certainly a vast and complex field to which I cannot do justice here. However, it must be acknowledged from the outset that 'a history' of any country or community is inevitably an interpretation that is never in fact completely objective. For example, as was eloquently argued recently by Huw Pryce (2019), 'the history of Wales' has always been conditioned by varying philosophies and values of different authors, and by a range of ideologies and beliefs popular at the time of writing.

---

1   This chapter is based on fieldwork conducted in Chubut Province, Argentina, in 2016 for a pilot study that forms part of a larger ongoing project on language contact and dialect contact phenomena in relation to Patagonian Welsh. This fieldwork was made possible by a small grant from the Coleg Cymraeg Cenedlaethol and it subsequently led to the development of an educational online resource that aims to introduce the traditional dialect forms of Patagonian Welsh to teachers working in the province (see Rees 2017). The detailed linguistic data upon which the findings of this chapter are based are presented and analysed fully from a contact linguistics perspective in Rees (2021).

The same is surely true in the case of the history of the Welsh colony in Patagonia. R. Bryn Williams's, for instance, concludes that the so-called Welsh colony is 'one of the most glorious failures of the Welsh nation' (Williams 1962: 298).[2] Geraldine Lublin's recent literary investigation of identity construction based on a detailed analysis of four memoirs published in the second half of the twentieth-century by Patagonians of Welsh extraction provides a thought-provoking response to Williams's assertion:

> Though a big question mark still hangs over the future of the [Welsh] language in Chubut, a lot more than the reminder of a glorious failure can be found in present-day Chubut. Welshness in Patagonia is still relevant and vibrant as a flexible, multifaceted phenomenon constantly evolving in new directions and responding to a full range of different dynamics.
>
> (Lublin 2017:193)

It could certainly be argued that both interpretations are valid as far as they depend on one's precise definition of 'Welshness' or even *Y Wladfa*. Although R. Bryn Williams's perspective may appear rather gloomy to us today, it is nevertheless consistent with other studies conducted in the second half of the twentieth-century (e.g. Davies 1976; Williams 1975, 1991). The state of the Welsh language and culture in Chubut has been portrayed negatively by each of these Welsh scholars. A continuous decline in the use of Welsh and the social status of its speakers from the 1920s onwards, ultimately leading to a general lack of intergenerational transmission of the language, has been a common theme. However, these accounts predate the so-called 'revival' (*adfywiad*) or 'awakening' (*deffroad*) of the 1990s, defined by Johnson as:

> a growing interest in the language and Welsh culture among the inhabitants of the region, reflective of curiosity regarding the origins of the original settlers and of the greater freedoms allowed since the restoration of democracy to Argentina and devolution of powers to individual provinces.
>
> (Johnson 2009:142)

Without the benefit of hindsight, it is worth bearing in mind that the authors of the more pessimistic interpretations of *Y Wladfa* evidently could not foresee the gradual revitalization of Welsh (mainly as a second language) that Chubut Province has witnessed since the 1990s. Conversely, it could be argued that it is largely because of this 'revival' that Lublin's viewpoint is strikingly more optimistic in relation to earlier accounts of the Welsh colony.

---

2   All translations are my own.

Furthermore, bearing in mind that Lublin is a native of Argentina, it is also plausible that her study's emphasis on the contribution of the Welsh colony in Patagonia as an integral part of Argentina, as opposed to its imperative role in the development of Welsh nationalism and the history of Wales generally, accounts in part too for its relative positivity. Indeed, Johnson even suggested that the recent 150th anniversary of the Welsh colony in Chubut was celebrated for wholly distinct reasons on both sides of the Atlantic:

> The celebration in Wales is largely of the unique survival of the Welsh language and culture in an exotic outpost far from home. In Patagonia, the celebration is of the successful settlement of the territory and how the Welsh made the otherwise barren area fertile and possible to inhabit through the irrigation of the fields surrounding the River Chubut. We should, of course, question both myths.
>
> (Johnson 2015)

Be that as it may, by acknowledging from the outset that historical interpretations of *Y Wladfa* (or *la colonia galesa del Chubut*) are bound to vary according to the national background of their authors and their dates of publication, what follows in the next section is a schematic and brief summary of some of the most unambiguous facts pertaining to the Welsh colony in Chubut, coupled with an overview of the development of the Welsh language and culture in the region. In this initial summary, I will attempt to demonstrate that the case of Patagonian Welsh is particularly interesting from the perspective of language contact generally since it has witnessed considerable (and some unexpected) changes in terms of its status, domains of use and the nature of its contact with Spanish.

This general outline will then be followed by a reflection on the fieldwork that I have conducted in various communities in Welsh Patagonia and the various methodological issues that have arisen accordingly. I will then proceed to summarize the main findings of a pilot study of an ongoing project that examines the effects of social and cultural developments in Chubut on the use of various linguistic features in contemporary Patagonian Welsh, a surprisingly understudied variety of Welsh. The general linguistic trends revealed in this section will draw on comparisons with previous data obtained by R.O. Jones (1976, 1984, 1988), following his fieldwork in the lower Chubut Valley in the early 1970s. The final part of this chapter will explore the repercussions of the findings yielded so far for future projects, including possible anthropological avenues of research.

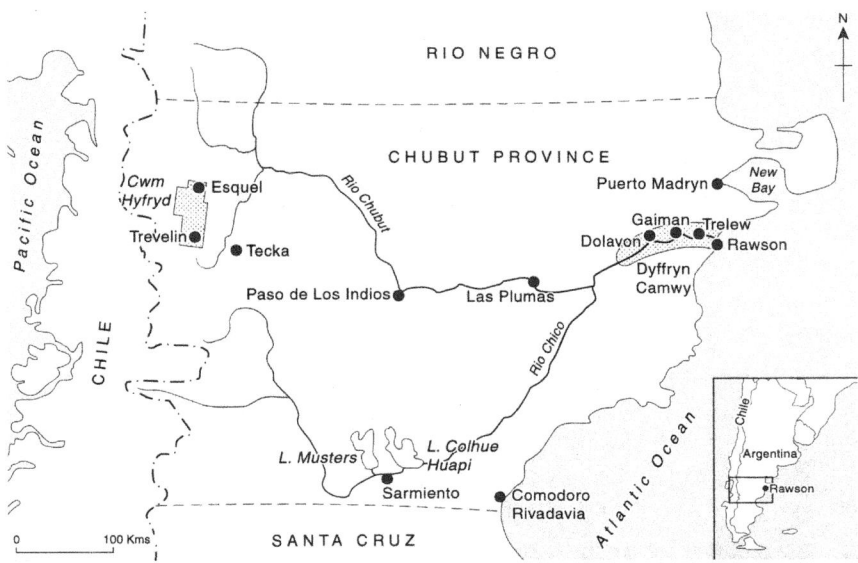

Figure 1 Map of Chubut Province, including places in the Welsh colony (from R. Jones 1998:296).

Historical background of the Welsh colony in Chubut

As mentioned above, the Welsh colony in Patagonia, or *Y Wladfa* (*Gymreig*), is found in Chubut Province, southern Argentina. The colony does not consist of the entire province however, and today it is generally considered that *Y Wladfa* is confined to two distinctive parts of Chubut, namely the lower Chubut Valley (*Dyffryn Camwy* in Welsh), which extends from Rawson to Dolavon in the east of the region, and the Cordillera de los Andes region (*Godre'r Andes* in Welsh), which borders Chile and comprises Esquel and Trevelin (see Figure 1). Although separated by over 550 kilometres, family connections and Welsh cultural links remain between these two major districts.

The term *Y Wladfa* (*Gymreig*) probably reinforces the widely held belief that it represents the first and only attempt by the Welsh to establish a distinctively Welsh colony. However, as both R.O. Jones (1998:289–92) and MacDonald (2015:3–4) point out, this common perception is by and large erroneous because several previous attempts were made by groups of Welshmen to colonize parts of the Americas. The first of these can be traced back as far as 1617 when William Vaughan of Golden Grove (*Gelli Aur*), Carmarthenshire, founded Cambriol or New Cambriol in Newfoundland.

This episode in the history of Welsh colonization is documented as a spectacular failure since it appears that the harsh weather conditions of one winter in Newfoundland, coupled with the resentment of some neighbouring French settlers, were enough to send most of the Welsh colonists back home.

Later attempts to establish Welsh settlements include Morgan John Rhys's Cambria in the Allegheny Mountains of west Pennsylvania (founded in 1798), New Cambria in Nova Scotia (established in 1818), Cardigan in New Brunswick (founded by a Welsh company in 1819), as well as Thomas Benbow Phillips's endeavour to set up the Welsh-speaking colony of Nova Cambria in the Rio Grande do Sul region of Brazil in 1850 (the closest in terms of proximity and chronology to *Y Wladfa*). As MacDonald highlights, these previous attempts to found Welsh colonies can collectively be described as 'a series of catastrophic failures' (MacDonald 2015:3). Indeed, R.O. Jones implies that it is in relation to these unsuccessful ventures that the significance of *Y Wladfa* becomes clear:

> although Welsh was to be supplanted to a large extent by Spanish [after the second and third decades of the twentieth century], it is highly significant that there are still Welsh speakers in Patagonia to this day [i.e. at the end of the twentieth century] – the fourth and fifth generation for whom Welsh is the mother tongue. The language has not survived in any other settlement or colony established by Welsh speakers. In every other instance outside Wales success has been achieved only in the short term.
>
> (R.O. Jones 1998:288)

Despite substantial emigration from Wales in the mid-nineteenth century, especially to North America (Jones and Jones 2001), Welsh is not commonly regarded as a colonizer language. Bearing in mind that Welsh has today become a minoritized language in Wales itself, with around 19 per cent (562,000) of the country's population being able to speak it according to the 2011 UK census (ONS 2012), it is all the more astonishing that the Welsh language has existed continuously in Patagonia since the establishment of *Y Wladfa* over 150 years ago. The exact number of Welsh speakers in Chubut is in fact not known, but recent sources suggest that some 5,000 people still speak Welsh in the province today (Anon. 2019; James 2014).

Another crucial question is how *Y Wladfa* came into existence in the first place. On 28 July 1865, 153 Welsh emigrants, most from the coalfields of south-east Wales and English urban centres, arrived in Patagonia aboard the *Mimosa*, a converted tea clipper. The establishment of a Welsh colony in this remote region of South America was not only in response to the increasing dominance of the English language and of the Anglican Church in Wales (Jones 2009; Williams 1991:23), but also resulted from concerns that considerable emigration from Wales in the mid nineteenth century, mainly to North America, ultimately led to the loss of Welsh speakers' language, culture and religion (Johnson 2009: 141). Indeed, Michael D. Jones, the Welsh

Congregationalist minister and principal of a theological college who was key to the idea and implementation of the Welsh colony, had previously spent some years in the United States, where he had observed that Welsh immigrants tended to assimilate very quickly compared with people of other nationalities (R.O. Jones 1998:291–2; Williams 1991:22–6). Consequently, he believed that it was necessary to establish a Welsh colony in a more isolated location away from the influence of the British Empire where Welsh immigrants could preserve their language, culture and religion. Eventually, the Argentine government's offer of the lower Chubut Valley was accepted in exchange for the Welsh settlers' occupation of the land, which would ultimately secure Argentine sovereignty over the region (Coupland and Garrett 2010:8).

Around 3,000 Welsh emigrants travelled to Patagonia between 1865 and 1911, but immigration from Wales ceased thereafter (Johnson 2009:142), largely because of the outbreak of the First World War. Initially, the Welsh colony was largely self-sustaining and independent, and it managed its own education system, its own local political and legal institutions, its religious buildings, and its own economic cooperative company and irrigation society (R.O. Jones 1998:297–307). Unsurprisingly, Welsh was established as the exclusive language of all these establishments, and it cannot be overemphasized how revolutionary this sudden and substantial expansion in the language's domains of use was, bearing in mind that Welsh was to a great extent confined to the home and the chapel in Wales until the second half of the twentieth century. Moreover, several Welsh-language newspapers were published regularly soon after the establishment of *Y Wladfa* (Brooks 2012; Williams 1962:123–6, 169, 198), and the early Welsh settlers even had their own constitution written in Welsh (R.O. Jones 1998:298).

The domination of Welsh in all domains of public and personal life was not to continue however, and by the end of the nineteenth century, the Argentine state increased its pressures on the Welsh community to integrate into the wider community, and education through the medium of Spanish became a legal requirement for all public schools. Gaiman was the only area which came into direct confrontation with the Argentine government over the education issue, but even here, the government finally took over the school in 1899. Another consequence of this resistance by the Welsh community was that Welsh-speaking teachers were relocated away from lower Chubut Valley to other regions in Argentina (Coupland and Garrett 2010:9).

Nevertheless, instruction through the medium of Welsh did not cease to exist completely in the twentieth century since a campaign got under way for an independent secondary school, which was eventually opened in Gaiman in 1907, and remained operative until 1947. As R.O. Jones points out, Ysgol Ganolraddol y Gaiman (the Gaiman Intermediate School) was pioneering in that 'its syllabus was patterned on that of the British grammar school system but the education was trilingual – Welsh, Spanish and English in contrast to the English monoglot education current at the same period in Wales' (Jones 1984:239).

It could therefore be interpreted that a reluctant acceptance of Spanish coincided with a degree of anglicization, at least in the case of the school in Gaiman. Incidentally, it is noteworthy that Brooks's recent study of Welsh print culture in *Y Wladfa* concludes that 'an almost total adherence and sense of belonging to an international British community' can be seen from the pages of *Y Dravod*, a local newspaper, from the advent of the First World War until 1920 (Brooks 2012:14). Similarly, Williams also highlights that certain members of the Welsh ethnic group (especially those who had migrated from the lower Chubut Valley to Buenos Aires) tended to align themselves with the Anglo-Argentine community during this period, and thereby emphasizes the irony that 'Britishness assumed a respectability which their forefathers had found repugnant and oppressive' (Williams 1991:246–7).

It appears that the Argentine education system was successful in its attempt to Hispanicize the children of the Welsh settlers. Interestingly, during his visit to Chubut in 1971/2, Davies (1976: 77) observed that levels of bilingualism varied among female speakers, specifying that several women over the age of seventy hardly had any knowledge of Spanish, whilst generally those under the age of seventy were able to communicate fluently through the medium of Argentina's national language. He also claims that the same levels of difference were not observed among male speakers due to the influence of Argentina's compulsory military service (from 1901 onwards).

It follows that all members of the Welsh community in Chubut were not necessarily Hispanicized after the turn of the twentieth century. Indeed, this initial period of the colony has even been described as 'the period of independence for the Welsh language' (ibid.:69). However, Davies concludes that an influx of immigrant groups other than the Welsh during the first decades of the twentieth century was ultimately the most effective medium to Hispanicize the Welsh colony in Chubut Valley, remarking that 'the older generation can still remember the time when almost all of the natives were Welsh, referring to the odd Italian shopkeeper in Gaiman, or even in Trelew, who would also learn a bit of Welsh for commercial purposes' (ibid.:77).

A substantial increase in the non-Welsh population was not the only factor that contributed to the decline of the Welsh language in Chubut, however. Because of economic developments in Argentina between the 1920s and 1930s, the Welsh settlers also witnessed a decline in their political influence. Williams, for instance, states that the Welsh settlers 'lost their institutional power base through the collapse of the Co-operative Society, the nationalization of the Irrigation Society, the Railway Company, and the flour mills and their loss of control of the local municipalities' (Williams 1991:156). Moreover, intermarriage became increasingly common too, leading to a reduction in the intergenerational transmission of the language. After the Second World War, as the Argentine government promoted monolingualism in the country, Welsh became increasingly restricted to Welsh-speaking families and religious meetings.

Even attendance at Welsh-speaking chapels fell since their function as local welfare agencies became less necessary due to the Argentine government's introduction of medical insurance for the self-employed from the 1940s onwards (ibid.:126–7, 257). Ultimately, a conflict concerning the involvement of missionaries from the Methodist Episcopal Church from the United States, who encouraged the use of Spanish as the medium of communication, served to practically separate the remaining members of the Welsh chapels into two factions in the early 1960s (ibid.:127–32). As Williams highlights, '[c]ertainly the conflict served to speed up the process of cultural assimilation by further reducing the Welsh-language domains and by weakening the internal cohesion of the ethnic group in formal institutional terms' (ibid.:131–2).

However, it is claimed that the 1965 centenary of the establishment of the Welsh colony led to an improvement in attitudes towards the Welsh ethnic group, as well as a renewed interest in the Welsh language and culture (Brooks and Lublin 2007; Coupland and Garrett 2010:9; Johnson 2009:142). The *Eisteddfod*, a competition-based Welsh cultural festival dedicated to literature, music and dance, was revived during the celebrations of the 1965 centenary for instance. However, it was not until the early 1990s that the Welsh language seemed to be on the increase (Jones 1996), largely due to the support of voluntary Welsh-speaking teachers from Wales.

This revived enthusiasm for Welsh ultimately led to the initiation of a formal project to promote the language in Chubut in 1997 funded by the Welsh Office (now the Welsh Government), the British Council and the Wales–Argentina Society. Over twenty years later, the 'Welsh language project in Chubut' is reported as being an astounding success, with the highest ever number of learners being noted in its 2016 annual report (Arwel 2016). The most recent milestone in the project's development has been the establishment of Ysgol y Cwm in 2016, Chubut's third Welsh–Spanish bilingual primary school. Since the inception of the project in 1997, three teachers from Wales have been assigned to different regions of Chubut each year to teach Welsh to adults and school pupils at various levels, as well as to coordinate cultural activities through the medium of Welsh.

However, despite the growth of Welsh language classes in the province, Welsh speakers still constitute a small minority of the 500,000 plus inhabitants of Chubut today (as noted above, the exact number of Welsh speakers in Chubut is not known). The long-term future of Welsh as a heritage language is far from clear, and interestingly, Birt suggests that '[l]earning Welsh in Patagonia is not an attempt at reversing language shift but rather, [a means of] enabling participation in Welsh-language cultural events' (Birt 2005:148). Nonetheless, several children claimed in interviews with me to have acquired Welsh (partly) at home, and it remains to be seen whether the transmission of the language will be common among future generations.

Fieldwork and methodological issues

The fieldwork relating to the findings of this chapter was conducted in Chubut Province, Argentina, in 2016 for a pilot study upon which a larger project on language contact and dialect contact phenomena may be based. The simple aim of this field trip was to record a range of Welsh speakers from a variety of linguistic backgrounds to establish the degree and nature of language variation present, not only between different speaker types but also within the language of individual speakers.

Informants were selected in different areas of Chubut using the 'friend of a friend' technique that enabled me to draw on people's pre-existing social relationships (Milroy 1987:66).[3] Contact was thus made with prominent local community members who agreed to function as 'brokers' in the area and helped me to persuade suitable speakers to participate in interviews with me. The brokers explained to the participants that I was a native speaker of Welsh from Wales seeking conversations with Welsh speakers in Chubut. In this way I was able to access local social networks, and to be recognized primarily not as a researcher but as an acquaintance of the 'brokers' who was from Wales.

It must be acknowledged, however, that this technique was not completely successful in persuading every person contacted to take part in my research: claims of inability to speak 'proper Welsh' or even to remember the language were the most common reasons for such refusals. Future work on the sociolinguistics of Welsh in Chubut should bear this challenge in mind, especially when the objective is to obtain representative samples of the Welsh-speaking population in these communities. Random sampling was not used in this study: as noted above, Welsh speakers constitute a very small minority of the population of each community in the Welsh settlement, and sociolinguists working on varieties of Welsh in Wales have found this technique to be

---

3   This technique has previously been used in several sociolinguistic studies around the world, e.g. in Wales (Jones 1982; M. Jones 1998), England (Britain 1997), New Zealand (Holmes *et al.* 1991), Austria (Lippi-Green 1989), Australia (Horvath 1985) and Brazil (Bortoni-Ricardo 1985).

impractical in the context of a minority language (e.g. M. Jones 1998:49; Thomas 1998:92).

For the purpose of this pilot study, and due to time limitations, an accurate representative sample of the whole Welsh-speaking population in Chubut was not considered to be practical nor necessary; rather, the aim was to record a cross-section of speaker types. As for the classification of speakers, I decided to distinguish between 'heritage speakers' (including 'heritage learners'), defined by Polinsky and Kagan as 'people raised in a home where one language is spoken who subsequently switch to another dominant language' (Polinsky and Kagan 2007:368), and second-language learners of Welsh (L2 learners henceforth) who have been raised through the medium of Spanish only.[4]

The advantage of engaging with the concept of heritage speakers, rather than employing the more superficial term 'first-language speakers' (L1 speakers), is that it acknowledges the considerable inter-individual differences that exist among this group of speakers. Indeed, Polinsky and Kagan (ibid.:370–2) have proposed a continuum of speaking abilities among heritage speakers that ranges from 'acrolectal' (high-proficiency, near-native) speakers to 'basilectal' (lowest-proficiency) speakers. Although placing various heritage speakers on the continuum goes beyond the scope of this pilot study, it should be borne in mind that the heritage speakers of Patagonian Welsh are not uniform in terms of their speaking competencies and that a mixture of 'heritage speakers' (who have never formally been educated in Welsh) and 'heritage learners' (that is, heritage speakers who follow Welsh courses, often accompanied by L2 learners of Welsh) can be found today in Chubut.

Ultimately, thirty-five speakers were interviewed, and divided into four specific types of speaker according to the way in which they had acquired Welsh (see Table 1). For this specific study however, only six of these speakers form the basis of my analysis; three from group A (heritage speakers), one from group B (a type a heritage learner who had the opportunity to study Welsh in Wales in the 1990s), and two from group C (L2 adult learners).[5] Members of group D – namely L2 pupils currently learning Welsh (mainly) at bilingual schools – are not included in this study; these speakers were recorded conversing with their peers and Welsh teacher at Gaiman's secondary school, Colegio Camwy, but further individual interviews would be required for the

---

4   In the context of language learning, 'second language' (L2) can also refer to a third, fourth and fifth language (and so on) that the learner is learning or has learnt.

5   It is worth highlighting that heritage learners who have studied Welsh in Chubut only were not included in this pilot study but would be useful in future work for assessing the extent to which the 'Welsh language project in Chubut' is influencing heritage speakers' use of Welsh.

Speaker types	No. of speakers
A – Heritage speakers; raised through the medium of Welsh; received no formal Welsh education	12
B – Heritage learners; (some) Welsh during upbringing; followed Welsh courses in Chubut and/or Wales	10
C – L2 adult learners; followed Welsh courses in Chubut and/or Wales	9
D – L2 pupils currently learning Welsh in Chubut	4

Table 1   The number of speakers interviewed in each group.

data of this group to be comparable with the results obtained for the other speaker types.

Further details of each individual speaker interviewed are found in Table 2, where it is shown that male and female informants are included within groups A and C. Despite gender and age differences within the sample, speakers' mode of acquisition was considered the most pertinent factor in the investigation of linguistic variability. As for the single individual in group B, it was originally intended to include her in group A; however, it became apparent that this speaker, who claimed to have always spoken Welsh to her grandmother (but mostly Spanish to her parents), had spent two years studying in Wales. Interestingly, she was able to distinguish between words that she used with her grandmother during her childhood and other forms that she believed to have acquired whilst studying in Wales. It was thus decided that this speaker would be very appropriate as a representative of an intermediary group – that is, a type of 'heritage learner' between the two main groups. As for the other two groups, it should be emphasized that differences relating to the use or experience of Welsh exist within the same category of speakers. For instance, the two female speakers of group A (A1 and A3) were noted to be more involved in local Welsh-language activities than male speaker A2. In the same way, among the L2 learners of group C, speaker C1 is an experienced tutor and one of Chubut's early learners who started learning Welsh in the early 1990s, whilst speaker C2 had been studying Welsh for less than five years at the time of the interview.

The decision to focus on a relatively small sample of speakers reflects the fact that a holistic approach to language variation was adopted in this study; the aim was simply to identify as many relevant linguistic features as possible across the various speaker types.[6]

---

6   A detailed description of all the linguistic features identified (most of which are phonological/phonetic in nature) and the way in which they were transcribed and analysed can be found in Rees (2021).

Group	Speaker	Male/Female	Living in/Brought up in	Date of birth
	A1	F	Esquel / Trevelin	10/03/1928
A	A2	M	Esquel / Bryn Gwyn (near Gaiman)	12/01/1943
	A3	F	Gaiman / Bryn Gwyn	21/06/1927
B	B1	F	Gaiman / Treorci (near Gaiman)	23/02/1965
	C1	M	Gaiman	25/04/1971
C	C2	F	Gaiman / Buenos Aires and Gaiman	17/11/1967

Table 2   Informants' details.

The main findings

As noted above, the full detailed results of each individual speaker for every linguistic feature examined (most of which are phonological and/or phonetic in nature) will not be presented in this chapter but are analysed in detail from a contact linguistics perspective in Rees (2021). Rather, the aim of this section is to summarize the main general findings of the results and thereby explore the social and cultural implications of the linguistic phenomena apparent today among Patagonian speakers of Welsh.

The first subsection below will explore the relationship between degrees of linguistic Hispanicization and recent changes to the type and density of social networks in which Welsh speakers in Chubut have participated. The second subsection will then investigate the effects of language standardization, which largely emanates from the British Council's 'Welsh language Project in Chubut' and more generally from increased transnational contact, on the use of Spanish and English loanwords that are common in heritage speakers' traditional varieties of Patagonian Welsh. In each of these cases, comparisons will be drawn with previous data obtained by R.O. Jones following his fieldwork in the lower Chubut Valley in the early 1970s.

Linguistic Hispanicization

The relationship between the use of traditional dialect features and the density of social networks is succinctly summarized in the following hypothesis by Milroy and Milroy: 'the degree to which individuals approximate to a vernacular speech norm seems to correlate to the extent to which they participate in close-knit networks. It should not be surprising that a close-knit group tends to be linguistically homogeneous' (Milroy and Milroy 1978:23). By including the retention of linguistic features originating from Wales as examples of the 'vernacular speech norm' as opposed to later innovations arising due to the influence of the dominant Spanish language, it is certainly possible to apply this theory to the case of Patagonian Welsh over the last fifty years or so. R.O. Jones (1984), for example, based on his fieldwork in the town of Gaiman in the early 1970s, attempted to examine the relationship between linguistic variation and the social stratification of Welsh in the community. A random sampling technique was applied, based mainly on speakers' gender and age, but their cultural orientation was also considered. The latter social dimension considered speakers' religious and educational background, as well as their cultural affiliation.

Table 3 is included in this section despite its phonetic nature: not only is it useful in giving linguists an idea of some of the phonetic features involved in both R.O. Jones's study and my own, but it will also be of interest to non-linguists since it illustrates neatly how clear-cut some intergroup differences were in the 1970s (as opposed to the situation today). In Table 3, the Welsh-speaking sample obtained is divided into four main age-groups. It is also shown that group II has been further divided into two subgroups according to their cultural orientation: category A speakers are more likely to be prominent members of a Welsh chapel, for instance, whilst category B informants tend to be more involved with Spanish-medium religious establishments. Significantly, R.O. Jones states that:

> social network patterns coincide with these social strata divisions in that
> informants A tended to socialize far more with other Group A speakers but
> not to the exclusion of rapport with Group B speakers or with non-Welsh
> speaking members of the community.
>
> (Jones 1984:245)

Without going into detail about the precise phonetic qualities involved in the case of each of the four features analysed by R.O. Jones, it is clear from Table 3 nevertheless that age played a crucial role in the patterns of variation obtained among younger speakers, who appeared to be much more likely to have incorporated Hispanicized variants in their Welsh than the older generation, who seemed to be identical to Welsh speakers in Wales. However, the differences between sub-groups IIA and IIB confirm that age was not the only relevant social factor in the early 1970s, and that speakers' cultural orientation, and thus their social networks, were also important elements that conditioned the extent of Spanish influence.

How does the older generation of the 1970s, characterized above by linguistic uniformity – that is, a consistent use of features associated with the homeland – compare with today's traditional heritage speakers (group A speakers as defined above)? My initial analysis has in fact revealed that linguistic uniformity is neither the norm within the language of single speakers nor that between different individuals. For example, intra-individual variation between homeland (ʃ) and Hispanicized (s) was common by female speakers

	I	II		III	IV
	Elderly (60+)	Middle-aged (45–60) A	B	Young Middle-aged (30–45)	Young (under 30)
chi 'you'	[χiː]	[χiː]	[xiː]	[xiː]	[xiː]
chwaer 'sister'	[χwaːir]	[χwaːir]	[xwaːir]	[xwaːir]	[xwaːir]
te 'tea'	[tʰeː]	[tʰeː]	[teː]	[teː]	[teː]
tân 'fire'	[tʰaːn]	[tʰaːn]	[taːn]	[taːn]	[taːn]
pont 'bridge'	[pʰontʰ]	[pʰontʰ]	[pont]	[pont]	[pont]
siŵr 'sure'	[ʃuːr]	[ʃuːr]	[siuːr]	[siuːr]	[siuːr]
siwgr 'sugar'	[ʃugur]	[ʃugur]	[siugur]	[siugur]	[siugur]
Spanish	[spaniʃ]	[spaniʃ]	[spanis]	[spanis]	[spanis]
machine	[maʃiːn]	[maʃiːn]	[masiːn]	[masiːn]	[masiːn]
mynydd 'mountain'	[mənið]	[mənið]		[minið]	[minið]
yn y tŷ 'in the house'	[ən ə tiː]	[ən ə tiː]		[ən ə tiː]	[in i tiː]
fy afal i 'my apple'	[ən aval i]	[ən aval i]		[ən aval i]	[in aval i]

Table 3   The realizations of four phonetic variables (adapted from Jones 1976:60).

A1 and A3, whilst the Hispanicized variant was used consistently by male speaker A2 (see details of the speakers in Table 2). This difference may well be related to the speakers' social networks and general usage of Welsh: the two female speakers (A1 and A3), for instance, participated regularly in Welsh-speaking and chapel events, and often encountered visitors from Wales; the male speaker on the other hand was very much on the fringe of Welsh-speaking networks and associated the language mostly with the past and his late mother, who had refused to speak Spanish to him during his childhood.

To sum up, whilst older speakers of Patagonian Welsh in the early 1970s seemed to exhibit a substantial degree of linguistic uniformity due to their retention of homeland-like phonetic features, it follows that an absence of such homogeneity among Chubut's present-day heritage speakers of Welsh strongly suggests that the close-knit Welsh social networks that existed a generation or so ago have ceased to be due to intense Hispanicization. In other words, the increased amount of variability seen among traditional speakers of Patagonian Welsh today certainly points to the fact that they engage mostly (if not exclusively) in Spanish-speaking communities of practice. This finding therefore concurs with Milroy and Milroy's hypothesis, cited above, but contrasts with Nagy's investigation of heritage languages in Toronto, in which no correlations were found between speakers' 'strength of ties to the outgroup and [contact-influenced] linguistic patterns in the heritage language' (Nagy 2017:101).

Finally, it is worth quoting an extract from my interview with a female traditional speaker (A3), who attributed her strong Welsh identity to a former 'Welsh circle' (sadly, she has recently died):

INTERVIEWER: Why did you like Wales so much?

A3: Well ... well, maybe because I felt homely there, like, the same kind of people as us [...] Because the Spanish people are different, aren't they?

INTERVIEWER: Do you feel more Welsh than ...

A3: Yes, yes. Well, I've had a Welsh home. And then ...

INTERVIEWER: But you wouldn't say ...

A3: And the circle in Gaiman, and in Bryngwyn too, it was a Welsh circle you could say, but that [circle], as other people are coming in, it's getting weaker, isn't it?

INTERVIEWER: Yes. Would you say that you are an Argentinian who speaks Welsh?

A3 [*laughs*]: Well, I am in Argentina of course. But there you are, I usually say that I'm ninety-nine and another nine per cent [i.e. 99.9 per cent] Welsh. Yes.

INTERVIEWER: Welsh?

A3: Almost a hundred.

Certainly there can be no doubt that this specific qualitative evidence reinforces my interpretation of the linguistic data that a reduction in close-knit Welsh-language social networks has coincided with an increase in linguistic Hispanicization generally.

Standardization

Patagonian Welsh is also a fascinating subject area from a dialect-contact perspective. Indeed, between 1865 and 1911, Welsh speakers from all parts of Wales (the industrial south-east, south-west and north of the country) migrated to Patagonia, and as is common in *tabula rasa* colonial settings (see e.g. Trudgill 2006), a new 'colonial' variety of Welsh was formed as a natural consequence of this mixture of dialects. The phenomenon of 'dialect levelling', defined by Williams and Kerswill as 'a process whereby differences between regional varieties are reduced, features which make varieties distinctive disappear, and new features emerge and are adopted' (Williams and Kerswill 1999:149), seems to resonate with R.O. Jones's interpretation of the way in which Patagonian Welsh was formed:

At the beginning of my analysis I believed the northern dialects had prevailed. However, after having examined the data more thoroughly, we see that it is the linguistic patterns of the Bible and the public speech patterns of the pulpit ... which account for the [early] fusions [i.e. the dialect levelling] and standardization.

(Jones 1987:21; see also Jones 1974)

Standardization is thus not a recent phenomenon in relation to the development of Patagonian Welsh; however, it should be borne in mind that this supposed chapel-based standardization that occurred early in the history of *Y Wladfa* was merely partial and that, consequently, the use of non-standard forms, including loanwords from Spanish and English alike, are still common today among some Welsh speakers in Chubut.

How then does the use of loanwords vary according to the different speaker types noted above in Tables 1 and 2? The results for eight lexical variables were obtained from speakers' responses to eight separate pictures, and a glance at the data reveals a stark and categorical contrast between the heritage speakers of group A and the L2 speakers of group C who have learnt Welsh as adults. Simply, loanwords are used constantly by the traditional speakers but are always replaced by standard Welsh words by the L2 learners. Four of the variables yielded a combination of English and Spanish loanwords by group A speakers ('strawberries' and *frutilla*; 'stairs' and *escalera*; 'sweets' and *caramelos*; 'plums' and *siniguelas*); two variables had English variants only ('carrots', pronounced as [karɔts] or [karɛts]; 'cabbage', pronounced as [kabɛts]) and the other two had Spanish loanwords only (*galpón* and *carbón* for 'shed' and 'coal' respectively).

However, the data obtained from informant B1 (a heritage learner) are valuable in that she was able to distinguish between the words that she would use when conversing with her grandmother during her childhood on the one hand, and the forms that she claims to have used regularly following her time studying in Wales. What is striking about the results of speaker B1 is that most of her childhood forms mirror those obtained from group A speakers; conversely, her self-reported current usage of standard Welsh words seems to connect her with the adult learners of group C. Consequently, the similarities seen between B1's 'new forms' and the standard Welsh words used by group C speakers appear to confirm that Welsh language instruction is a significant factor insofar as lexical variation and change in contemporary varieties of Welsh spoken in Chubut is concerned.

The clear pattern of decline that is seen in the use of Spanish and English loanwords is undoubtedly an indication of the language standardization (or further standardization) that is taking place amid L2 and heritage learners of Welsh as a result of Welsh language lessons (in both Chubut and Wales). In this respect, it is worth highlighting that a shift towards lexical standardization appears to coincide with an increased level of phonological Hispanicization among new speakers of Patagonian Welsh. It is also noteworthy that this recent instance of standardization appears to derive mainly from linguistic norms determined and imparted by institutions in Wales. The British Council has worked closely with the Welsh for Adults sector ever since the inception of their 'Welsh language project', for instance, and the newly established National Centre for Learning Welsh is involved in developing new educational resources specifically for learners in Chubut. Certainly, this contrasts sharply with the language standardization that took place early in the history of *Y Wladfa* since this was entwined to a great extent with establishments and initiatives founded in the Welsh colony itself (see above for details).

Conclusion

The empirical evidence presented above allows us to explore the way in which the significant social and cultural changes that Welsh speakers in Chubut Province have experienced correlate to a great extent with various linguistic phenomena. The first of these phenomena, namely linguistic Hispanicization, can certainly be attributed to a decline in the existence (if not disappearance) of close-knit Welsh-language social networks over the last fifty years or so. This considerable social development could also explain to some degree why the intergenerational transmission of Welsh is generally low among most of the traditional heritage speakers that remain in Chubut today, although there are exceptions to this trend. More generally though, there can be no doubt that the increased linguistic Hispanicization that has been observed is in fact a reflection of the Welsh ethnic group's gradual integration into wider Argentinean society. In a way then, *Y Wladfa* has eventually succumbed to the same destiny as other Welsh communities in diaspora, despite the early Welsh pioneers' belief that assimilation was not inevitable.

On the other hand, the notion of language standardization has been shown to be prevalent among both heritage learners and L2 learners of Welsh in Chubut. Clearly then, the instruction of Welsh, mainly by means of the British Council's 'Welsh language project', has influenced the use of certain lexical features in contemporary varieties of Patagonian Welsh. It therefore follows that the standardization observed in the case of loanwords is indicative of the wider revival of the Welsh language and culture in Chubut that has accelerated in the province since the early 1990s.

Be that as it may, the significant linguistic differences that have been shown to exist between traditional heritage speakers and L2 learners of Welsh certainly raise important questions about the way in which heritage languages generally are taught and promoted in postcolonial contexts. Indeed, further research is required in order to determine the extent to which the needs of learners from all language backgrounds in Chubut are accommodated in the classroom, and whether the use of non-standard features by heritage learners (for example, the use of English loanwords which are in fact perceived as Welsh words by some traditional speakers) are not undermined by linguistic norms perpetuated in Wales.

Finally, it is worth highlighting that the analysis provided above has focused solely on the linguistic repercussions of certain social developments in Chubut. There remains ample potential therefore to conduct other studies from a more anthropological perspective in order to show how social phenomena, such as general Hispanicization, transnational contact and tourism (see e.g. Johnson 2010), bilingual education and so on have also influenced a whole raft of cultural and religious customs and practices. For instance, to what extent has the linguistic assimilation observed above or the lack of intergenerational transmission of the language among members of the Welsh ethnic group in Chubut coincided with religious changes, including conversion to Catholicism? Similarly, in what ways has an increase in transnational contact, including short-term tourist visits and longer-term engagements of teachers from Wales, resulted in adapting or changing Welsh Patagonian cultural events or institutions such as *Eisteddfod y Wladfa*, *Gorsedd y Wladfa*, folk music and dance societies as well as local choirs?

It is hoped that this study will thus inspire researchers from a variety of backgrounds to explore the ever-changing and multifaceted phenomenon of Patagonian Welshness, for example, as a Welsh-language utopia or as in more recent Spanish-language representations. Furthermore, this study will also illuminate future investigations of the interplay of the role of place and the concept of Welsh identity. In this respect, this unique diasporic situation lends itself to further academic study as it concerns a complex relationship between (at least) two contrasting localities (Wales and Patagonia/Argentina) and identities (Welsh and Argentinean/Hispanic).

Acknowledgements

I thank the University of Wales Press for permission to reproduce the map in Figure 1, the Coleg Cymraeg Cenedlaethol for the grant that made my visit to Argentina possible and, of course, the members of the Welsh-speaking community in Chubut who gave of their time to help me with this project. I am also indebted to Professor Emeritus W. John Morgan not only for the invitation to share some of my findings at the joint symposium 'Social anthropologies of the Welsh: past and present' held at Cardiff University, but also for encouraging me to contribute to this volume.

References

Anon. 2019. 'Argentina'. In D.M. Eberhard, G.F. Simons and C.D. Fennig (eds), *Ethnologue: Languages of the World*, 23rd edn: www.ethnologue.com/ country/AR/languages (accessed 17 December 2019).

Arwel, R. 2016. 'Welsh language project in Chubut: 2016 annual report'. British Council Wales: wales.britishcouncil.org/sites/default/files/welsh_language_ report_english.pdf (accessed 17 December 2019).

Birt, P. 2005. 'The Welsh language in Chubut Province, Argentina'. In D. Ó Néill (ed.), *Rebuilding the Celtic Languages: Reversing Language Shift in the Celtic Countries*, pp. 115–51. Talybont: Y Lolfa.

Bortoni-Ricardo, S.M. 1985. *The Urbanization of Rural Dialect Speakers: A Sociolinguistic Study of Brazil*. Cambridge: Cambridge University Press.

Britain, D. 1997. 'Dialect contact and phonological reallocation: "Canadian raising" in the English Fens'. *Language in Society* 26:15–46.

Brooks, W.A. 2012. 'Welsh print culture in Y Wladfa: the role of ethnic newspapers in Welsh Patagonia, 1868–1933'. PhD thesis. Cardiff: Cardiff University.

Brooks, W.A., and Lublin, G. 2007. 'The Eisteddfod of Chubut, or how the reinvention of a tradition has contributed to the preservation of a language and culture'. *Beyond Philology* 4:245–59.

Coupland, N. and Garrett, P. 2010. 'Linguistic landscapes, discursive frames and metacultural performance: the case of Welsh Patagonia'. *International Journal of the Sociology of Language* 205:7–36.

Davies, G.A. 1976. *Tan Tro Nesaf: Darlun o Wladfa Gymreig Patagonia*. Llandysul: Gomer.

Holmes, J., Bell, A. and Boyce, M. 1991. *Variation and Change in New Zealand English: A Social Dialect Investigation*. Wellington: Victoria University.

Horvath, B.M. 1985. *Variation in Australian English*. Cambridge: Cambridge University Press.

James, E.W. 2014. 'Viewpoint: the Argentines who speak Welsh'. *BBC News*, 16 October: www.bbc.co.uk/news/magazine-29611380 (accessed 17 December 2019).

Johnson, I. 2009. 'How green is their valley? Subjective vitality of Welsh language and culture in the Chubut Province, Argentina'. *International Journal of the Sociology of Language* 195:141–71.

——— 2010. 'Tourism, transnationality and ethnolinguistic vitality: the Welsh in Chubut Province, Argentina'. *Journal of Multilingual and Multicultural Development* 36(6):553–68.

——— 2015. 'Patagonia: no Welsh Shangri-La'. *IWA*, 12 June: www.iwa.wales/ click/2015/06/patagonia-no-welsh-shangri-la (accessed 17 December 2019)

Jones, A. and Jones, B. 2001. *Welsh Reflections: Y Drych and America 1851–2001*. Llandysul: Gomer.

Jones, A.E. 1982. 'Erydiad Geirfaol: Astudiaeth Ragarweiniol'. *Cardiff Working Papers in Welsh Linguistics* 2:25–42.

Jones, M.C. 1998. *Language Obsolescence and Revitalization: Linguistic Change in Two Sociolinguistically Contrasting Welsh Communities.* Oxford: Clarendon Press.

Jones, R.O. 1974. 'Amrywiadau Geirfaol yn Nhafodieithoedd Cymraeg y Wladfa'. *Studia Celtica* 8/9:287–98.

——— 1976. 'Cydberthynas Amrywiadau Iaith a Nodweddion Cymdeithasol yn y Gaiman Chubut – Sylwadau Rhagarweiniol'. *Bwletin y Bwrdd Gwybodau Celtaidd* 27:51–64.

——— 1984. 'Change and variation in the Welsh of Gaiman, Chubut'. In M.J. Ball and G.E. Jones (eds), *Welsh Phonology: Selected Readings*, pp. 237–61. Cardiff: University of Wales Press.

——— 1987. *Yr Efengyl yn y Wladfa.* Pen-y-bont ar Ogwr: Llyfrgell Efengylaidd Cymru.

——— 1988. 'Language variation and social stratification: linguistic change in progress'. In M.J. Ball (ed.), *The Use of Welsh: A Contribution to Sociolinguistics*, pp. 289–306. Philadelphia: Multilingual Matters.

——— 1996. 'A report on the Welsh language in Argentina's Chubut Province 1996/ Adroddiad ar yr iaith Gymraeg yn nhalaith Chubut, yr Ariannin 1996'. Cardiff: British Council.

——— 1998. 'The Welsh language in Patagonia'. In G.H. Jenkins (ed.), *Language and Community in the Nineteenth Century*, pp. 287–316. Cardiff: University of Wales Press.

Jones, R.T. 2009. 'Michael D. Jones a Thynged y Genedl'. In E.W. James and B. Jones (eds), *Michael D. Jones a'i Wladfa Gymreig*, pp. 60–84. Llanrwst: Gwasg Carreg Gwalch.

Lippi-Green, R.L. 1989. 'Social network integration and language change in progress in a rural Alpine village'. *Language in Society* 18:213–34.

Lublin, G. 2017. *Memoir and Identity in Welsh Patagonia: Voices from a Settler Community in Argentina.* Cardiff: University of Wales Press.

MacDonald, E. 2015. 'Y Wladfa 1865–2015: Dathlu Beth?' Llyfrgell Adnoddau'r Coleg Cymraeg Cenedlaethol: llyfrgell.porth.ac.uk/View. aspx?id=1571~40~oojXKuy3 (accessed 17 December 2019).

Milroy, J. and Milroy, L. 1978. 'Change and variation in an urban vernacular'. In P. Trudgill (ed.), *Sociolinguistic Patterns in British English*, pp. 19–36. London: Edward Arnold.

Milroy, L. 1987. *Observing and Analysing Natural Language.* Oxford: Basil Blackwell.

Nagy, N. 2017. 'Cross-cultural approaches: comparing heritage languages in Toronto'. *University of Pennsylvania Working Papers in Linguistics* 23(2):95–103.

ONS (Office for National Statistics). 2012. '2011 census: key statistics for Wales':
    www.ons.gov.uk/peoplepopulationandcommunity/populationandmigration/
    populationestimates/bulletins/2011censuskeystatisticsforwales/2012-12-11
    (accessed 17 December 2019).

Polinsky, M. and Kagan, O. 2007. 'Heritage languages: in the "wild" and in the
    classroom'. *Language and Linguistics Compass* 1(5):368–95.

Pryce, H. 2019. 'Why write the history of Wales – then and now?' O'Donnell Lecture,
    Cardiff University, April 2019.

Rees, I.W. 2017. 'Cyflwyno Tafodieithoedd Cymraeg y Wladfa'. Llyfrgell Adnoddau'r
    Coleg Cymraeg Cenedlaethol: llyfrgell.porth.ac.uk/Default.aspx?catid=528
    (accessed 17 December 2019).

——— 2021. 'Hispanicization in the Welsh settlement of Chubut Province, Argentina:
    some current linguistic developments'. In D. Perez and E. Sippola (eds),
    Postcolonial Language Varieties in the Americas. Berlin: De Gruyter.

Thomas, A.E. 1998. 'Ynys Fach o Gymreictod: Astudiaeth Sosioieithyddol o'r
    Gymraeg ym Mhont-rhyd-y-fen'. PhD thesis, Cardiff: University of Wales,
    Cardiff.

Trudgill, P. 2006. *New-Dialect Formation: The Inevitability of Colonial Englishes*.
    Edinburgh: Edinburgh University Press.

Williams, A. and Kerswill, P. 1999. 'Dialect levelling: change and continuity in Milton
    Keynes, Reading and Hull'. In P. Foulkes and G. Docherty (eds), *Urban
    Voices*, pp. 141–162. London: Arnold.

Williams, G. 1975. *The Desert and the Dream: A Study of Welsh Colonization in
    Chubut 1865–1915*. Cardiff: University of Wales Press.

——— 1991. *The Welsh in Patagonia: The State and Ethnic Community*. Cardiff:
    University of Wales Press.

Williams, R.B. 1962. *Y Wladfa*. Caerdydd: Gwasg Prifysgol Cymru.

7

Community studies and twentieth-century social change

Perspectives on Welsh society

GARETH REES

Introduction

This chapter explores a series of remarkable social anthropological studies that were conducted in Wales during the decades preceding and immediately following the Second World War. They were self-consciously 'community studies', focusing on the analysis of social relations in specific localities, predominantly (although by no means exclusively) in rural Wales. However, despite this local focus, it will be argued that they provide a unique set of insights into the character of Welsh society midway through the twentieth century. Given this, it is perhaps surprising that they are not better known by today's scholars.

It is also noteworthy that these studies reflected the institutional contexts in which they were developed. In what follows, three groups of studies are distinguished, each associated with a specific academic environment, at what were then respectively the University College of Wales, Aberystwyth, the University of Manchester and the University College, Swansea.[1] Table 7.1 lists the studies produced by each of the three 'schools' of research, indicating the localities and dates of the studies, and the dates when the results were published. It will be argued that these schools of research were characterized by distinctive analytical approaches that were shaped by the intellectual currents that predominated in their specific academic environments. In turn, the studies contributed significantly to the further development not only

---

1   The two Welsh institutions were the forerunners of the present-day Aberystwyth University and Swansea University respectively.

Study	Date of publication	Locality	Date of fieldwork
Aberystwyth School			
Rees, *Life in a Welsh Countryside*	1950	Llanfihangel-yng-Ngwynfa, Montgomeryshire	1939–46
Davies and Rees, *Welsh Rural Communities*	1960	Aber-Porth; Tregaron; Aberdaron; Glan-Llyn.	1945–50
Jenkins, *Agricultural Community in South-West Wales at the turn of the Century*	1971	South-west Cardiganshire	1958–61 (oral history & historical sociology)
Manchester School			
Frankenberg, *Village on the Border*	1957	Glynceiriog, Denbighshire	1953
Emmett, *North Wales Village*	1964	'Llan', Merionethshire	1958–62
Swansea School			
Brennan, Cooney and Pollins, *Social Change in South-West Wales*	1954	various local communities of the Swansea sub-region	1949–53
Rosser and Harris, *Family and Social Change*	1965	urban villages, Swansea	1960
Charles, Davies and Harris, *Families in Transition*	2008	ethnographic areas, Swansea	2002

Table 1   Three schools of community studies.

of their local intellectual contexts, but also to that of social anthropology generally (e.g. Cohen 2005; Frankenberg 1966). Less well known are the significant consequences of these studies for the growth, both institutional and intellectual, of the social sciences in Wales. Indeed, this is a topic which is worthy of much more systematic analysis than is possible here.

The principal aim of this chapter is expository. It sets out to provide an account of the content of these three groups of community studies and to compare the analytical approaches they adopt. In doing so, questions are raised about the nature of the insights they provide into the character of Welsh society in the middle of the twentieth century. Hopefully, this might stimulate interest among today's scholars in these now sadly neglected studies. More generally, albeit more briefly and tentatively, the chapter also explores the influence that these studies have had on the ways in which Welsh society is conceived outside the narrowly academic realm. How Welsh society is understood more popularly is of crucial importance to contemporary political and cultural debates. It is, therefore, a matter of importance as to how our understandings of these issues have been shaped by academic studies of the kind that are considered here.

The 'Aberystwyth School': rural *Gemeinschaft*

The prime mover in the development of the 'Aberystwyth School' of community studies was Alwyn D. Rees. During the years preceding and immediately following the Second World War, Rees organized a programme of research involving broadly ethnographic studies of a series of small localities within what was unambiguously rural Wales. Indeed, Frankenberg (1966:45– 65) subsequently used these studies to illustrate what he termed the 'truly rural' in his discussion of a 'morphological continuum' of community types in Britain (and Ireland). Whilst Rees's programme was only partially completed, the studies that were conducted provide a coherent and cumulative account of social relations in rural Wales at this time.

The initial study was Rees's own of Llanfihangel-yng-Ngwynfa, in Montgomeryshire, a rather isolated, upland settlement, albeit not far from the border with England (Rees 1950). His research was begun in 1939 and eventually completed in 1946, following the significant interruption of the Second World War. During the immediate post-war years, further studies were conducted by Rees's postgraduate students, in a variety of locations in Mid and North Wales. Four of these were published in a volume edited by Alwyn Rees and his colleague Elwyn Davies (Davies and Rees 1960). Finally, one of these postgraduate students, David Jenkins, who had remained at Aberystwyth, carried out an interesting study in south-west Cardiganshire between 1958 and 1961, around the small village of Rhydlewis, in which respondents were asked to reflect back on the nature of social life in the locality some half a century previously (Jenkins 1971).

The intellectual context for this work was provided by the then Department of Geography and Anthropology at Aberystwyth, where innovators such as Daryll Forde and H.J. Fleure were pioneering anthropological research. The former was instrumental in supporting Alwyn Rees in developing the programme of ethnographic community studies, as was the then principal of the University College of Wales, Aberystwyth, Ifor Evans (Carter 1996:3). This institutional environment, in turn, goes some way towards accounting for the wider theoretical framework within which the studies were conducted, as well as, perhaps more directly, the specific perspective from which the social relations of Welsh rural society were viewed. It is also worth remarking that both Alwyn Rees and David Jenkins became long-term members of the academic staff of the Department of Extra-Mural Studies at Aberystwyth (in fact, Rees eventually became its director in 1949). It was working with adult classes, drawn from local areas external to the university, that provided both these authors with the primary subject matter for their principal studies (Jenkins 1971; Rees 1950).

It is fair to say that the analytical strengths of the 'Aberystwyth School' do not lie in major theoretical development. Indeed, later commentators have argued that Rees's study adopts no explicit theoretical framework for the analysis (Carter 1996; Owen 1986). In fact, he does draw on the social anthropology that was conventional for the period (at least as this was conveyed in the Department of Geography and Anthropology at Aberystwyth, where he had been a student). However, there are certainly no real claims to wider theoretical innovation (Rees 1950:162–5). Moreover, the studies whose publication followed are even more reticent about their theoretical framing and do not draw explicitly theoretical conclusions (Davies and Rees 1960; Jenkins 1971). What these studies do provide, however, are richly empirical accounts of the social relations characteristic of the localities that were investigated. What emerges is a coherent picture of Welsh rural communities that share a common way of life, despite the differences in their geographical locations and economic circumstances.

Accordingly, relations of economic production (predominantly in agriculture, but also embracing other activities such as fishing) are described as overwhelmingly cooperative; families and neighbours collaborate to sustain effective economic activity, especially at key periods of the year such as harvest time. Indeed, more generally, interactions based on kinship and neighbourliness are seen to be central to maintaining the close social relationships that pertain within these communities. Religious institutions and the beliefs which they foster play an integral role in social life, with both the churches and, more especially, the Nonconformist chapels providing not only a focus of belief and worship but also a major contribution to a range of social and cultural activities (such as *eisteddfodau*, debates and so forth). The influence of Nonconformism, moreover, is reflected in what is portrayed as a shared set of social values, prioritizing self-discipline, industriousness and the importance of educational achievement and upward occupational mobility. The indispensable mode of communication that underpins the wider cultural system of these communities is the Welsh language. Those who are not able to use the language are, in effect, excluded from participation in the everyday life of the community, which on occasion may give rise to tensions between the diverse groups of residents.

Overall, however, social conflicts were largely absent. In particular, class relations are described as almost wholly collaborative.[2] Following the demise of the landed gentry during the early decades of the twentieth century, relationships between the remaining class groupings – farmers and labourers – are based upon cooperation in the sphere of production and joint participation in the social institutions that are central to community life. Indeed, Jenkins (1960) notably proposes a system of attributing social status alternative to that based on occupation or wealth, which largely avoids social

---

2   There are clearly echoes here of the debates about the notion of the *gwerin* (Day 2002).

conflicts. Hence, for Jenkins, status derives from contrasting modes of living: *Buchedd A*, entailing individual (or family) respectability and conformity with the normative expectations of religious institutions; and *Buchedd B*, which involves a much more secular and somewhat hedonistic lifestyle.[3]

The Aberystwyth studies present Welsh rural society in terms that closely reflect Tönnies's celebrated depiction of *Gemeinschaft* (Tönnies 1955), a type of society built upon small-scale communities, intimate social relationships of kinship and neighbourliness, shared values rooted in characteristic religious observance and an absence of fundamental social conflicts, especially those based on class differences. This characterization, in turn, was consistent with the conventional wisdom of the social anthropology of the 1950s, which was dominated by functionalist forms of analysis (Cohen 2005:606–7).

However, whilst conventional in many respects, these studies also adopted a specifically Welsh perspective. The scholars who undertook them were self-consciously 'insiders', whose understanding of the communities they researched was enhanced by their own access to the Welsh language and their life-time of personal experience of the way of life they describe. Moreover, their accounts are underpinned by a largely unexamined conceptualization of the social relations they outline as constituting an 'essential Wales' and, by extension, an exclusive definition of what Welshness comprises. Hence, the consensual, intimate, linguistically homogeneous communities they depict are simultaneously deeply rooted in a relatively unchanging past and under threat from modernizing and anglicizing influences from across the border with England. To undermine the stability of Welsh rural life, as they see it, is to threaten the very core of Welshness itself. These are arguments which will be revisited later; but before doing so, it is necessary to explore a radically different account of Welsh rural society.

The Manchester School: class and social conflict

Dominating the work in Wales of the Manchester School is Frankenberg's study of Glyn Ceiriog, a village in Denbighshire, near to the border with England (Frankenberg 1957). The Manchester School of social anthropology is, of course, more widely celebrated as a key influence on the development of the discipline in Britain and elsewhere. During the years following the Second World War, a group of scholars came together in Manchester and, under the leadership of Max Gluckman, pioneered anthropological studies of industrialized societies (including Britain), placing a much greater emphasis on conflictual social relations than had hitherto been the norm (Cohen 2005:609–11). This intellectual environment powerfully influenced

---

3   For a well-argued critique of this argument, see Day and Fitton (1975).

Frankenberg's approach when he joined the Manchester department to conduct postgraduate research. Moreover, he brought with him a well-founded familiarity with Marxist theoretical ideas, as well as a strong practical commitment to left-wing politics. Indeed, he had been debarred from undertaking fieldwork in both what was then Northern Rhodesia and St Vincent in the West Indies in circumstances related to his membership of the Communist Party of Great Britain.[4] By electing to conduct fieldwork in north-east Wales, Frankenberg met the condition imposed by the university vice-chancellor in light of his earlier difficulties of being within easy reach of Manchester, and the disciplinary expectation of studying in a place where a language other than English was used (ibid.:605).

Not surprisingly, then, the initial emphasis of Frankenberg's account of Glyn Ceiriog is the locality's economic circumstances. The surrounding areas are described as being dependent on agriculture, but the village itself has an industrial history, based upon quarrying and agricultural processing. It is the demise of these industries in the area that constitutes the essential material conditions that shape local social relations. As a result, the bulk of the working-age men of the village are obliged to commute daily to employment outside the local area, many travelling to towns over the border with England. It is the women who spend the main part of their daily lives at home and, thereby, are the essential actors in everyday social interaction. This gender divide lies at the heart of the community's social life.

It is also striking that, whilst Frankenberg's account identifies many of the key social institutions that feature in the Aberystwyth studies (kinship and neighbourliness, chapels and churches, the role of the Welsh language and so forth), his analytical focus is on the structuring of local social relations in terms of endemic conflicts between social groups. These conflicts are sometimes seen as structured around differentiations of class, most clearly illustrated in the account of local politics, where wealthier interests dominate the more powerful echelons of local government. However, other dimensions of social differentiation are also significant. Hence, the protracted disputes over the organization of leisure activities in the community – in the football club and the annual carnival – can be understood only by reference to the underpinning tensions in gender relations. Conflicts between 'locals' and 'outsiders' or 'strangers', which often map on to distinctions between Welsh-speakers and English-speakers, are also a key element in the social dynamics of

---

4   Frankenberg was a member of the Communist Party from the early 1950s until the Hungarian uprising in 1956. Max Gluckman, Victor Turner and Peter Worsley, all senior members of the Department of Social Anthropology at Manchester, were also party members at the time (Cohen 2005:605).

the community as Frankenberg describes it. Indeed, somewhat paradoxically, it is the capacity of 'outsiders/strangers' to provide a means of defusing community conflicts by deflecting 'blame' from local protagonists that the locality's social cohesion can ultimately be maintained.

Emmett's study of an isolated locality in the uplands of north-west Wales (Emmett 1964) also highlights the importance of conflictual relations, in this instance between the Welsh and 'ruling England'.[5] In particular, she describes the ways in which local young people are required to negotiate complex pathways between 'opposing prestige ladders' (ibid.:43), between remaining loyal to the Welsh values that are intrinsic to the community on the one hand, and, on the other, responding to the obvious material advantages to be gained through education and upward social mobility, but which can only be accessed through the English language and, frequently, in England itself. Here, too, the social role of the 'outside' (conceived by locals in terms of the 'English') is, again somewhat paradoxically, to affirm the coherence and integrity of the characteristic social values of the local community.

In short, then, the studies produced by the Manchester School provide an account of Welsh rural communities that is quite different from that of the 'Aberystwyth School'. Ostensibly, the localities that they explored are rather similar in geographical scale and type of location. They also share key social institutions, amongst which kinship and religious institutions are especially prominent, and the Welsh language is recognized as playing a key role. However, as has been seen, the two groups of scholars conceive of the social relations that characterize their communities in sharply distinctive terms. Where Rees and his colleagues depict communities characterized by collaboration and consensus, Frankenberg and Emmett emphasize conflict and dissent. This analytical divergence, in turn, begs the obvious question of how to account for these manifest differences.

'Insider' and 'outsider' perspectives

For Rees and his colleagues, this conundrum of divergence can be resolved by reference to the nature of the researchers themselves. Hence, for example, in their editorial preface to the collection of community studies conducted by postgraduate researchers, Davies and Rees address the issue directly. They explain:

> The authors are all natives of rural Wales, who speak its language and are
> familiar with its ways; the author of the essay on Aberporth was, in fact,

---

5   The study was conducted before Emmett joined the Manchester group. However, she acknowledges the latter's influence in shaping her analytical perspectives.

brought up in the village about which he writes … [F]undamentally, these
are studies of a culture 'from within', the Welshman as he sees himself …
The things which are emphasized are those to which the greatest value was
attached in the societies in which the authors were reared … For the student
who approaches the culture from without, these things are for the most part
inaccessible.

(Davies and Rees 1960:xi)

In contrast with the authors of the Aberystwyth community studies, it
is argued by Davies and Rees, that Frankenberg (and, by extension, Emmett)
was not nurtured within the social and cultural system characteristic of Welsh
rural society. In consequence, and despite his immersion in Glyn Ceiriog for an
extended period of fieldwork (for more than a year), Frankenberg was unable
to access the 'essentials of the culture' and was diverted into a consideration
of peripheral social phenomena, such as the football club, the carnival and
local government. The essential nature of Welsh rural communities can be
grasped only by those who are themselves 'insiders' by virtue of their own life
experience.

This issue of the effects of the standpoint of the researcher on the results
of research is, of course, a familiar one, not only within social anthropology
but more widely across related social sciences too. There is no need to
rehearse these general arguments here. However, it is appropriate to make
brief observations on the tensions between the 'Aberystwyth School' and its
Manchester counterpart. First, it is noteworthy that the 'insider'/'outsider'
distinction is rather less sharply drawn by the direct protagonists than has
been suggested by subsequent commentators (e.g. Williams 1983). Davies
and Rees, having drawn attention to the distinction, aver that '[b]oth the
internal and the external points of view are relevant to a fuller understanding
of the culture' (Davies and Rees 1960:xi). Likewise, Frankenberg (1957:vii)
acknowledges the support provided to a researcher newly arrived in Wales by
Alwyn Rees, critically based on his expertise on matters pertaining to Welsh
rural society. He also writes quite warmly about the Aberystwyth research in
his later overview of community studies in Britain (and Ireland) (Frankenberg
1966).

Nevertheless, it is undeniable that significant differences, especially in
terms of theoretical orientation, do exist between the 'insider' and 'outsider'
perspectives. Perhaps the most perceptive summary of the differences
between the two groups of studies is provided by Frankenberg himself in a
review of David Jenkins's study of south-west Cardiganshire (Jenkins 1971).
Frankenberg says:

> I thoroughly enjoyed reading the book but it left me sadly contemplating the paradox of Welsh studies, that those who understand the culture best, are inhibited from analysing the society, while those of us who are largely cut off from the culture are left to carry out the social analysis.
>
> (Frankenberg 1972:179)

Frankenberg was strongly influenced by Marxist analysis and this was dramatically different from the largely unacknowledged functionalism of Rees and his colleagues. Moreover – and perhaps more importantly – he did not share the general approbation accorded by the Aberystwyth scholars to the social relations characteristic of Welsh rural communities, at least as they understood them. Secondly, the categories of 'insider' and 'outsider' are by no means wholly unambiguous. Hence, it is somewhat ironic that, unlike his postgraduate researchers, Alwyn Rees himself was not a 'native ... of rural Wales' (Davies and Rees 1960: xi). He was instead born and brought up at Gorseinon in the west of the South Wales coalfield and was the son of a miner. Whilst this part of the coalfield retained elements of its rural past, his own engagement with exclusively rural Welsh society was presumably initiated in later life, especially through his work in mid Wales for the Department of Extra-Mural Studies at Aberystwyth. Undoubtedly, however, he shared with other members of the 'Aberystwyth School' key elements of social experience, especially as expressed through religious Nonconformism and the Welsh language.[6]

Likewise, it was noted earlier that the 'outsider' studies were based on extensive fieldwork. Frankenberg and his wife lived in Glyn Ceiriog for an extended period and became involved – even adopting leadership roles – in local activities (Frankenberg 1957:119). Isobel Emmett provides an especially interesting case here. Her study was based in a village to which she had moved not to carry out an anthropological study initially but rather to live there with her husband, who had been brought up there and whose family were long-term locals (Emmett 1964:xii–xiii). The question posed here, therefore, is exactly what sorts of relationships with a community are necessary to qualify for 'insider' status?

---

6   It is perhaps worth observing that I share this sort of background. Indeed, my family home is close to the village of Aberporth, which was the subject of Jenkins's initial community study. Despite this geographical proximity and our shared 'insider' status, there are features of his account that I do not recognize from my own experience. It may be, of course, that differences in the period at which we acquired our 'insider' status underpin this dissonance.

It may well be that a crucial consideration in this context is the ability to use the Welsh language. Certainly, all the contributors to the 'Aberystwyth School' were native speakers of the language. It is less clear whether either Frankenberg or Emmett became fluent Welsh-speakers. Hence, there are indirect indications that Emmett learned enough to understand informal conversations but not to participate actively in social interactions conducted through the Welsh language. As for Frankenberg, his choice of a locality in north-east Wales in which to conduct his research was partly determined by the widespread use of Welsh in everyday life. He certainly provides a brief but insightful account of the complexities of Welsh-language use in Glyn Ceiriog and the surrounding area (Frankenberg 1957:29–33). How far he himself mastered the language is more difficult to determine. In a letter to his mentor, Max Gluckman, dated 24 March 1953, he wrote:

> We intended to telegraph back in Welsh but as the only thing we can say and write fluently is 'I am going to the village to sing' and this seems hardly relevant, so we did not. You can gather from this that the work is going slowly but I am beginning to grasp some Welsh.[7]

Clearly, then, if he did become fluent in Welsh (and he subsequently claimed to have done so),[8] he worked very hard at it during the few months between writing this letter and beginning systematic fieldwork in the summer of 1953. Moreover, he makes it clear that, irrespective of his own facility in the Welsh language, residents overwhelmingly avoided using it in his presence. Not having full access to the Welsh language (for whatever reason) inevitably restricted the engagement of the Manchester School researchers with key domains of social life. It is not surprising, for example, that Frankenberg (1957:67) very largely ignores the role of religious institutions, where activities were conducted wholly in Welsh. Undoubtedly, the Welsh language constitutes a key dimension of the 'insider' and 'outsider' distinction and, hence, the differentiation between the Manchester and Aberystwyth schools.

Communities and social change

A wholly alternative explanation of the contrasting accounts of characteristic local social relations provided by the two schools is that there were real

---

7   Letter, Frankenberg to Gluckman, 24 March 1953, Gluckman papers, RAI archives. I am indebted to Professor John Morgan for alerting me to this correspondence.

8   Frankenberg made the claim in conversation with Professor Pat Caplan (Pat Caplan, personal communication, 1 May 2019). I am grateful to Professor Caplan for this information.

differences between the communities they studied. Hence, for example, everyday life in Llanfihangel-yng-Ngwynfa could be differentiated from that in Glyn Ceiriog because, despite their somewhat similar geographical locations near to the border with England, the two localities had experienced widely different historical trajectories of economic and social change. The former, for instance, remained dependent upon largely traditional forms of agriculture adapted to upland conditions, whilst the latter had undergone very substantial economic changes as a result of the closure of local quarries and the plants processing wool and other agricultural products. These economic changes, in turn, had important consequences for local employment and for class and gender relations, as well as for other aspects of the community's social structure and interactions.

Viewed in this rather more sociological way, the social relations observed in local communities should be understood as being shaped by the working out of wider historical processes of economic and social change in ways specific to localities. Accordingly, whilst commonalities between different communities may be expected, there are significant differences too. What is crucial is that both shared features and those specific to particular localities are understood through sustained analysis of the interactions between the local social system and wider economic and social developments.[9]

The scholars of the 'Aberystwyth School' acknowledge these interactions, but only to a limited extent. It is true that there are passing references to the impacts of, for example, the Second World War and the rising prosperity of the post-war years; changes in the organization of agricultural production are also acknowledged. However, major historical shifts of this kind are not integral to their account of local communities. In fact, social change is conceptualized in a specific way. The only historical shifts that are recognized as being of major significance entail the imminent threat posed to the established social order of Welsh rural communities by the impacts of increasing secularization, materialism, commercialization, urbanization and linguistic decline. Moreover, these are viewed as alien intrusions, originating from outside Welsh rural society, especially from England and the anglicized regions of Wales. As Rees puts it:

> In more general terms, the little community of Llanfihangel, through
> accepting current values and becoming part of the contemporary economic

---

9   For a very clear review of this sort of analytical approach in a Welsh context, see Day (2002).

system, is already in the initial stages of the social atomisation which is
general in Western Civilisation.

(Rees 1950:168)

Hence, traditional social relations that have been relatively unchanging
over an extended period are portrayed as being in decline because of
external influences. What is striking here, moreover, is the normative basis
of the analysis. The social order under threat is seen as a uniquely valuable
expression of the established virtues of Welsh rural society. Not only are the
local communities studied taken to be representative of Welsh rural society,
but also to reflect the best features of Wales more widely. Accordingly, what is
at stake for the 'Aberystwyth School' is the survival not simply of the estimable
way of life that characterizes rural communities, but thereby of the essence
of Welshness itself. In this way, as Graham Day has succinctly put it, 'the
interpreters of Welsh community are also its advocates' (Day 2002:145).[10]

Clearly, for all the sensitivity with which Frankenberg (1957) depicted the
values embraced by the residents of Glyn Ceiriog and its surrounding areas, he
did not share this view of the value of the way of life of rural communities in
Wales – and similar arguments can be made about Emmett's (1964) study too.
There is ample evidence of his empathy with the people of the community,
but he did not understand their circumstances in terms of the threat to an
'essential Welshness' that underpins the Aberystwyth accounts.

Rather, as was noted earlier, Frankenberg's (1957) study provides an analysis
that explores in directly empirical terms the relationships between local
social processes and wider patterns of economic and social change. Indeed,
methodologically, he followed his mentor, Max Gluckman, in conceiving
of the fine-grained analysis of such local social processes as the necessary
route to the understanding of wider patterns of social change (Charles and
Davies 2005). Substantively, moreover, as his subsequent reflections on his
study of Glyn Ceiriog make clear (see Frankenberg 1966:88–92), he sees the
gradual undermining of established social relationships based on kinship,
religion and language as the local outcome of the wider restructuring of
economic production and the assertion of the general class relations that the

---

10   It is worth remembering that not all 'insider' observers shared this highly
     positive evaluation of the way of life described by the 'Aberystwyth School'. The
     writer Caradoc Evans, who was raised in Rhydlewis in Cardiganshire, provides
     an acerbically critical account of many of the same features of rural Welsh life,
     especially in his renowned (or notorious, depending on your viewpoint) collection
     of short stories, *My People* (Evans 1915). I am grateful to Dr Lynn Williams for
     pointing out this contrast.

latter embodies. He views local social relations as being shaped by societal processes; and the latter are understood – albeit largely implicitly – in terms of the broader context of British society or of an even wider comparative framework, rather than as being specifically Welsh.

This analysis undoubtedly provides powerful insights. It is limited, however, in that the detailed character of economic and social change is largely inferred. Hence, data on shifts in local social relations are based on Frankenberg's direct observations over only the single year that he spent conducting fieldwork in Glyn Ceiriog. Evidence of longer-term changes must be gleaned from indirect sources, such as the recollections of established residents. Likewise, the impacts of wider patterns of societal change cannot be directly substantiated based on a study conducted at, in effect, a single point in time. Indeed, evidence used to describe the character of these wider patterns is derived from earlier histories, rather than from primary sources. In fact, analysis of the relationships between changes in local social relations and these wider shifts owes as much to the theoretical perspectives that Frankenberg brought with him to his study as to robust empirical investigation (and, of course, his study is by no means unique in this regard).

In summary, an examination of the ways in which the community studies produced by the Aberystwyth and Manchester schools deal with historical change reveals highly instructive differences. The former adopts a perspective that emphasizes relatively homogeneous social relations that are viewed as characteristic of Welsh rural communities. These social relations, in turn, constitute an 'essentially Welsh' way of life that has endured for an extended period, but is increasingly under existential threat from alien influences, originating externally. For the latter, local social relations reflect the working out of trends of economic and social change that operate across British society as a whole and, indeed, even more widely. This approach opens the possibility of different forms of social relations, dependent upon the specific interactions between local circumstances and more general structural shifts. However, the emphasis on the precise forms of interaction between the local setting and wider restructuring entails very stringent requirements in terms of the types evidence that are necessary to sustain a plausible analysis in these terms.

The 'Swansea School': continuity and change

The third group of community studies to be examined in this chapter is comprised of those conducted by scholars of the 'Swansea School'. As with the other two schools, the institutional context of this work was significant, in that the studies were closely associated with the development of the social sciences at what was then University College, Swansea, eventually leading to the establishment of an independent Department of Sociology and

Anthropology, whose sad demise was announced in 2004 (Charles, Davies and Harris 2008:xiii). Initially at least, the aim was to provide a vehicle for the university to contribute to the analysis of the economic and social conditions of the region in which it was located (Brennan *et al.* 1954:vii). This meant, of course, that the setting for the Swansea research was quite different from that of the studies considered so far. The work of the 'Swansea School' focused on local social relations in the urban and industrial environments in and around Swansea itself.

The principal study here is that conducted by Rosser and Harris and published in 1965 (although the fieldwork was done a little earlier, during 1960). They viewed Swansea as a 'confederation' of local communities, which they described as 'urban villages', a concept they derived from the work of the distinguished American sociologist, Herbert Gans (1965). More specifically, they set out to explore the extent to which the central role of extended families and wider kin that had been identified in Bethnal Green, in the east end of London, in the 1950s by Young and Willmott (1957), was replicated in the rather different circumstances of Swansea. In doing so, they provided, in effect, a comprehensive account of the way of life characteristic of the 'urban villages' they identified (much as Young and Willmott had done previously), although they were unable to replicate the fine-grained, ethnographic analysis of the rural community studies. They concluded that far from being in decline, extended families and kin were integral to the local social relations they described, especially in the more working-class communities of Swansea. This was despite the latter's markedly different occupational structure and cultural make-up when compared with Bethnal Green (Rosser and Harris 1965).

To an even greater extent than Frankenberg's study, this Swansea-based research is thus self-consciously concerned with issues that resonate much more widely than the local communities ('urban villages') that provide their empirical focus. Certainly there is no suggestion that what they discover is in any way specific to Welsh society (in the manner of the 'Aberystwyth School'), although due reference is made to the linguistic and cultural dimensions of Welshness and the specificity of their manifestations in Swansea. Indeed, based on the similarity of the findings of the Bethnal Green study and theirs in Swansea, Rosser and Harris pose the question of whether 'we have a regularity of behaviour which is a common feature of urban kinship in Britain' (ibid.:228).

Intriguingly, a study conducted by Swansea researchers some forty years after Rosser and Harris completed their research also reports crucial similarities to these findings (Charles, *et al.* 2008). This new study, the fieldwork for which was conducted in 2002, was explicitly designed as a restudy of Rosser and Harris's original (and Chris Harris, although officially retired, participated in the research too). It focuses on 'ethnographic areas' within Swansea, which are broadly comparable to the 'urban villages' identified in the earlier study by Rosser and Harris (1965). Moreover, the authors conclude that the structure of families across generations and the nature of the social relationships they sustain are remarkably like those described by Rosser and Harris in the working-class areas of Swansea in 1960. In important respects, therefore, there appears to be 'a regularity of behaviour' not only between various parts of Britain, but also across historical epochs too.

This is not to suggest, of course, that Swansea is immune to social change. Hence, Charles *et al.* (2008:54–8) emphasize that residents of Swansea in 2002 form households much later than their equivalents in 1960, and they are substantially less likely, on average, to be living in families with children. For those people who are in families, they are likely to experience familial social relations like those of previous generations, but there are far fewer individuals who live in households with children at all. These differences, in turn, reflect wider changes in, inter alia, gender relationships, class relations and forms of economic activity and employment over the forty years or so separating the two studies.

Rosser and Harris (1965) were also clear that the communities they studied were undergoing significant economic and social change. Their principal point of reference in this regard was provided by what may be considered the first of the community studies carried out by the 'Swansea School' by Brennan *et al.* (1954). This was undertaken between 1949 and 1953 by a research unit specially created by the university to investigate economic and social change within the Swansea region.[11] Although it was concerned with the region around Swansea as a whole, it identified some fifty-five local communities, each with a clear and bounded social identity. Here, the authors describe a distinctive framework of social institutions, based upon tightly integrated linkages between chapels, trade unions and political associations, sustained by overlapping leadership groups.

A relatively homogeneous and stable population provides the basis for a way of life characterized by shared social values and strong codes of behaviour, based around Nonconformism and norms of close family and neighbourly interaction. The echoes of the social world delineated by the 'Aberystwyth School' are clear, despite the extended history of industrial activity in the area (although this coexists with the maintenance of rural activities).[12] Here too,

---

11 The researchers also made extensive use of the university's extra-mural classes to collect data, in ways comparable to key members of the 'Aberystwyth School' (Brennan *et al.* 1954).

12 The Swansea researchers also reference the work of Alwyn D. Rees (1950), although somewhat in passing.

moreover, a distinctive way of life and local culture is seen to be declining in the face of secularization, rising standards of living and a variety of what are described as 'English influences' (ibid.:6–8).

In part at least, Rosser and Harris's (1965) later study can be understood as providing confirmation of these trends. By 1960, they argue, significant elements of the traditional, working-class way of life described by Brennan and his colleagues had disappeared. Local communities in Swansea were much more socially heterogeneous and geographically fluid than they had been, as economic shifts created new educational and employment opportunities. Shared social values were much weakened and attitudes had become substantially more individualistic and inward looking; certainly, class solidarities were less secure than hitherto. In making these arguments, Rosser and Harris were again pointing to the ways in which changes in local communities in Swansea reflected wider developments in British society (and more widely), rather than uniquely Welsh social phenomena. Unsurprisingly, these wider trends attracted considerable sociological interest at the time, although this research suggested that patterns of change were somewhat more complex than portrayed in the Swansea study (Goldthorpe *et al.* 1969).

What is perhaps most striking about the work of the 'Swansea School' is the cumulative character of its empirical investigations. Three substantial studies – one of which is a formal restudy – together provide an account of developments in the social structure of local communities in Swansea and its environs over at least a fifty-year period, from the middle of the twentieth century to the beginning of the twenty-first. More effectively than either the Aberystwyth School or the Manchester School, the Swansea studies were able to present a direct examination of both the significant continuities over this period, as well as the manifest changes that had taken place. In doing so, their analytical strengths lie in their acute delineation of the ways in which wider patterns of social and economic change impact in specific ways in the local communities that are the primary focus of their research. However, this ambitious analytical approach is achieved at the expense of the richly ethnographic accounts that are central to the approach of the Aberystwyth and Manchester researchers.

Conclusion

It is unfortunate that – apart from the Swansea restudy (now nearly twenty years old) – there are few present-day equivalents of the twentieth-century community studies considered in this chapter. Despite the manifest and, in many instances, catastrophic fractures that have occurred in the structures of Welsh society over recent decades, social anthropologists (and social scientists more widely) have largely eschewed the study of local communities in Wales.

Hopefully, the preceding discussion has demonstrated the potential of this sort of approach to generating an improved understanding of the social worlds that people in Wales now inhabit. Crucially, however, what would be most effective here would be a thoroughgoing synthesis of richly fine-grained ethnographic research at the local level, with sophisticated analysis of wider historical shifts in economic and social conditions. Undoubtedly this is a demanding agenda, but its promise is equally rich.[13]

This is a matter of more than narrowly academic interest. This chapter has touched upon the relationships between the community studies undertaken and wider political and cultural perspectives on Welsh society. Hence, for example, the resonances between the account of the 'Aberystwyth School' of an 'essential Wales' under threat from 'anglicizing influences' and versions of popular, nationalist views of Welsh society are apparent. Indeed, Alwyn Rees himself was active in Cymdeithas yr Iaith Gymraeg, the Welsh language society, and became a long-term editor of the Welsh-language magazine *Barn*. Likewise, the emphasis of both the Manchester and Swansea schools on understanding local social relations in terms of the effects of economic and social shifts at the level of wider British society may be seen has having implications for how Wales may be understood more popularly.

It is not suggested that these sorts of relationships between academic research and more popular understandings are straightforward. However, given the current plight of so many Welsh communities, there is an urgent need for analysis based on systematic research to inform contemporary debates within the political sphere and civil society more widely. Properly construed, community studies provide a fertile means of achieving this.

References

Brennan, T., Cooney, E.W. and Pollins, H. 1954, *Social Change in South-West Wales*. London: Watts.

Carter, H. 1996. 'Life in a Welsh countryside: a retrospect'. In A.D. Rees, *Life in a Welsh Countryside*, pp. 1–10. Cardiff: University of Wales Press.

Charles, N. and Davies, C.A. 2005. 'Studying the particular, illuminating the general: community studies and community in Wales', *Sociological Review*, 53 (4), 672-690.

Charles, N., Davies, C.A. and Harris, C. 2008, *Families in Transition: social change, family formation and kin relationships*, Bristol: Policy Press.

---

13   The Wales Institute of Social and Economic Research, Data and Methods (WISERD) aims to generate something approaching this sort of synthesis. Some of its work is reported elsewhere in this volume.

Cohen, A.P. 2005. '*Village on the Border*, anthropology at the crossroads: the significance of a classic British ethnography'. *Sociological Review* 53(4):603–20.

Davies, E. and Rees, A.D. (eds). 1960. *Welsh Rural Communities*. Cardiff: University of Wales Press.

Day, G. 2002. *Making Sense of Wales: A Sociological Perspective*. Cardiff: University of Wales Press.

Day, G. and Fitton, M. 1975. 'Religion and social status: *buchedd* and its lessons for concepts of stratification in community studies'. *Sociological Review* 23(4):242–52.

Emmett, I. 1964. *A North Wales Village: A Social Anthropological Study*. London: Routledge and Kegan Paul.

Evans, C. 1915. *My People: Stories of the Peasantry of West Wales*. London: Andrew Melrose.

Frankenberg, R. 1957. *The Village on the Border: A Social Study of Religion, Politics and Football in a North Wales Community*. London: Cohen and West.

——— 1966. *Communities in Britain: Social Life in Town and Country*. Harmondsworth: Penguin.

——— 1972. Review of Jenkins (1971). *Man* 7:(1):178–9.

Gans, H. 1965. *The Urban Villagers*. Glencoe, IL: Free Press.

Goldthorpe, J., Lockwood, D., Bechhoffer, F. and Platt, J. 1969. *The Affluent Worker in the Class Structure*. London: Cambridge University Press.

Jenkins, D. 1960. 'Aber-Porth: a study of a coastal village in south Cardiganshire'. In E. Davies and A.D. Rees (eds), *Welsh Rural Communities*, pp. 1–66. Cardiff: University of Wales Press.

———1971. *The Agricultural Community in South-West Wales at the Turn of the Twentieth Century*. Cardiff: University of Wales Press.

Owen, T.M. 1986. 'Community studies in Wales: an overview'. In I. Hume and W.T.R. Pryce (eds), *The Welsh and their Country*, pp. 91–133. Llandysul: Gomer.

Rees, A.D. 1950. *Life in a Welsh Countryside*. Cardiff: University of Wales Press.

Rosser, C. and Harris, C. 1965. *The Family and Social Change: A Study of Family and Kinship in a South Wales Town*. London: Routledge and Kegan Paul.

Tönnies, F. 1955 [1887]. *Community and Association*. London: Routledge and Kegan Paul.

Williams, G. 1983. 'On class and status groups in Welsh rural society'. In G. Williams (ed.), *Crisis of Economy and Ideology: Essays on Welsh Society 1840–1980*, pp. 134–46. Bangor: BSA Sociology of Wales Study Group.

Young, M. and Willmott, P. 1957. *Family and Kinship in East London*. London: Routledge and Kegan Paul.

8

Exploring civil society through the lens of place

Illustrations from a post-industrial Welsh village

ROBIN MANN, DAVID DALLIMORE,
HOWARD DAVIS AND MARTA EICHSTELLER

Introduction

Drawing on fieldwork in a deindustrialized Welsh village, we make the case for a place-based understanding of civil society at local levels. We attempt to provide an approach for researching local civil society ethnographically, based on the analysis of four inter-linked components of place. These include sites of participation; the role of individual agents in leading and running local civil society groups and organizations; the presence of local civil society organizations themselves; and the opportunities for association and collective action through events. These components, we would argue, are integral to understanding civil society practices across a range of socio-spatial contexts. They emerge out of the process of embarking on ethnographic fieldwork and the initial analytical reflections on how a broad range of civil society activities take form over local socio-spatial terrains.

The term 'civil society' has several meanings and is most often thought of as a diverse space of communication and solidarity (Cohen and Arato 1994). It is most often examined in terms of its relationship with the state – whether this be challenging the state through movement, resistance or representation of plural interests, or through engaging in a social contract with the state – in pursuit of the greater good. But there is also a rather different, and much broader, definition of civil society to be had, evident in both anthropological and sociological studies (Hann and Dunn 1996; Svendsen 2006), and which sees civil society as grounded in everyday associational practices. From this viewpoint, participation in civil society continues to be defined, to a large degree, by the tangible social relations between people within specific places.

This resonates with Putnam's social capital thesis, which has a focus on local clubs and associations (Putnam 2000). However, Putnam's conceptualization of social capital has been widely criticized for failing to acknowledge the uncivil side of associational life. And, in any case, Putnam's version of social capital is much more suited to the quantitative analysis of civil society (e.g. Li *et al.* 2005) than to its ethnographic documentation. Instead, we would suggest that the study of local civil societies be located within anthropological and sociological studies of place. Participation in local associations is itself linked to performances and practices of place (Benson and Jackson 2013). Further, as Savage *et al.* have argued, there is a need to recognize 'the myriad kinds of association, their different dynamics and constituencies, to develop a more nuanced and adequate account of their importance … seeing how associations are implicated in the routine social relations of neighbourhoods' (Savage *et al.* 2006:74).

Rhosllannerchrugog ('Rhos')

In what follows we draw on fieldwork examining continuity and change in participation in civil society in a large, deindustrialized village in north-east Wales, Rhosllannerchrugog ('Rhos').[1] The aim of the project was to develop understandings of how changes in associational forms and the experiences of local civil society participants are shaped by local contexts. By spending extended periods of time in Rhos between 2015 and 2016 we were able to gather a variety of data, including fifteen biographical narrative interviews with individuals in key roles within different local groups and organizations, members of the community council and the local MP. Interviewees were selected based on their leading role within local groups, and the aim was to interview actors across a wide range of contrasting activities taking place across different local spaces in Rhos.[2] In addition to these interviews, field notes were made at various meetings and events such as community council meetings and local public events and exhibitions. We also conducted face-to-face, questionnaire-based, interviews with 101 residents. These were collected in different public places, including the library, along the high street and at the different local events. Informal conversations were also held with people in Rhos in different public settings such as the library, cafes and shops. Finally, we collated a variety of documentary material such as historical archives

---

1   The paper presented at the original symposium offered a comparison of Rhosllanerchrugog with the predominantly anglicized small town of Overton on-Dee (Welsh: Owrtyn), also in north-east Wales.

2   Pseudonyms are used for interviewees throughout.

and internet sources, which were particularly important in providing further documentary evidence in support of individual narrative accounts.

Rhos is a former coal-mining village with a population of just under 10,000 (ONS 2013). It falls within the jurisdiction of Wrexham County Borough Council in the north-east of Wales and is six miles from the large town of Wrexham itself, which has a population of 61,000 (ibid.). Since the mid nineteenth century, Rhos's fortunes have been heavily linked to the rise and subsequent decline of heavy industries, both in the village and in the broader north-east Wales area. Located within Rhos itself was the Hafod coal mine, while the larger Bersham and Gresford mines lay in the wider locale; together, these were the major sources of employment for people living in Rhos from the second half of the nineteenth century and for much of the twentieth century.

Alongside the mines were other heavy industries in the Wrexham area, including iron and steel production, quarrying, and brick and tile manufacturing. After the Second World War, the north-east Wales area experienced a growth in employment in chemical, plastic and other light manufacturing industries in surrounding villages, small towns and in new industrial estates. This diversification of industry had a considerable influence on patterns of settlement and mobility in and around Rhos. Adjacent to Rhos is the village of Johnstown, which grew in population in the second half of twentieth century as an overspill for Wrexham. As will be shown below, these historical changes relate to the sense of an 'old' or 'proper' Rhos, which refers to the original village, and a 'new' Rhos, which includes the more recent settlement in Johnstown. The industries each have their own trajectory, but by the end of twentieth century all would either have ceased operations or undergone a significant reduction in the number of people employed.

Rhos is also defined by religion and its historical connection to Welsh liberal Nonconformism. The village was a centre of the Welsh religious revival of 1904/5, and at least twenty-one chapels were recorded in 1905 (CHS n.d.). In many ways, the chapels were in tension with industrial workers and their regard for public houses and the sale of alcohol. Over the course of the nineteenth century, chapels in Wales became sites for the assertion of Welsh nationalist consciousness, as well as for local association. They also provided opportunities for political leadership, which were otherwise denied by the Acts of Union of 1536 and 1542, which excluded Welsh-speaking people from political and institutional roles.

This relationship between chapels and Welshness was a central feature of Alwyn Rees's seminal study of Welsh community life (Rees 1950). According to Emmett, Rees made a frank claim: 'if the chapel dies, Welsh culture dies … and the chapel is dying' (Emmett 1982:168). In Rhos, the establishment of the

Welsh-language community newspaper (*papurau bro*) *Nene* in the 1970s was a response to concerns for sustaining the local distinctiveness of the Welsh language, albeit in a period that saw significant developments in Welsh media and Welsh medium and bilingual education at the national level. But a legacy of chapel culture is that the use of Welsh as the language of daily interaction in the village has continued into the twenty-first century. Contemporary data (ONS 2013) shows that while Rhos has a higher proportion of Welsh speakers than either Wrexham or Wales as a whole, these differences mainly derive from the older age groups. The roots of Welsh within Rhos are strongly linked to the growth of industry, which brought Welsh-speaking workers from other parts of Wales to settle in the village. Today there are two primary schools in the village – one where Welsh is the medium of instruction, and another where it is predominantly English, reflecting one of the main fault lines that run through the village.

Local civil society and sociological studies of place

Within the UK, there is, of course, a rich body of place-based ethnographies, including those drawing on the concept of community, which illustrate how local attachments and ties can shape people's involvement in local associational life (see Day 2006). Studies conducted during the 'heyday' of British community studies (1950 to 1970) contain lengthy illustrations of local associations across a variety of geographical contexts.

Amongst other things, this literature emphasizes how participation is linked to sociability and to informal social support, and, therefore, has relevance for Tocquevillian and Putnamesque understandings of civil society as a kind of associational life (see also Svendsen 2006). Examples include Frankenberg's study of local community relations on the Welsh-English border (Frankenberg 1957), Jackson's research into working men's clubs and bowling clubs in Huddersfield (Jackson 1968) and Williams on local associations in the village of Gosforth (Williams 1956:121–36). During this period, Pahl also found how middle-class incomers to rural and suburban areas established different kinds of local association and societies – for example, residential associations and village preservation societies – in which their distinctive imaginings of the village ideal are performed and acted out (Pahl 1965). As Savage *et al.* (2006:87) observe, these associations were key to how communities were organized based on insiders and outsiders, and they were commonly marked by class, gender and racial distinctions.

By the beginning of the twenty-first century, Savage *et al.* (2004) concluded that local places had undergone a more wholesale transformation: the symbolic capital that residents acquired from defining who is 'local' was now being challenged by middle-class incomers who could claim local belonging based on how choices over where to live fulfilled material and symbolic needs. Looking across several case studies, we see how the investments people make into maintaining local associations and groups are an indicator that community is not only 'symbolic' (Cohen 1985) or 'in the mind' (Pahl 2005) but is also practised and performed (Benson and Jackson 2013). For example, Neal and Walters (2008) show how participation in organizations – namely the Women's Institute and Young Farmers Association – play a role in producing community feeling and belonging in areas of rural England . Likewise, in their research across different urban and commuter locations, Benson and Jackson (2013) show how involvement in local clubs, the village fete, parish council and amateur dramatics society are key to the 'doing' of the local, and moreover that belonging to a place can lead to a sense of moral responsibility towards maintaining associations (ibid.:804).

We touch on this body of work simply to highlight how place-based studies have provided a lens through which to understand civil society on the ground. However, whilst sociological studies of place have tended to focus on associations, they have had less to say about other aspects of local civil society, for example, the way the 'local' represents both site and focus, for activism, protest and grassroots mobilization, a pattern most evident in local civil society organizations with a gender, human rights or migration focus (Diani 2005). For example, Sassen (2002:235) refers to diasporic networks as representing 'micro-sites' in global civil society. McIlwaine (2007), meanwhile, looks at how migrant-based local associations, formed to provide support for locally residing migrants, increasingly operate on a transnational level by providing support for migrants to maintain contact and send money to family in their home countries. These insights illustrate how the understanding of civil society is shifting from 'a locally and nationally bounded notion, towards more spatially porous global and transnational conceptualisations' (ibid.: 1253).

There are also considerations to do the working of the interface between civil society and the state at local levels that are not necessarily dealt with in the community studies literature. Of relevance for us is the re-territorializing of local civil society arising from the governmental turn towards empowering communities through agendas of civic participation and localism (Stokke and Mohan 2001). Whether it be the former New Labour government's 1997 New Deal for Communities, the Welsh Government's Communities First programme or David Cameron's idea of the Big Society, governments across the UK and elsewhere are increasingly looking to draw on people's capacity for association and organization.

According to Milligan and Fyfe (2004), the professionalization of the voluntary sector has also led to its re-territorializing at broader scales of locality through formal volunteer centres and larger third-sector organizations. Third-sector research has also begun to focus on small, locally orientated 'below the radar' voluntary activity (McCabe and Phillimore 2009; Soteri-Proctor *et al.* 2013), highlighting the role of key individuals working at community levels as well as the importance of sites, or hubs, that act as shared spaces for local groups to meet in. However, people's sense of place is rarely coterminous with locality, in the territorial sense. And as a range of critical studies have shown, efforts to address deficits in civic participation often fail because of their reliance on predefined, territorially bounded areas that simply do not correspond to where, and with whom, people participate (Telfer 2013).

Boundaries, flows and local civil society

If all this makes the case for studying local civil society, there remains the question of how this should proceed ethnographically through a focus on specific places. As much as we stress the ongoing importance of place, we also need to address the ways in which local civil society activities cut across boundaries, as well as the way state and civil society intersect at local levels. There is a need to examine 'how participation "flows" through and across different spaces and places and how participants navigate through these' (Brodie *et al.* 2011:16).

It would be impossible to understand civil society in Rhos without encountering boundaries of various kinds – place/locality, civil society/state as – well as boundaries between established/outsiders and Welsh/English. Rhos is situated within a specific locality, being on the outskirts of a larger town, through which it is subject to governmental efforts to foster local community engagement. The absence of any formal charitable or third-sector organizations in Rhos is itself not surprising in the context of an increasingly 'governmentalized' third sector. Such organizations are typically based in larger towns and urban contexts, even when their work and activities take place elsewhere, especially in areas of high deprivation (NVCO 2016). Finally, its connection to Welsh-language culture, as well as its proximity to the Welsh border, provides specific insights into the idea of a Welsh national civil society and how this takes shape within the context of post-devolution, multi-level governance.

As Burrell (2009:183) observes, within contemporary ethnographic research there has been a preference for virtual and networked field sites through which the influences of wider socio-spatial terrains can be mapped. The emergence of this preference was partly in response to macro-level transformations and the increase in the scale, complexity and interconnectedness of social processes under conditions of late capitalism. It was also prompted by methodological interrogations concerning the way research sites based in small places like villages and towns were taken to be spatially bounded (ibid.:183). Of course, this is the basis of the critique made against the community studies conducted in the 1950s and 1960s, and we see this emphasis on networked, multi-sited and virtual methodologies in recent community research also. As far as place-based research is concerned, there is a clear case for field studies designed to capture parts and components rather than wholes (Marcus 1998). One strategy for so doing, Burrell suggests, is to see place-focused field sites as providing 'entry points' (Burrell 2009:189), rather than as constituting a bounded location, with the next step, upon entry, being to follow up on how the social phenomena in question flow across meaningful local contexts, and through relationships with the state and market.

We argue that the analysis of the four components provides a way of anchoring research within the particularities of place, whilst also being open to exploring connections and movements across wider socio-spatial contexts. Each of the four components presents avenues for pursuing the relational, and potentially fluid, nature of local civil society, whilst also recognizing the ongoing significance of place for association. Specific sites of participation – chapels, community centres, parks – are often synonymous with people's emotional attachments to place, and they may be what they associate with that place the most. But sites are also transformed through their use by, and dependency upon, the state. Alongside this, across a wide variety of places we find a set of local civil society actors making considerable investments in the running of groups and associations. The time and labour they put into these activities are sustained by their attachment to place as well as by the status they hold on account of their community leadership. In many cases the biographies of these actors reveal both past and present experiences of civic engagement. Civil society groups and events may be in specific places, but they still depend upon membership and audiences from further afield to remain sustainable.

Components of local civil society in Rhos
Sites of participation
To begin with, it made sense to identify the range of sites in Rhos in which participation takes place. By 'sites' we are referring to buildings or other physical spaces, and they correspond to what Studdert refers to as 'spaces of appearance' (Studdert 2016:629). In Rhos, the most important sites include the Miners' Institute (the 'Stiwt', built in 1926), the Hafod working men's social club, the library, the community café, the local primary school, and chapels, churches and public houses. These are essentially the buildings in Rhos in which we know some form of civil society group activity occurs. In addition to these, outside spaces are used by local sport or leisure-based groups and for community events as well. These include the bowling green and club house, and the recreational park (the 'Ponciau Parks'). Other groups meet in

more personal and private settings; for example, the local Welsh-community newspaper, *Nene*, is essentially run from the home of the editor.

These sites have importance for understanding local civil society on a number of levels: as already indicated, they represent 'entry points' for accessing groups and organizations; people attach meanings to sites that reflect continuities and changes in their purpose and use within the community; residents hold strong views on what certain sites should or should not be used for; and they have specific spatial and geographic features that also shape what forms of participation are possible. The Stiwt, the library and chapels symbolize the rise and fall of Rhos as a community. Cai, for example, illustrates how the Stiwt today is impacted negatively by traffic flows within the village:

> Rhos, visually I feel it's looking very grey and it's looking broken ...
> Simple things, such as making a one-way system in the village, I feel has
> had a detrimental effect on businesses, the theatre. There used to be a
> thoroughfare to the village where people would promenade up and down,
> that doesn't happen anymore ... There's no point having a poster this size
> outside the Stiwt over here when everybody's walking up and down over
> there ... So why not use a billboard on the side of one of the shops down
> Hall Street to say what is happening at the Stiwt because now the one-way
> system happens and people tend to not walk past the theatre ... But people
> tend not to use the local shops as much, only for little bits and bobs. They'll
> go and do their major shops outside.

The above passage illustrates how local civil society in Rhos can be shaped by the various entanglements between people and the materiality of participatory spaces (Amin 2006). Residents' views of the Stiwt also provide indications of their 'conviviality' – how welcoming they are to strangers, and if they provide opportunities for chance, serendipitous encounters. As described below, sites in Rhos vary considerably in the degree to which they are used for group and organizational activity. Sites also represent spaces in which local civil society interacts with state institutions and formal third-sector bodies. In particular, the Stiwt and the library are used for local government activities like council meetings and drop-ins. On the one hand this helps to maintain these sites by providing a source of regular income. On the other, this was perceived by some interviewees as the local council using community facilities 'on the cheap'.

There is a clear theme of competitiveness in our interviewees' accounts of sites, whereby civil society activities in Rhos competed with each other, and with the development of Wrexham as a civic and cultural hub: 'I don't think it helps that the council are intent on an arts hub in Wrexham and therefore have not invested as they should have done in the Stiwt'. The sense of imposition in these accounts exemplifies how relations between local associations and the local authority are shaped by agendas of localism and the inherent contradictions between people's attachments to place and locality as a territorial unit (Clarke and Cochrane 2013; Mohan and Mohan 2002).

Arguably, the legacy of local civil society in the form of both Nonconformism and working-class association has left Rhos with an 'over supply' of 'ill-suited' sites for community activity and consequent disuse of the many chapels and public houses. For example, at its peak in the 1950s, the Stiwt represented the location for a wider variety of civil society activities, including chess clubs, snooker, art and dramatics, a silver band, a library, choirs as well as a cinema (see Hall 2016).

The sites that do remain active are those that receive support from the local state, but which are also suited for groups focused on an ongoing or growing interest in sport, being active and healthy, music and drama groups, local history and language learning, and intergenerational learning activities. Currently the bowling club building is used for various community activities. It serves as the clubhouse, a multi-use learning centre, polling station and a venue for private hire for events like birthday parties.

At the same time there is an absence of sites that may be more apparent in other places. Indeed, there is no village or town hall in Rhos, although the Stiwt does take on this role to a significant extent. According to the then local MP, Alison, the Bethel Chapel school room 'now has some twenty something groups using it, you know, like keep-fit or choirs and all sorts'. For some, the grandeur of the Stiwt, in its appearance and structure, makes it less accessible and more expensive for hosting group activities. A visible public online presence is also limited, although civil society groups based in Rhos have Facebook pages, and the Rhos community council, and some churches, have websites that provide information on local events.

Individuals and leadership within groups and organizations

The second component in the analysis concerned the backgrounds, activities and networks of the actors involved in running groups in Rhos. Our biographical interview respondents were all selected based on their role in organizing, and in cases establishing, local civil society groups. They do unpaid work, which involves considerable time and sometimes financial investment on their part. In this respect, they are more than simple volunteers in that they have a strong sense of ownership over the activity or group in question – establishing and running the community newspaper, setting up the community cafe, maintaining religious services or an ongoing commitments to the Stiwt or community council. The sense of ownership over the group is intimately connected to the strength of attachment to place. Each of the Stiwt volunteers to whom we spoke had long family histories in Rhos over several generations, and this does generate a sense of obligation to keeping groups running. As one volunteer explained, 'perhaps we're stupid ... You've just got to do it.'

As is the case with certain types of local voluntary activity, the individuals running local civil society groups in Rhos are relatively old and the majority are retired. For instance, Dafydd, who is a trustee of the Stiwt, is seventy-seven; Ifor, who runs *Nene*, the Welsh-language community newspaper, is seventy-nine; Gwilym, the minister of the Bethel Chapel, is eighty; Henry and William, who are members of the Hafod social club, are seventy and sixty-six; Sally and Hilda in the bowling club are in their sixties; and Peter, who is a community councillor, is sixty. These and other respondents raise concerns and fears over succession and the failure of younger cohorts to take over key organizational and leadership roles. Only two of our biographical interviewees were under sixty: Aled, forty-two, a teacher in the Welsh-medium school and secretary to the community choir; and Joan, forty-five, who runs the community cafe. All but one of our interviewees were born and brought up either in Rhos itself or within the Wrexham locality, the one exception being Joan in the community cafe, who had moved to Rhos ten years ago. However, their accounts also point to both previous and current involvement in multiple groups, which sometimes links them to other places. This is evident in Henry's account of his previous involvement in UK-wide trade union and labour movement activity. We interviewed two individuals who were raised in Rhos and have moved away, but who have continued to be actively involved community groups through their profession.

One example of this is the then local MP, Alison, who divides her time between London and Rhos.

> ALISON: It just felt right – I'm from here, I'm from Rhos.
> DAVID [*laughs*]: There must have been something more to it than that!
> ALISON: Not really, no. You've spoken to people, there is no more than that,
> is there... Like a typical Welsh person I've never really been away. I used to
> come back a lot, and because I am from here. It's not as though I'd just come
> back having not been here for three years or something – it wasn't like that.

As Alison stresses, these continuing returns to where she is from are an important way in which she establishes her legitimacy in a context where she knows long-standing commitments to place matter a great deal. But there are also interesting cases of locally raised individuals who have left but remain engaged from further afield due to the emotional attachments they have for the place. This includes the case of Cai, currently residing in Cardiff, who has been pivotal in organizing theatrical and musical performances at the Stiwt.

> I knew the people before, they knew me. I was bringing television cameras and something that they as a community were benefiting from. A lot of people turned up and signed up to the idea, but it was very much a smaller group that carried it through.

Cai's case contains features of the wider social mobility of highly educated young people from Welsh-speaking families in the second half of the twentieth century (Baker and Brown 2008). For such actors, their continued engagement needs to be understood in terms of the symbolic value of and emotional attachments to place. They indicate the esteem through which some places may come to be known – Rhos for its chapels, choirs and singing; the distinct local Welsh dialect – and which may continue to maintain some long-standing civil society activities, albeit in new ways.

Of course, the key individuals we highlight here can be described as being at one end of a continuum of local civil society involvement. At the other end of the spectrum are the residents and other people whose engagement is principally as users, or participants as audience members. Key individuals did recruit and manage volunteers within their group. For example, Joan in the community cafe told us of her experiences of using young volunteers recruited through volunteer centres, whereas Ifor described his use of Welsh-speaking school students for producing the community newspaper. Peter, the local councillor, spoke of struggles to recruit new, younger members to the community council. On the other hand, Hilda, in the case of the bowling club, and Aled, that of the choir, gave accounts of increasing levels of participation among locals, both as members and audience.

Associational presence

Our third component is the profile of civil society groups and associations that were active at the time of fieldwork in Rhos. We have already alluded to these via our discussion of sites and individual actors. They include a number of active choirs (the Rhos Male Voice Choir and its subsidiary Rhos Boys Choir; there is also the Rhos Orpheus Choir, the mixed Cantorion Choir, a ladies choir as well as two school choirs). Also currently active and based in Rhos are the Welsh-language community newspaper, a bowling club, working men's social club, and senior and junior football and rugby teams; additionally, there is a local history group, a Welsh learners group, an 'old photos and memories of Rhos' Facebook group, and a caged-bird society. Both the Stiwt and Ponciau

Park referred to above have status as charitable organizations as Friends of the Stiwt and Friends of the Ponciau Parks. There are also parent and toddler groups and after-school clubs linked to, but independent of, local schools.

The focus on local associations leads us to consider questions of both space and time. The choirs mentioned above represent some of the most long-standing groups in Rhos. They hold rehearsals in Rhos. The male voice choir rehearsals take place both in the Stiwt and the Hafod social club, primarily to support both sites, whilst the Cantorion choir rehearses in the Bethel Chapel. But as successful choirs, their performances, and thereby their audiences, are both national and international in scope.

> ALED: It's the area, the chapels and mines – singing was a way of life.
> DAVID: Its funny, the chapels are in real decline, the mines have gone, yet the choirs remain?
> ALED: There are still members of the choirs who were either colliers themselves or come through chapel. But now with younger members there isn't that grounding in choral music.
> DAVID: So where are the current members drawn from?
> ALED: The person who travels furthest is from the Wirral. Also from Anglesey – he used to come once a week rather than twice. But most are from general Rhos, Wrexham area.

In this passage Aled describes the importance of the older members alongside younger members in the functioning of the choir. He also indicates that the choirs bring people to Rhos from further afield. This contrasts with other forms of volunteering and civil society activity in which the direction of flow is away from Rhos, often to Wrexham. As Cai remarks on why people would go to Rhos: 'they'll go to join a choir. They wouldn't go shopping, maybe for a walk in the mountains, but you wouldn't go shopping'. Several of the Stiwt volunteers who are from Rhos also volunteer in Wrexham – for example, in charity shops and in the hospital. Moreover, a few groups that were previously based in Rhos have moved to Wrexham.

This is the case for the Rhos and District Silver Band, which was known up until 1968 as the Hafod Colliery Band, and which changed its name to Wrexham Brass in 2001 and now rehearses in Wrexham, a few miles away. The reasons for moving to Wrexham are obvious in terms of maximizing audience and convenience for participants and members. Other groups and organizations are based in the adjacent villages of Johnstown and Penycae, including the British Legion and Scout group in Penycae and the Women's Institute branch in Johnstown. These distinctions between places are more important for certain respondents than others. Even though forms of civil society flow from a given village or town, there are still limits to the spatial terrain over which an activity might successfully operate.

There are clear individual linkages that connect groups with each other. As mentioned, Aled, the leader of the Rhos choir, grew up in the village. He then went away to university before returning to live there, and is now a Welsh-speaking teacher in the primary school. Another example is Hilda, who was involved in establishing the women's bowling team, and who, along with others, had previous experience of bowling with the Rhos and Johnstown Women's Institute. Alongside the links between groups are the organizational connections between informal Rhos-based groups and formal third-sector volunteer providers located in Wrexham town centre. For several groups, the recruitment and role of volunteers is key to their sustainability, although this is not without problems, which resonate with wider concerns about the changing nature of volunteering.

Since the 1990s, obtaining grants from the Big Lottery Fund has profoundly altered the way local groups operate. Amongst our respondents these funds are viewed positively overall, but with concerns over the declining availability of grants for future sustainability. The Welsh-language newspaper forms part of the national network of *papurau bro* across Wales, and receives funding from the Arts Council of Wales. Relations with local authorities (in this case Wrexham Borough Council) are more ambivalent and sometimes viewed with suspicion, and some accounts, as mentioned above, hint at an 'exploitative' relation whereby the council would make use of the Stiwt in order to run some of its services in relation to housing.

Events for collective association and action

Our fourth component is events which, for our purposes, refer to collective activities that involve the participation, at least in the form of attendance, of residents and others for a common purpose. Sampson *et al.* (2005) argue that 'collective action events' should be considered alongside individual civic participation in debates about civil society. For these authors, 'non-routine' collective events are an important indication of a neighbourhood-based civil society. Such events, they argue, are empirically observable and can range from protest events to more community-orientated ones like local fundraising events, street parties or ones which 'blend' protest and community, like action against library closures or demands for new playground facilities.

Certainly there are historical collective-action events that continue to have symbolic significance for some residents. The playground and park are etched into local memory for being the site where miners dug for coal during the 1926 strike. Subsequently, during the 1930s, the Miners' Institute committee and volunteers worked to turn the pits into a park, with help from students across Europe from the International Voluntary Society for Peace, who volunteered at Ponciau between 1932 and 1934.

Perhaps the most pertinent example was the local mobilization in response to the proposed demolition of the Miners' Institute building through the 'Save the Stiwt' campaign in 1985. The campaign consisted primarily of local community leaders, especially former teachers, and was able to mobilize considerable local support from residents. Dafydd recalls how the local council, prior to the planned demolition, had opened the doors of the Stiwt for locals to have one last look around: '3,000 people came through the doors, and that's when the Save the Stiwt committee was established ... Public opinion would not allow it ... it had come close to the heart of the community'.

The current position of the Stiwt remains precarious, but there is little likelihood of a repeat of the 'Save the Stiwt' movement, which was, at the time, bolstered by a large group of early-retired teachers. Instead there is a keen sense of resignation in the face of both lack of funding and a perceived lack of local interest. That said, there are presently efforts by key individuals to save Rhos library, which is also currently faced with the prospect of either closure or relocation. This has not taken the form of a movement, as was the case with the Stiwt, but the aim is to draw to Wrexham Borough Council's attention to the loss it would represent for the village.

Our own fieldwork encounters centred on annual or one-off fundraising activities, as well as more routine events that take place on a regular, sometimes weekly, basis, with groups organizing events to raise money. Some are annual events, such as Park Day in the summer and the Christmas procession and fair in the winter; fund-raising for park facilities such as benches beside the bowling greens; annual community fun days; live music events, family fun days, arts and craft activities and sports coaching. In relation to these, Alison said: 'When they're doing the Christmas lights you can have a thousand people here. So, there's big things happening, the Remembrance Day parades and things involve several hundred people'. An exhibition of old photographs of Rhos held at the Stiwt was attended by around sixty people. Examples of routine weekly events include Welsh language classes or parent and child craft workshop, both of which take place in the community cafe. The cafe is one of the few spaces in Rhos where informal interaction takes place across generations. In addition, St David's church, which appears to be the most active of the churches and chapels in Rhos, holds weekly events including coffee mornings and a toddler group.

Conclusion

Through field research at one deindustrialized village in North Wales, we have sought to describe key elements – sites, actors, organizations, and events

– that anchor civil society to places. We only provide a general sketch of the make-up of these elements here, in part for reasons of space, but also because our intention is to demonstrate the wider analytical value of a place-based approach for civil society studies. We have argued that place-based studies have continuing relevance for exploring the way some local civil society actors, groups and spaces are being influenced through mobility, networks and new ways of belonging, changes to third-sector organizations, as well as through governmental efforts to reorganize different kinds of social and civic participation at broader levels of territory (Clarke and Cochrane 2013).

Of particular importance here are the ways in which the four components described interconnect. The choir holds its rehearsals in the Stiwt and in the Hafod social club, and this is in part a commitment on the part of the organizers to support both local sites, as well as an awareness of the historical tension between them. The choir holds events like performances in the Stiwt, but also in the school and in other places, that engage with other residents and schools as an audience. We do find evidence of local civil society stretching away with activities, which used to take place in and through Rhos, now spilling out beyond the geographical borders of the village. But we would also add that local civil society continues to be framed in relation to the imaginations and materialities of place, and we should be cautious of drawing too sharp a distinction between boundedness and porousness. This is especially the case with the Rhos choirs, which rehearse in Rhos, and for whom 'Rhos' continues to represent a symbolic resource, but whose members and audiences are not physically or emotionally connected to Rhos in the same way that they once were. As we have discussed, the availability of, and attachments towards, certain local sites of participation continue to anchor certain groups and organizations to place. Alongside this, we encounter the role of key individuals whose motivations and actions are, in part, linked to their emotional and material attachments to place.

We have also argued how a place-based approach can contribute to wider debates concerning the changing relationship between civil society and the state. Places themselves constituted spaces in which civil society and state actors interact. The way local voluntary groups are increasingly embedded in relations with the state has been a central issue in third-sector research but has been largely neglected within community studies. In Rhos, it would be impossible to consider the patterns of participation in local civil society activities without reference to state funding regimes. For certain groups, Heritage Lottery Fund (HLF) grants stand out as having helped to sustain sites as important centres of community, associational and self-organizing activity.

HLF grants are administered by local authority councils, and these also employ key staff to animate community activities and attract further grants, as well as manage the spaces. Thus, the local authority is a key player; but there are complex intersections between the 'civic' and the 'civil' at the very local level. There are close personal and working links between council employees, elected representatives and volunteers. Friends of the Stiwt and the bowling club are evidence of this symbiosis. Governmental efforts to reorganize civic activities across broader levels of territory often came into conflict with local civil society actors' attachments to place, and sometimes seem to undermine the activities taking place in Rhos.

Civil society activity means flows between places, whether this be the ongoing involvements of non- or former-residents, or Rhos residents volunteering in Wrexham and elsewhere. By attending to these four components, we have tried to show how researching civil society through place can proceed in ways that avoid bounded conceptualizations of place and that take seriously the cross-boundary nature of participation. The approach stands in contrast with previous community studies mentioned earlier, in which the emphasis was on capturing wholes, and where the analysed was organized according to distinct social spheres – family, leisure, work, religion. Local civil society groups based in specific places are shaped by larger systems governing civic, social and cultural participation at local territorial levels. Our focus on components of civil society provides one way to pursue the cross-boundary nature of the local.

References

Amin, A. 2008. 'Collective culture and urban public space'. *City* 12(1):5–24.

Baker, S. and Brown, B.J. 2008. 'Habitus and homeland: educational aspirations, family life and culture in autobiographical narratives of educational experience in rural Wales'. *Sociologia Ruralis* 48(1):57–72.

Benson, M. and Jackson, E. 2013. 'Place-making and place maintenance: performativity, place and belonging among the middle classes'. *Sociology* 47(4):793–809.

Brodie, E., Hughes, T., Jochum, V., Miller, S., Ockenden, N. and Warburton, D. 2011. 'Pathways through participation: what creates and sustains active citizenship?'. National Council for Voluntary Organizations, Institute for Volunteering Research, and Involve: www.involve.org.uk/sites/default/files/uploads/Pathways-Through-Participation-final-report_Final_20110913.pdf (accessed 16 October 2020).

Burrell, J. 2009. 'The field site as a network: a strategy for locating ethnographic research'. *Field Methods* 21(2):181–99.

CFHS (Clwyd Family History Society). 2012. 'Denbighshire collieries'. Clwyd Family History Society: www.clwydfhs.org.uk/miscellanea/dencollieries.htm (accessed 16 October 2020).

CHS (Chapels Heritage Society). n.d. 'Rhosllannerchrugog'. Chapels Heritage Society: www.capeli.org.uk/uploads/local_05_Rhosllannerchrugog.pdf (accessed 16 October 2020).

Clarke, N. and Cochrane, A. 2013. 'Geographies and politics of localism: the localism of the United Kingdom's coalition government'. *Political Geography* 34:10–23.

Cohen A. 1985. *The Symbolic Construction of Community*. London: Routledge.

Cohen, J. and Arato, A. 1994. *Civil Society and Political Theory*. Cambridge, MA: MIT Press.

Day, G. 2006. *Community and Everyday Life*. London: Routledge.

Diani, M. 2005. 'Cities in the world: local civil society and global issues in Britain'. In D. Della Porta and S. Tarrow (eds), *Transnational Protest and Global Activism*, pp. 45–67. Lanham, MD: Rowman and Littlefield.

Emmett, I. 1982. 'Fe godwn ni eto: stasis and change in a Welsh industrial town'. In A. Cohen (ed.), *Belonging: Identity and Social Organisation in British Rural Cultures*, pp. 165–98. Manchester: Manchester University Press.

Frankenberg, R. 1957. *Village on the Border: A Social Study of Religion, Politics and Football in a North Wales Community*. London: Cohen and West.

Hall, R. 2016. 'Being a man, being a member: masculinity and community in Britain's working men's clubs, 1945–1960'. *Cultural and Social History* 14(1):73–88.

Hann, C. and Dunn, E. (eds). 1996. *Civil Society: Challenging Western Models*. London: Routledge.

Jackson, B. 1968. *Working Class Community*. London: Routledge and Kegan Paul.

Li, Y. *et al.* 2005. 'Social capital and social trust in Britain'. *European Sociological Review* 27(2):109–23.

McCabe, A. and Phillimore, J. 2009. 'Exploring below the radar: issues of theme and focus'. Third Sector Research Centre, Briefing Paper No. 8: www. birmingham.ac.uk/Documents/college-social-sciences/social-policy/tsrc/working-papers/working-paper-8.pdf (accessed 16 October 2020).

McIlwaine, C. 2007. 'From local to global to transnational civil society: reframing development perspectives in the non-state sector'. *Geography Compass* 1(6):1252–81.

Marcus, G. 1998. *Ethnography through Thick and Thin*. Princeton, NJ: Princeton University Press.

Milligan, C., and Fyfe, N.R. 2004. 'Putting the voluntary sector in its place: geographical perspectives on voluntary activity and social welfare in Glasgow'. *Journal of Social Policy* 33(1):73–93.

Mohan, G. and Mohan, J. 2002. 'Placing social capital'. *Progress in Human Geography* 26(2):191–210.

NCVO (National Council of Voluntary Organisations). 2016. 'The UK civil society almanac'. London: NCVO.

Neal, S. and Walters, S. 2008. 'Rural be/longing and rural social organizations: conviviality and community-making in the English countryside'. *Sociology* 42(2):279–97.

ONS (Office for National Statistics). 2013. 'Neighbourhood statistics': www. neighbourhood.statistics.gov.uk (accessed 16 February 2016).

Pahl, R.E. 1965. 'Class and community in English commuter villages'. *Sociologia Ruralis* 5(1):5–23.

——— 2005. 'Are all communities, communities in the mind? *Sociological Review* 53(4):621–40.

Putnam, R. 2000. *Bowling Alone: The Collapse and Revival of American Community*. New York: Simon and Schuster.

Rees, A.D. 1950. *Life in a Welsh Countryside*. Cardiff: University of Wales Press.

Sampson, R.J., McAdam, D., MacIndoe, H. and Weffer-Elizondo, S. 2005. 'Civil society reconsidered: the durable nature and community structure of collective civic action'. *American Journal of Sociology* 111(3):673–714.

Sassen, S. 2002. 'Global cities and diasporic networks: microsites in global civil society'. In H. Anheier *et al.* (eds), *Global Civil Society*, pp. 217–40. Oxford: Oxford University Press.

Savage, M., Bagnall, G. and Longhurst, B.J. 2004. *Globalization and Belonging*. London: Sage Publications.

Savage, M., Li, Y. and Tampubolon, G. 2006. 'Rethinking the politics of social capital: challenging Tocquevillian perspectives'. In R. Edwards, J. Franklin and J. Holland (eds), *Assessing Social Capital: Concept, Policy and Practice*, pp. 70–94. Newcastle: Cambridge: Cambridge Scholars Publishing.

Soteri-Proctor, A., Phillimore, J. and McCabe, A. 2013. 'Grassroots civil society at the crossroads: staying on the path to independence or turning onto the UK Government's route to localism?' *Development in Practice* 23(8):1022–33.

Stokke, K., and Mohan, G. 2001. 'The convergence around local civil society and the dangers of localism'. *Social Scientist* 2 (11/12):3–24.

Studdert, D. 2016. 'Sociality and a proposed analytic for investigating communal beingness'. *Sociological Review* 64(4):622–38.

Svendsen, G.L. 2006. 'Studying social capital in situ: a qualitative approach'. *Theory and Society* 35(1):39–70.

Telfer, S. 2013. 'What makes effective place-based working?' Joseph Rowntree Foundation: www.jrf.org.uk/report/what-makes-effective-place-based-working (accessed 16 October 2020).

Williams, W.M. 1956. *The Sociology of an English Village*: London: Routledge.

9

Making sense of welfare reform

History, community and kinship in the South Wales Valleys

HELEN BLAKELY

Introduction

Ideas of 'community' might be said to have held a salience for many years for those anthropologists and sociologists working in Wales, in part at least because of the prominence afforded to the concept by activists and policymakers (Charles and Davies 2005). In terms of academic scholarship, as Rees outlines in this volume, there are several notable Welsh works that can be viewed as part of the tradition of classic community studies, including those of Rees (1950) Frankenberg (1990) and Rosser and Harris (1983). Typically, scholarship of this type has focused on the sense of belonging to a local community that can be constructed through ties of kinship (see, for example, Strathern 1981). These studies assume an anthropological sensitivity, whereby 'the discussion of small segments of society in detail is used to throw light on the general' (Frankenberg 1990:187). The contention here is that through a fine-grained analysis of the local complexities and particularities of social relations, it is possible to develop a more general commentary relating to the social world more broadly.

This approach is adopted here to consider the everyday interactions between a group of welfare-reliant single mothers, the 'Lifeline girls', and the pervasive mechanisms of street-level welfare governance in one community in the South Wales Valleys, known here as Valleyside. By situating these encounters within a local, social and economic structure and the wider institutional context of market and state, we can attempt to grasp their significance for the formation of social relations more broadly. The implications of recent and far-reaching welfare-state reforms are of particular interest:

firstly, in terms of the dispersal of welfare governance to new sites of practice in the field of community development and specifically here to Lifeline, a community education project; and secondly, through the extension of the moral imperative of employment to those traditionally assumed to be outside the labour market, and notably lone parents. The Lifeline girls were key targets of this restructuring, and the significance of the repositioning of this group of women within new symbolic and material constraints and opportunities for kinship practices is a central focus here.

Making sense of the Valleys in recent times necessitates understanding the implications of processes of economic and political restructuring and the associated recomposition of social relations. This was achieved through a multi-method ethnographic approach that considered welfare-state restructuring from its rhetorical imaginings to the situated action and meaning-making found in one site of practice. The data presented in this chapter emerged through ethnographic fieldwork within community development projects in Valleyside between 2007 and 2010, including a six-month period that focused closely on the Lifeline project. Here, there is an emphasis on attending to those extra-local political and economic systems that relate to and permeate the local site of ethnographic inquiry (Burawoy 1998, 2009; Burawoy *et al.* 2000).

In this context, the history of the Valleyside community and the South Wales Valleys more broadly, as well as the ideological framework of emerging welfare-state reform in the contemporary era, become important analytical touchstones for ethnographic engagement with street-level welfare-state governance. Each is discussed in turn briefly below to contextualize narratives and practices of kinship, and particularly those of motherhood, produced through the context of a radically restructuring welfare state. The negotiation of street-level welfare governance was associated with emergent patterns of kinship relations quite distinct from those of the past, as the Lifeline girls increasingly identified with a moral rationality that emphasized undertaking paid employment as an integral part of being a 'good' mother. The research contributes to the limited academic knowledge of the lives of women in communities experiencing the legacy of industrial decline and the implications of welfare-state restructuring.

This account of Valleyside and the Lifeline girls develops a detailed analysis of the negotiation of these developments when and where the presence of both was becoming acutely felt. Many earlier studies concluded that for poor women the responsibility to care for others outweighed the obligation to enter the labour market, and that many prioritized caring over paid employment (see e.g. Duncan and Edwards 1999; Lewis 2002, 2005). By focusing on the impact of the most recent welfare reform on its targets, we recognize here that this is a fast disappearing 'choice' for welfare-reliant lone mothers. This highlights the importance of appreciating the extent and rapidity of social change in relation to the welfare state and its impact on welfare-reliant single mothers.

The Valleys

The South Wales Valleys cover around 500 square miles and are home to approximately 1 million people. The broad brush strokes of the history of the Valleys are well known: it is the story of the rise and decline of the extractive, heavy industries of iron and coal, the associated industries of steel and rail, and the social relations these industries created and sustained (Day 2002). Industrialization began with the emergence of the iron industry in the first half of the nineteenth century along the northern edge of the Valleys. This was followed by the development of steel manufacturing and the expansion of coal production in the latter half of the nineteenth century. By the early twentieth century, this relatively narrow industrial base produced and sustained a set of social relations textured by a sense of shared experience, as often single industry settlements emerged and organized around places of work. These communities were characterized by a set of distinctive and widely recognized features: a strong working class and an associated form of collective solidarity manifest in institutions of political and civil society including the Nonconformist chapel, the trade union and the Labour Party.

While it is important to guard against the impression of the Valleys as a uniform or homogenous entity, the economic base that developed was one of primary production, marked by a reliance on the globalized demand for raw materials, which was to prove critical to its subsequent fortunes.[1] The collapse of this economy during the Great Depression, and the failure to secure the manufacturing or commercial activity that were an increasingly significant component of the wider economy, was to have a significant impact. This was an era characterized by industrial dispute and mass migration from the coalfields, which has long been understood as having a legacy for the working-class people of the Valleys (ibid.). During the post-war period, the loss of traditional forms of work continued, although for a time the impacts of the contraction of the coal and steel industries would be mitigated by the advent of manufacturing industries. However, a manufacturing sector of any significant scale failed to develop in the Valleys, and as the century progressed,

---

1   The Valleys were home to several different industries with contrasting working structures, relations and fortunes over time. While there were significant differences between industries, they were broadly comparable and undifferentiated in terms of their conditions and control (Day 2002).

and deindustrialization took hold again, it was increasingly apparent that the structural weaknesses of the local economy were deeply entrenched.

By the mid 1980s, the accelerated loss of new forms of manufacturing employment had combined with the ongoing demise of traditional industries to produce significant economic contraction and social decimation. As the central significance of male manual labour – so critical to the set of social relations characteristic of the Valleys –disintegrated, so too did the hitherto characteristic features of those communities defined largely by the nature and rhythms of the workplace. The economy of the late twentieth century was increasingly characterized not just by the emergence of significant unemployment but also the erosion of the family wage and changes in what employment was available: part-time, unskilled and non-unionized. This marked the beginning of a period where a flexible, casualized and insecure workforce was considered part of a normal and functioning labour market, both in the Valleys and beyond (Beynon 2019).

In this context, and of interest here, is the changing position of women in the labour market in the Valleys over time. In the industrial Valleys there was a hugely significant working-class presence. At its core was a gendered division of labour, the dominant features of which – men's largely manual wage labour and women's confinement to the domestic sphere – were firmly established for more than 100 years. While, the economic contribution of women in Wales in the past has been less visible and relatively undocumented historically, there were comparatively low levels of paid work for women in the Valleys in comparison with elsewhere in Britain – the midland potteries and the textile belt, for example (ibid.).[2] And while accounts of the feminization of the labour force may be somewhat exaggerated (Day 2002; Rees, Gorard and Fevre 1999; Winckler 1985), it remains the case that numbers of women in paid employment rose significantly over the latter half of the twentieth century. The rise of manufacturing, the later expansion of the service sector and the associated transformation in patterns of occupations and skills afforded women far more opportunities for employment (Massey 1983). However, these developments meant that women were more likely to work for lower wages and under less favourable terms and conditions than both their male counterparts locally and other working women further afield (Day 2002; Rees, Gorard and Fevre 1999; Winckler 1985). There are also important local variations in patterns of employment that merit further investigation and require careful consideration. This chapter marks an attempt to grasp the specificity, complexity and particularities of these processes through detailed

2   The contribution of women's unpaid care work in the domestic sphere remains largely unrecognized.

investigation within one community, a housing estate in the South Wales Valleys known here as Valleyside.

Valleyside

The historical overview above supports Massey's contention that 'much of the history of capitalist societies so far has consisted of the opening, domination, and subsequent desertion of areas by industries' (Massey 1984:100). The Valleys consists of places made for and by industry – places that are now far removed from sites of wealth production both spatially and temporally. Historical narratives and representations of the Valleys are well established, and these understandings are of course useful if we are to comprehend the nature of social change – those processes and practices produced through and productive of social change.

Day (2002) reminds us that historical representations of life in the Valleys inevitably cohere into an ideal type constructed through understandings of a working class dominated by the manual labour of the male breadwinner and an associated collective form of consciousness. The same may be said of those emergent representations of the contemporary era. Critically here, a caricature forms around the juxtaposition of the industriousness of the past, with the sense of obsolescence that is a feature of representations of the Valleys in the present. The remnants of industries have all but disappeared, and now assume an ongoing material presence 'only' as the object of preservation efforts through the heritage industry (Dicks 2000). Inevitably then, a great deal of the more recent discussion of the Valleys tends to position the place as comprised of either deeply troubled or troublesome communities.

One such community is the Valleyside estate, which sits on the periphery of a town in the upper reaches of the South Wales Valleys, a product of the slum clearances of the 1920s and 1930s when the housing built by iron masters and colliery owners was deemed uninhabitable. Geographically relatively isolated and populated by predominantly white, working-class people, Valleyside, like many of its neighbouring local communities, has fallen victim to continuing economic contraction. It is a community that ranks consistently highly in the Welsh government's index of multiple deprivation, which includes measures relating to employment and income, and over time has become a key target for policymakers across multiple layers of governance.[3]

---

3   The Welsh government's index of deprivation: gov.wales/welsh-index-multiple-deprivation-full-index-update-ranks-2019 (accessed 20 October 2020). Beatty et al. (2019) analyse the current state of the former coalfields and point to commonalities in experiences but also divergences in fortunes, and there is

For many within the community that I met and spoke with there was a perception that the few good local jobs that there were (such as those answering the phones in call centres) go to outsiders, and that the closest that you could come to work in an office was working in its canteen or cleaning its floors in the early hours. Women were much more likely to pick up poorly paid work, although wages for both men and women were poor. Few of those living in Valleyside were employed as managers or more senior officials, compared to Wales as a whole, but also to other communities in the Valleys. In contrast, the number of residents working in elementary occupations were disproportionately high in comparison both to surrounding areas and further afield. Many in the community understood this 'new work', which was predominantly within the service sector, to be for 'for women'. The increase in the number of women entering the labour force was welcomed by a few as a break from 'old-fashioned' values and an opportunity for women to pursue new life chances; but more often it was seen as an attempt by women to hold together the community as best they could in the face of adversity.

Either way, the young women who had entered the workforce were often hailed by the older generations as stoic heroes, in contrast to many of the men of the community, who were the object of contempt at worst and dismay at best. One resident memorably described the contemporary era as one populated by a generation of 'missing men'. Another stated that it is 'the contribution of women ... that is striking', in contrast to the men who had gone 'AWOL'. While this development was a fleeting subject of discussion, less worthy of comment was the traditional domestic division of labour within Valleyside that nonetheless remained firmly entrenched.

Valleyside has long had the reputation of being a tough place, and an awareness of a form of territorial stigmatization was widespread amongst residents, often fleetingly acknowledged and dismissed in casual conversation through mild references to the proverbial 'bad apples' of the estate. In this way, many spoke of a neighbour who was 'trouble', referencing 'drug dealing in the house opposite' or 'fiddling benefits over the road'. However, the stories of child abuse, drug addiction, incest, infanticide, suicide and depression that I was also told were more troubling and have added to the notoriety of the place. A tough place indeed where people needed to be tough to survive. For the most part, the story of Valleyside is one of unemployment and under-employment, and people simply trying to make the most of the 'hand they had been dealt'. A significant element of the narrative framing Valleyside and its residents, many of whom are seemingly living the stereotype of welfare

---

evidence that the South Wales coalfields continue to experience disproportionately high levels of deprivation even in comparison to other former coalfields.

dependency, was constructed through its representations in both popular and political discourse, not least those related to the welfare state. In order to make sense of the political and economic imperatives at work here it is also necessary to consider the role of the state, and specifically the motivations of policymakers and those constructions of political ideology that relate to practices of forms of street-level state governance.

State intervention: welfare reform

A welfare state can be conceptualized in two distinct ways: as a redistributive mechanism of material rewards, and as a symbolically interpretive apparatus constructed through knowledge, norms and identities (Clarke 2004; Haney 2000). Understood in these ways, the welfare state not only provides economic relief for the poor by redistributing wealth, but also constructs historically contingent representations and interpretations of who the poor are and how best to regulate them. Any prevailing welfare contract has a clear moral dimension defining what it means to be a 'good' citizen and endorsing assumptions pertaining to, for example, who should enter the workforce and who should take on care roles within the home, as well as how and why this should happen. In Valleyside, welfare reform had made its presence felt in (at least) two important ways: through interventions intent on targeting types of people, and through interventions intent on targeting specific places.

Historically, welfare-state relief was extended based on a set of assumptions relating to the gender roles of a household, whereby men were tasked with earning while women were to care for the young and old. The birth of the welfare state presupposed that certain aspects of welfare could and should be provided by women within the domestic sphere, rather than through public provision (Pateman 1989). The dependency of women was at the core of a welfare settlement built on the foundation of full male employment and a one-wage stable family unit. Therefore, while the 'settlement at the heart of the modern welfare state was between capital and labour ... there was a second key settlement between men and women' (Lewis 2001:152).

In recent times, one of the most significant policy interventions targeting types of people was evident in the extension of the moral imperative of employment to those traditionally assumed to be outside the labour market. Of interest here was the targeting of lone parents through reforms that endorsed a welfare-state contract, which meant citizenship was increasingly synonymous with participation in the labour market. The governments of New Labour (1997 to 2010), the coalition (2010 to 2015) and the Conservatives (2015 to 2019) have repeatedly stressed that work is the best route out of poverty (see e.g. DWP and DCSF 2008).

This promotion of an adult-worker model of citizenship fundamentally reconfigured the nature of the welfare regime and the gender regime of which it was a key element. It is worth noting that while the number of lone parents recorded as such has risen in recent years across the Great Britain, at the time of the most significant shift in policy targeting lone parents, the number in this group claiming Income Support stood at approximately 650,000.[4] Given the popular and political attention given to this group, we would be forgiven for thinking this figure was far higher.

One of the key policy's was New Labour's New Deal for Lone Parents, which saw an increase in the conditionality of welfare aid for lone parents. The introduction of biannual welfare eligibility interviews, non-attendance at which risked financial sanction, was a particularly significant marker of a radically reforming welfare state. Created to facilitate the move of lone parents into the labour market, the interview was designed to engender transformations in the behaviour, attitudes, values and beliefs of its targets who had come to be positioned as the undeserving poor. Claimants were expected to actively participate in these interviews: answering questions about qualifications, previous work experience and childcare responsibilities, as well as having to provide evidence of having undertaken work-related activity. The welfare eligibility interview was spoken of by the women I met in Valleyside as a grinding humiliation with transgression meaning a risk of financial sanction. Concurrently, parenting itself had become a significant policy issue (Braun *et al.* 2008; Gillies 2004, 2005). For the most part it was those reliant on welfare who were understood to need specific guidance through policy interventions intent on improving parenting practices (Gillies 2004, 2006). Policy emphasized that childcare in the marketplace is as good, if not better, than that provided in the home by lone parents (see e.g. DWP 2006).

The mechanism of economic citizenship outlined here implicitly created a moral dichotomy between the 'inactive' and 'active' citizen. Lone parents became failures in moral self-governance through a welfare policy that focused on a psycho-social dimension: it was aimed at reforming pathological behaviour, values, attitudes and beliefs. The symbolic positioning of people claiming welfare in this way drew on a moral underclass discourse of deservingness that can be traced back to nineteenth century concepts of the 'deserving' and 'undeserving poor' (Morris 1994). Lone parents claiming welfare thus became both a threat and a burden to the state and wider society. Welfare dependency became the target of political reform rather than poverty

---

4   www.ons.gov.uk/employmentandlabourmarket/peopleinwork/
     employmentandemployeetypes/timeseries/j9cn/lms (accessed on 27 November, 2020).

per se as policy was aimed at breaking what was perceived as the 'clear link between benefit dependency and hardship' (DWP 2006:19).

Also significant were those policy interventions intent on tackling poverty by targeting places. Over the course of time, the decline of the traditional economic base prompted new forms of place-based state intervention in the Valleys and Wales more broadly. This included a period of regional development and industrial policy relating to the distribution of private industry, and an expansion in public sector employment through the relocation of significant state departments. Over the course of the latter half of the twentieth century this form of British regional policy would come to be replaced by economic development interventions directed by the European Union and, in the post-devolution era, by the Welsh government. Our interest here in part lies in these more recent interventions, which can be viewed as one aspect of a broader process of a radically restructuring welfare state in recent decades, one which has come to assume significance for many of those living in the Valleys.

Recent decades have seen the dispersal of welfare-state governance to new sites of practice amongst civil society actors within the field of community development. The basic premise of these types of place-based community development approaches was that local people were well placed to produce solutions to local problems. In theory at least, this state-sponsored community development approach afforded the capacity to focus on the institutional deficiencies of more mainstream policy implementation. In Valleyside, this approach was evident through various policy interventions, including the Welsh government's Communities First programme and the European Commission's Equal initiative.

The Welsh government privileged an ideal of community in policy initiatives designed to generate grassroots activity within local areas. In this regard, ideas of community, suggestive of what Srnicek and Williams (2015) refer to as a kind of 'folk politics', characterized by small scale and authentic responses to public issues, might be said to be part of the political imaginary of Wales. It was often the case that the ways in which these community development initiatives were embedded within the dominant welfare regime were textured by political imperatives that privileged an approach to unemployment. This strand of community development policy was preoccupied with enhancing the employability of groups that historically had not participated in the labour market. It was the concept of employability, - that is, the qualities a worker possesses, their attitudes to work and skills, but also their expectations regarding working conditions and rewards (Peck and Theodore 2000) – that dominated policymaking.

The restructuring of the welfare state was also evident through these distinct approaches to tackling poverty: a mainstream 'welfare to work' agenda and more localized community development interventions. It is possible to argue that these arms of the welfare state share common principles insofar as both promoted an active model of citizenship whereby the responsibility or capability for tackling poverty was understood to lie with either poor people or poor places, which become 'both the problem and the solution' (Fremeaux 2005:271). This policy rhetoric was accomplished through the normalization of meritocratic principles: the expectation was that people and poor communities were at liberty to determine their futures for themselves, although this was to occur through normatively restrictive channels.

It is of course possible to identify disjunctures between the prescriptive rhetoric of policymakers and those practices of street-level of governance (Korteweg 2006; Lipsky 2010; Massey 2010; Wacquant 2008). For community development workers within Valleyside, it was clear that there was a strong feeling that the far-reaching and radical welfare reform emanating from central government of the type detailed above was having a significant impact within the community. For the same community development workers, it was also certainly clear that the policy position outlined above obscured the structurally grounded inequalities that dramatically curtailed the extent to which people in Valleyside were free to pursue labour market opportunities. For them, the policy rhetoric offered only a 'thin' discussion of the distinct types of cultural, economic and social capital that mediate decisions both to work and care (and ensure 'choices' are encountered and 'risks' taken). Valleyside became home to a community education project, referred to here as Lifeline, which emerged in response to and through this context of welfare-state restructuring.

Lifeline

Lifeline was a community education project designed to protect lone mothers from what were perceived as the worst excesses of recent welfare-state reform, and specifically their coercion into vulnerable or precarious employment. The concern was that many living in the community were faced with no choice but to accept low-wage, short-term and non-unionized employment in the face of impending economic sanctions through cuts in their benefit entitlements. Lifeline was created to mitigate the worst excesses of this process, which was widely perceived within Valleyside as having a significant impact. In one meeting of community development workers, living with welfare reform was cited as the most significant challenge facing the community's residents.

The rationale for the Lifeline project was the understanding that given the opportunity and in the absence of reprisals from the state, lone mothers living in Valleyside would be able to reap the rewards of education and improve their employment prospects. Participating in Lifeline was constructed as a process of 'learning how to learn' as the project supported women on the path towards further and higher-level education by offering entry-level accreditation. The practices of support workers consisted of a series of psycho-social therapeutic interventions, a form of emotional labour (Hochschild 1979) focused on 'coaching' the Lifeline girls through the day-to-day challenges. As one Lifeline support worker commented of the typical Lifeline girl, 'she appreciates the fact that by doing this, it will give her a way out'. The principles and practices of Lifeline were positioned as quite distinct from those of the dominant forms of street-level governance of the welfare state. Indeed, the project's support workers explicitly positioned themselves in opposition to Jobcentre Plus's welfare workers to the extent that it was believed that 'they wouldn't understand this'.

Most Lifeline girls had working histories up to the point when they had their children (typically this was caring, cleaning or retailing). Poor academic records together with a paucity of work experience had restricted the Lifeline girls' movement in the labour market. This aside, few had time to establish a strong employment record before they 'caught' and fell pregnant, and many quickly learnt to suppress any childhood aspirations of pursuing 'careers'. While it was common to hear of grandfathers, and some grandmothers, who had enjoyed 'good' jobs within local factories and more traditional industries, mothers and fathers had often found themselves in a similar position to the girls, with opportunities confined to more low-paid, short-term and non-unionized employment at the periphery of the labour market. These girls were both geographically and economically located in the margins.

Historically, for the Lifeline girls, taking this kind of work simply did not add up financially. As one said of a job that she applied for at a local hotel, 'my money would go down, I did check that, by £5.50'. It was also the case that much of the available employment was inflexible, and did not complement the patterns, or compensate the costs, of childcare obligations. This circumstance was commonplace and led one support worker to surmise that until the advent of welfare reform, many of the girls had understandably concluded, 'if I just live on the dole for the rest of my life I can have my hundred-odd pound and as long as I live quite wisely and I don't take out too much debt, you know, I can get by'.

As key targets of welfare restructuring, the Lifeline girls were repositioned within new symbolic and material constraints and opportunities, subject to new pressures associated with different forms of welfare practice. In this new context, Lifeline's aim was to secure its participants' future social mobility through the pursuit of careers as professional carers – as nurses, health visitors and speech therapists, for example. On meeting the women that attended the Lifeline project, it was clear that caring for others and dealing with complex personal issues was often a feature of their everyday domestic life, be it family members with substance misuse issues, children with special educational needs or behavioural difficulties, or elderly relatives living with poor health.

Historically, the pursuit of a commitment to motherhood by 'being there' for children, at the school gate, the kitchen table and at the bedside held particular salience, and motherhood had become the primary means by which the girls, and many other women living in Valleyside, were able to value themselves. For the Lifeline girls, the 'naturalness of caring' was a strong motif in discussions around the rationale for the project simply because, in the words of one support worker, 'it's naturally what they do, it's what they have been doing all their lives'. Caring for those close to them was clearly an important part of the girls' biographies, and the project sought to transpose these caring roles from the domestic sphere to the labour market. Crucially, Lifeline also made provision for the fact that its participants were lone parents in receipt of welfare: attendance at the project in itself cost very little financially, and critically it was the first project in Valleyside to offer a crèche to support a learning activity. These developments were to have far-reaching implications for kinship practices.

Kinship practices

While earlier studies have played down the role of the welfare state in influencing values, attitudes and practices relating to motherhood (see e.g. Duncan and Edwards 1999), for the Lifeline girls, welfare reform made a commitment to time-intensive, 'being there' practices of motherhood increasingly difficult to sustain. This was a significant development, not least because it was well-established that women in 'different class positions, different household arrangements and living in different localities negotiate their respective responsibilities and moral obligations for caring and earning' in different ways (McDowell 2005:273). More specifically, the often poor material rewards of employment and the lack of provision of available and affordable childcare contributed to the preference of many working-class mothers to look after their own children rather than work outside the home (Crompton 2006). Historically, working-class women in the UK have consistently tended to prioritize mothering over paid work (Duncan and Strell 2004; Irwin 2005).

Within the contemporary welfare regime, the structural conditions under which choices relating to family and employment were made had altered. Entering employment had been identified as the path to full citizenship and self-fulfilment, and the choice of caring for children in the domestic sphere was no longer either materially tenable or symbolically legitimate. Certainly, amongst the Lifeline girls, roles as mothers caring in the domestic sphere came to be a defining feature of life as it was led in the past, relating to a set of values and practices in tension with contemporary arrangements. The prospect of complying with the work ethic necessitated the adoption of a new set of moral rationalities in relation to practices of kinship and the ethics of work and care. This process amounted to an act of reconciliation, whereby hitherto clearly opposed positions relating to the pursuit of a commitment to motherhood were made compatible with each other. Within Lifeline, this entailed the production and circulation of narratives motivated by the desire to become a 'good' mother and a 'good' citizen, which crucially could only be accomplished through participation in the labour market.

However, the switch of allegiance from what were fast becoming residual to more dominant modes concerning motherhood was at times fraught with tension. At times, the girls negotiated and navigated multiple and contradictory allegiances in relation to their commitment to motherhood. There were moments of doubt and concern when working motherhood was questioned and found wanting. On occasion, engaging in education was framed as a self-seeking or self-interested exercise, indulged in at the expense of the immediate needs of children. Over time, becoming a self-disciplined, self-governing citizen of the type advocated by welfare reform involved an implicit, and occasionally explicit, devaluing of past practices of 'being there' for children. Performances of motherhood, always motivated by the desire to be a good mother, oscillated between past and future practices of motherhood (between residual and what were fast becoming dominant moral knowledge of motherhood) that reflected doubts of moral self-worth. The targets of welfare reform were pulled in incompatible directions: rapid social change was visible in this form of emotion work and the 'new configuration of feelings' (Heller 1979).

One of the narratives invoked to resolve these tensions, between the practices and values of the past and those of the future, positioned working motherhood as an investment for both the girls and their children. As one Lifeline girl explained in relation to her son, 'I want for him to do well, I want more for him than I have had'. This kind of account, which draws on ideas of the intergenerational transmission of values, attitudes, beliefs and behaviour was motivated by a desire to secure both economic and moral responsibility for children and was commonplace amongst participants. One accounting device prominent in this narrative was the construction of the symbolic boundaries (Cohen 1985) of the Valleyside community. As entering the labour market began to lie at the heart of a commitment to motherhood, representations of Valleyside were produced to position the community as a place from which to escape, if not literally then certainly culturally. These representations of Valleyside were drawn through indicators of deprivation – for example, disproportionately high rates of welfare aid, young motherhood and poor educational attainment. Here, the norms of life in Valleyside were juxtaposed with the understanding of there being 'more to life out there' and the hope that their children would 'go that bit further' than those around them.

One feature of this process involved embracing the idea of spending 'quality time' with their children, in keeping with politically salient discourses relating to parenthood and actively encouraged by Lifeline's support workers. The girls began to speak of reading with their children and helping them with their homework, and talking to teachers who were no longer seen as intimidating – practices that were frequently contextualized by personal regrets over their own past experiences of compulsory education. This was often attributed to the new-found confidence this group of women had in their own skills. These 'integrations' of the roles of mother and worker allowed the girls to reconcile the tension between the dominant, community expectations of them in the past and the dominant welfare-state expectations of them in the future. Like many working mothers, the Lifeline girls increasingly identified with a moral rationality that emphasized undertaking paid employment as an integral part of being a good mother.

Conclusion

This chapter has attempted to develop an understanding of contemporary social change through the ethnographic study of street-level welfare governance. Following Frankenberg (1990), we suggest that the best way to understand general social processes is through the study of their manifestation in the detail of social life. The aim here was to forge linkages between local forms of 'situated action' and 'vocabularies of motive' (Mills 1940), and those institutions and structures that 'coprocess' them (Wacquant 2002:1480). The challenge facing the ethnographer is grappling with the nature or character of these connections. One of the interesting questions prompted by this approach is the extent to which it is possible to identify and draw on these linkages – to make more abstract inferences and claims while attending to local, concrete detail.

In this vein, we should consider the extent to which the South Wales Valleys experience of industrialization, deindustrialization and welfare-state restructuring can be placed within a wider model (Day 2002). We cannot necessarily assume that the set of social relations described here exists elsewhere and is widely distributed. There are of course important temporal and geographical variations associated with the localized, uneven and partial impacts of the geographies of capitalism, and specifically neoliberal reform (Clarke 2004; Massey 1984).

However, on some terrain we may feel more comfortable when speaking of generality than on others. It seems straightforward to suggest that in recent years the restructuring of the welfare state, including the dispersal of welfare governance to new sites of practice in localities beyond the core machinery of the welfare state, has had significant and widespread implications for social relations, including kinship practices. The manifestation of a 'welfare-to-work' policy orchestrated by the state and rolled out across Britain, meant lone mothers claiming welfare entitlements were increasingly faced with pressure to seek employment and childcare. The economic and political imperatives to becoming a 'good mother' and a 'good worker-citizen' were fundamental in shaping structurally embedded choices to enter the labour market.

It may also be the case that the analysis of the unusual – and distinctly unrepresentative – reveals general processes and lays bare structures and mechanisms that are normally hidden (Sayer 2010). Certainly, popular and academic discussion of the South Wales Valleys, both past and present, positions the locality as one possessing a distinctive character, borne of a set of socio-economic relations. It is also true that Valleyside was understood to be a distinctive place, both within and beyond its boundaries, and Lifeline itself was positioned by its creators as a 'bespoke' intervention quite removed from the mainstreamed mechanisms of welfare governance. The origins and evolution of this community education project were rooted in a revealing understanding of the mechanisms of the central welfare state as a coercive force that failed to acknowledge either the biographies of welfare claimants or the recent history and contemporary culture of the places in which they lived.

For community development workers in Valleyside, good practice necessitated attending to these local realities, which had a bearing on how a radically changing welfare state was negotiated by lone mothers: a depressed labour market, prevailing gender divisions, and cultural values and practices relating to care and work each assumed significance in the ways in which welfare-state reform played out at a community level.

There is a complexity at work here in terms of our commitments and capabilities relating to the ethics of work and care, and formations of class and gender, that is often overlooked in political and academic discourse. An ethnographic approach is a helpful way of making linkages between the practices at work in one site of street-level welfare governance and broader, ongoing debates in the public sphere. Welfare reforms inevitably rest on various shifting economic drivers and related conceptions and evaluations of deservingness. Assessments of this type, as far as they are produced and sustained in the field of public policy, have very real implications for the lives of people living in the South Wales Valleys.

However, there has been a lack of clear consensus within society regarding single parents and the obligation to enter the workforce. While there is general popular support for government initiatives that link single parents' receipt of welfare to the search for work, views about whether single parents should work tend to depend on the ages of their children. In 2010, again when the most significant welfare reforms were underway, only one in two people (52 per cent) thought a single mother with a child of school age had a 'special duty' to go out to work to support her child (up from 44 per cent in 1998) (Park *et al.* 2010). With popular opinion divided, the radical reform of the welfare state we have recently witnessed is contentious. In this context, studies of the struggles of women to be good citizens – that is, both good mothers and good workers – are important, highlighting the everyday practices of work and care in society and the implications of the changing norms that surround them.

References

Beatty, C., Fothergill, S. and Gore, T. 2019. 'The state of the coalfields, 2019: economic and social conditions in the former coalfields of England, Scotland and Wales'. Report. Centre for Regional Economic and Social Research, Sheffield Hallam University, and the Coalfields Regeneration Trust: www.coalfields-regen.org.uk/wp-content/uploads/2019/10/The-State-of-the-Coalfields-2019.pdf (accessed 22 October 2020).

Beynon, H. 2019. 'After the long boom: living with capitalism in the twenty-first century'. *Historical Studies in Industrial Relations* 40(1):187–221.

Braun, A., Vincent, C. and Ball, S.J. 2008. '"I'm so much more myself now, coming back to work": working class mothers, paid work and childcare'. *Journal of Education Policy* 23(5):533–48.

Burawoy, M. 1998. 'The extended case method'. *Sociological Theory* 16(1):4–33.

――― 2009. *The Extended Case Method: Four Countries, Four Decades, Four Great Transformations and One Theoretical Tradition*. Berkeley: University of California Press.

Burawoy, M., Blum, J.A., George, S.M., Gille, Z., Gowan, T., Haney, L. Klawiter, M., Lopez, S.H., Riain, S.O. and Thayer, M. 2000. *Global Ethnography: Forces, Connections, and Imaginations in a Postmodern World*. Berkeley: University of California Press.

Charles, N., and Davies, C.A. 2005. 'Studying the particular, illuminating the general: community studies and community in Wales'. *Sociological Review* 53(4):672–90.

Clarke, J. 2004. *Changing Welfare, Changing States: New Directions in Social Policy*. London: Sage.

Cohen, A.P. 1985. *The Symbolic Construction of Community*. London: Tavistock.

Crompton, R. 2006. *Employment and the Family: The Reconfiguration of Work and Family*. Cambridge: Cambridge University Press.

Day, G.A.S. 2002. *Making Sense of Wales: A Sociological Perspective*. Cardiff: University of Wales Press.

Dicks, B. 2000. *Heritage, Place and Community*. Cardiff: University of Wales Press.

Duncan, S. and Edwards, R. 1999. *Lone Mothers, Paid Work and Gendered Moral Rationalities*. Basingstoke: McMillan.

Duncan S. and Strell, M. 2004. 'Combining lone motherhood and paid work: the rationality mistake and Norwegian social policy'. *Social Journal of European Social Policy* 14(1):41–54.

DWP (Department for Work and Pensions). 2006. 'A new deal for welfare: empowering people to work': www.assets.publishing.service.gov.uk/government/uploads/system/uploads/attachment_data/file/272235/6730.pdf (accessed 22 October 2020).

DWP and DCSF (Department for Work and Pensions and Department for Children, Schools and Families). 2008. 'Ending child poverty: everybody's business'.: www.dera.ioe.ac.uk/7764/1/budo8_childpoverty_1310.pdf (accessed 22 October 2020).

Frankenberg, R. 1990. *Village on the Border*, 2nd edn. Prospect Heights, IL: Waveland Press.

Fremeaux, I. 2005. 'New Labour's appropriation of the concept of community: a critique'. *Community Development Journal* 40(3):265–74.

Gillies, V. 2004. 'In different worlds: what is damned as bad parenting is a product of poverty'. *Guardian*, 1 December: www.guardian.co.uk/education/2004/dec/01/schools.uk2 (accessed 31 December 2010).

——— 2005. 'Raising the "meritocracy": parenting and the individualization of social class'. *Sociology* 39(5):835–53.

——— 2006. 'Working class mothers and school life: exploring the role of emotional capital'. *Gender and Education* 18(3):281–93.

Haney, L. 2000. 'Global discourses of need: mythologizing and pathologizing welfare in Hungary'. In M. Burawoy *et al.* (eds), *Global Ethnography: Forces, Connections, and Imaginations in a Postmodern World*, pp. 48–74. Berkeley: University of California Press.

Heller, A. 1979. *A Theory of Feelings*. Assen: Van Gorcum.

Hochschild, A.R. 1979. 'Emotion work, feeling rules and social structure'. *American Journal of Sociology* 85(3):551–75.

Irwin, S. 2005. *Reshaping Social Life*. London: Routledge.

Korteweg, A. 2006. 'The construction of gendered citizenship at the welfare office: an ethnographic comparison of welfare-to-work workshops in the United States and the Netherlands'. *Social Politics* 13(3):313–40.

Lewis, J. 2001. 'The decline of the male breadwinner model: implications for work and care'. *Social Politics* 8(2):152–69.

——— 2002. 'Gender and welfare state change'. *European Societies* 4(4):331–57.

——— 2005. 'The gender settlement and social provision: the work-welfare relationship at the level of the household'. In R. Salais and R. Villeneuve (eds), *Europe and the Politics of Capabilities*, pp. 239–55. Cambridge: Cambridge University Press.

Lipsky, M. 2010. *Street-Level Bureaucracy: Dilemmas of the Individual in Public Services*. New York: Russell Sage Foundation.

McDowell, L. 2005. 'Love, money, and gender divisions of labour: some critical reflections on welfare-to-work policies in the UK'. *Journal of Economic Geography* 5(3):365–79.

Massey, D. 1983. 'The shape of things to come'. *Marxism Today* 27:18–27.

——— 1984. *Spatial Divisions of Labour: Social Structures and the Geography of Production*, London: Macmillan.

——— 2010. 'The political struggle ahead'. *Soundings* 45:6–18.

Mills, C.W. 1940. 'Situated actions and vocabularies of motive'. *American Sociological Review* 5:904–13.

Morris, L. 1994. *Dangerous Classes: The Underclass and Social Citizenship*. London: Routledge.

Park, A., Curtice, J., Thomson, K., Phillips, M., Clery, E. and Butt, S. 2010. *British Social Attitudes: Exploring Labour's Legacy*: www.methods.sagepub.com/book/british-social-attitudes-the-27th-report (accessed 22 October 2020).

Pateman, C. 1989. *The Disorder of Women: Democracy, Feminism and Political Theory*. Cambridge: Polity Press.

Peck, J. and Theodore, N. 2000. '"Work first": workfare and the regulation of contingent labour markets'. *Cambridge Journal of Economics* 24(1):119–38.

Rees, A.D. 1950. *Life in a Welsh Countryside*. Cardiff: University of Wales Press.

Rees, G., Gorard, S. and Fevre, R. 1999. 'Industrial south Wales: learning society past, present or future?' *Contemporary Wales* 12:18–36.

Rosser, C. and Harris, C. 1983. *The Family and Social Change*. London: Routledge and Kegan Paul.

Rowlingson, K. and Millar, J. (eds). 2001. *Lone Parents, Employment and Social Policy: Cross-National Comparisons*. Bristol: Policy Press.

Sayer, A. 2010. *Method in Social Science: A Realist Approach*. London: Routledge.

Srnicek, N. and Williams, A. 2015. *Inventing the Future: Postcapitalism and a World Without Work*. London: Verso.

Strathern, M. 1981. *Kinship at the Core*. Cambridge: Cambridge University Press.

Wacquant, L. 2002. 'Scrutinising the street: poverty, morality, and the pitfalls of urban ethnography'. *American Journal of Sociology* 107(6):1468–1532

——— 2008. *Urban Outcasts*. Cambridge: Polity Press.

Winckler, V. 1985. 'Tertiarization and feminization at the periphery: the case of Wales'. In Newby et al. *Restructuring capital: Recession and Reorganisation in Industrial Society*, pp. 179–220. London, Macmillan.

10

One Wales, one model?

Complicating ways of knowing Wales

ELAINE FORDE

Introduction: models and modes of knowledge

As one of the recurring themes in this volume is comparison, this chapter will explore the role of models and will ask how do socio-cultural models assist in the task of comparison? In the context of anthropological research and given the absence of any earlier objects for comparison, it is often models – abstractions of everyday observable phenomena – that emerge as comparative focal points. In this case, models at once do the work of foregrounding certain issues, while also eliding others. Models by their nature can only be fleeting representations, abstractions from real complexity; by rights they should not endure. The model examined in this chapter is Denis Balsom's 'three Wales' model (Balsom 1985). Balsom's model is a spatial representation of the map of Wales, depicting the interrelationship between language and national identity. Whether the 'three Wales' model somehow captured researchers' imaginations or tapped into some intuitive way of knowing about Wales is unclear. However, the model and versions of it have become remarkably ingrained in the body of knowledge about Wales, approaching what some scholars have called an orthodoxy (Scully and Wyn Jones 2012).

In seeking to know more about the 'three Wales' model, it may help to bear in mind Kirsten Hastrup's advice:

> To investigate a particular idea of knowledge, we must ... not only look
> at the object of interest, but also the mode of that interest, that is the

particular way of attending to the object and of organizing the information as knowledge.

(Hastrup 2004:456)

In the case of the 'three Wales' model, this chapter considers the routes by which the model has become portable and known through alternative 'modes'. In the case examined here, the 'three Wales' model itself is of course the object of knowledge with which I am concerned. To understand more about the mode of this model as knowledge, however, it will be helpful to situate the model in its own scholarly tradition, as well as in the diverse fields of social scientific and popular knowledge about Wales.

This chapter thus focuses on the 'three Wales' model but also explores other ethnographic models of Wales, examining how they have developed and how they interrelate as a way of accounting for a developing ethnographic mode of knowing Wales. This, I shall argue, at least partly demonstrates how Wales has come to be constructed as a fixed and static object. Alongside this academic process of object-making, a complimentary mode of knowing, of a more intuitive knowledge about Wales, is shown to reflect and distort other modes of knowing. Falling back on Hastrup's contention that knowledge is both relational and that known objects are integral to the conditions that produce them (ibid.:468), I use data about migration and ethnographic data about migrants in order to show how the models by which Wales is known can be challenged, developed and improved in dialogue with other modes of knowing.

Models and social anthropologies of the Welsh

In response to Nigel Rapport's contention that those with an anthropological interest in Britain 'had to blood themselves on exotica' before being permitted to work on seemingly rather more mundane home turf (Rapport 2002:5), an alternative approach has been to seek out the unusual or exotic at home (e.g. Okely 1983) or to mobilize exoticizing constructs such as the 'Celtic Fringe' (McKechnie 1993), or indeed *Y Fro Gymraeg* (Balsom 1985:6). 'The Celtic fringe' is part of a 'popular geography' according to Fernandez, one that contains common and widespread ideas and moral notions about relations between the centre (civilized) and periphery (barbarian) (Fernandez 2000:123–4), a relationship that is based on the 'creative re-conceptualization of that or those contained by a process of displacement' (ibid.:132). The idea of Wales's Celticism is something that has been seized upon by ethnographers of Wales from all disciplinary backgrounds. Wales, along with Ireland, Scotland and Brittany were subjects of early ethnographic interest in the Celtic Fringe, to be found in such works as Arensberg's study of County Clare (Arensberg

1937). Later, the genre became typified by ethnographies such as Fox's study of Tory Island (Fox 1978). In this ethnographic model, rural places functioned as the exotic in a centre/periphery dyad prevalent in social science both at the time and later.

The emergence of a body of ethnography of Wales since the mid twentieth century is therefore part of the development of the 'anthropology at home' approach, and of the ethnography of Europe more generally. It was largely the Aberystwyth school of the 1950s and 1960s that pioneered ethnographies of rural Wales, though Manchester and Swansea also played a role (see e.g. Emmett 1964, 1982a, 1982b; Frankenberg 1957; Jenkins 1971; Rees 1950; Rosser and Harris 1965). One of the important motifs that came to be synonymous with this corpus of work is the 'stasis-and-change' model. The Welsh community studies genre was one that exploited the timelessness (Fabian 1983) of the village vis-à-vis the upheavals and changes of the modernizing world. Since the centre/periphery model largely fell out of favour, language has become a focus in Welsh ethnography and broader schools of research that have sought to understand the culture and ethnolinguistic diversity of Wales. That is why Balsom's 'three Wales' model (Balsom 1985), based on the interplay of language and national identity, became such an enduring feature of social scientific research on Wales. Though it was originally developed to account for distinctive and other-than-class-based voting preferences in Wales, it became a useful model in ethnographies and geographies of Wales (e.g. Bowie 1993; Mars 1999; Osmond 2002). Even within the 'three Wales' model, however, what is constituted by the Welsh language can be fragmentary, as distinct dialects may also serve to demarcate the 'other' very plainly.

In Gwynedd, while being Welsh-speaking is regarded as being indivisible from being Welsh, the Welsh language is intertwined with other aspects of Welsh cultural life and cannot be analysed in isolation. Kin and *bro* have been themes in Welsh ethnographies, even those that have not overtly engaged with 'community'. In Rosser and Harris's picture of Swansea in the 1950s and 1960s, kinship is the primary social bond, and sharing the Welsh language (through chapel) augments the closeness of kin (Rosser and Harris 1965:11). Further, Trosset notes how the distinctiveness of the *bro* (a small region of 10 to 20 square miles) is a significant part of a Welsh person's sense of identity (Trosset 1993:9). For example, as well as having Welsh as a first language, being born in Wales and having reputable Welsh relatives are essential criteria for being regarded as Welsh: one or other of these categories is not enough (Bowie 1993:177).

Trosset's model of Welsh culture (Trosset 1993) does not focus solely on language. Instead, she suggests that Welshness is performative, and her ethnography of Gwynedd examines the affective roles and ways of being that comprise being Welsh: egalitarianism, martyrdom, emotionalism, performance and *hiraeth* (longing), as she sees it. Reconciling Bowie's observations with Trosset's performative model is problematic, however, if the ability to perform as a Welsh speaker, though apparently important, is perhaps less 'Welsh' than a connection to reputable Welsh people. As will be seen below, the somewhat new – or at least post-devolution – status of the Welsh language as a technical skill open to all to acquire further complicates the positioning of language as a purely cultural trait.

Balsom's model

The brief outline of key developments in the modes by which Wales has been conceptualized ethnographically presented above illustrates that, unusually among the various modes of knowing Wales, Balsom's model is remarkable as an example of a comprehensive model for understanding Welsh society and Wales as a whole. By contrast, the stasis-and-change model for example, was naturally restricted to isolated (whether by default or design) village-based studies. In large part this is due to how Balsom's model was conceived. Not as a model for cultural analysis or comparison as such but, in the intellectual tradition of political science, Balsom's own disciplinary trade, the model was an attempt to understand and predict voting behaviour in Wales, as distinct from England or Britain as a whole.

Balsom's analysis therefore primarily concerns partisanship, and Balsom suggests that this can be expressed according to the territorial diversity of three core identities in Wales: British Wales, Welsh Wales and *Y Fro Gymraeg*. In the model, these categories of identity are expressed spatially, according to an east–west–south divide, the exception being south Pembrokeshire. Balsom's model is notable as an attempt to look broadly at Wales as a society, and as such it differs markedly from the corpus of work on Welsh identities preceding Balsom, which had largely been confined to the Welsh community studies genre.

The 'three Wales' model originates in an article written by Balsom *et al.* (1983), in which the authors sought to develop an alternative to the 'British perspective' in predicting voting behaviour in Wales. The authors summarize the British perspective, when applied to Wales, as a largely class-based model, which attributes Labour voting (in Wales) primarily to the working class, the middle class located in working class areas and Nonconformists. However, Balsom *et al.* point out that this view understates the importance of third-party voting in Wales, and therefore they suggest that other cultural factors might be at play (ibid.:300).

In seeking to account for the predominance of Labour votes in Wales, Balsom *et al.* analyse interview data from 858 respondents interviewed between May and September 1979 as part of a Welsh election study conducted by Balsom and Madgwick. As part of the survey, voters were asked whether they identified as Welsh, British, English or something else, as well as questions about use of the Welsh language. From this data the authors identify four key criteria in order to arrive at a 'Welsh' perspective: a strong sense of Welsh identity; allegiance to the Welsh language; a radical political tradition; and cultural differences that produce a geographical division within Wales (ibid.:304). This Welsh identity is said to have an 'independent and pervasive effect' on all the other variables that could affect voting choice (ibid.:304). Identifying as British meant that voter preferences were much more closely aligned to the typical British response, particularly in terms of middle-class Labour voters. In this respect, the 'British' in Wales behave like the British at large (ibid.:304).

But what does it mean to be Welsh in this model? To examine the interplay of Welshness, voting behaviour and culture, the authors used an eight-point 'cultural attachment scale' (CAS hereafter) to explore how the notion of culture is understood, as it is acknowledged that the ability to speak Welsh is not by itself the only, or indeed primary, measure of Welshness.

The CAS used eight criteria: facility in Welsh; linguistic environment of the home; parental linguistic background; adherence to Nonconformism; Welsh-medium education; residence in North or West Wales or upper South Wales; reading a Welsh-oriented daily newspaper; and watching Welsh TV news at least occasionally (in English or Welsh). Respondents gained a point if they possessed a specific attribute. Points were added up to indicate high (4 to 8) or low (0 to 3) cultural attachment (ibid.:306). In this model, it is possible to be Welsh, but it is possible to be less or more culturally attached to being Welsh. It is not made clear in the article exactly how these criteria were arrived at, though they can be seen to cover aspects of key institutions such as education, the family and the media, along with more nuanced cultural categories. Regardless of the methodological rigour of arriving at these criteria, Balsom *et al.* used them to show that Plaid Cymru voters almost always identified as Welsh and had 'high' cultural attachment (ibid.:312).

Balsom's later exploration of the 'three Wales' model (Balsom 1985) focuses almost entirely on the interplay of language and identity, and as such is a much less detailed exploration than the earlier study of Balsom *et al.* (1983). The aim of the later exploration seems be to visualize the data collected in 1979. While the visualization consists of three demarcated zones and appears to be divisive, Balsom does note commonality – for instance, that Welsh identifiers have more in common with other Welsh identifiers regardless of where they are physically located or where they place themselves in terms of speaking Welsh (Balsom 1985:6).

Summing up, Balsom states that the prognosis for the durability of the 'three Wales' model is bleak, predicting a heightening of linguistic conflict in Welsh identities (ibid.:16). With hindsight, quite the reverse set of circumstances have occurred. Despite being published thirty-five years ago, Balsom's model has remained steadfast in the face of changes within Wales and Welsh society, most notably the ongoing processes of political, jurisdictional and fiscal devolution. Even a most cursory literature search yields scholars still using the model in 2019. Before turning to examine the model in anthropological terms, it would be useful to look more closely at the work of those scholars that are still using Balsom's model, and to think about how the knowledge represented by the model itself has filtered out to influence other modes of knowledge about Wales.

Applying the 'three Wales' model

Scholars using Balsom's model have used it for a range of purposes, which were probably never foreseen by Balsom himself. While the conflation of identity and politics is common in literature on devolution in the UK (Pearce 2019:7), in political science the 'three Wales' model gained almost mythic status. For instance, Scully and Wyn Jones (2012) claim to be submitting the 'orthodoxy' of the 'three Wales' model to detailed scrutiny for the first time – in twenty-seven years. According to Scully and Wyn Jones however, the model contains critical flaws that mean it has not remained useful or accurate for the purpose it was intended.

The authors argue that the 'three Wales' model's theoretical foundation – social background – ignored other factors that played a more substantive role in electoral decision-making and outcomes. Their choice-based explanation for voting, based on valence theories, states that voters assess the relative competence of political parties and leaders. In defence of the cultural frame used by Balsom, the exploration of the interplay between culture, identity, class and partisanship was notably detailed (ibid.:657). Perhaps this is an indication of the model's relative portability across social scientific research in, on and of Wales.

Scully and Wyn Jones are extremely critical of Balsom *et al's* CAS (1983:306). Perhaps this is due in part to their general critique of Balsom's work as representing what they present as a rather more 'sociological' form of political science. This seemed to have fallen out of favour by the 1980s to be replaced by more 'directly political' analyses of voting behaviour. Even from the British perspective, argue Scully and Wyn Jones, 'class voting' had become old fashioned with 'issue voting' and 'valence' becoming far more useful explanations for voter choice (Scully and Wyn Jones 2012:659).

On the matter of the CAS though, Scully and Wyn Jones are particularly scathing. Having examined bivariate correlations between CAS criteria, the authors note that the categories lack value as they are too closely correlated. This is particularly the case with the linguistic criteria – for example, they find that the ability to speak Welsh correlates too closely with whether Welsh is spoken at home and thus the same data is counted twice. At the same time, other variables are only peripherally connected, such as geographic location and whether respondents read a daily Welsh newspaper, and, more surprisingly, geographic location and whether respondents were taught Welsh in school (ibid.:659–60). If CAS does not offer a very 'compelling and valid measure' of Welsh cultural attachment (ibid.), we might, as anthropologists, consider what criteria do? For example, we might consider how the categories employed by Trosset (1993) align with or augment these criteria. For instance, could *hiraeth* (longing) stand in place of a residential-location category that has been complicated by generations of in- and out-migration? And where is the sort of information that Bowie (1993) highlights, about being born in Wales and having a reputable Welsh lineage?

Scully and Wyn Jones retest Balsom's data against their own choice-based approach, and cross-reference this with data from their own 2011 Welsh Assembly election survey. They conclude that Balsom's sociological model is not an adequate predictor of voting behaviour, and was not particularly dependable when developed. Instead, they put forward what they consider a more dependable 'valence politics' approach (Scully and Wyn Jones 2012:665). A word of caution: by 2011, the Welsh electorate had had a range of elections in which to indicate their partisanship. A peculiarity of the Welsh Assembly voting system is the form of proportional representation that allows voters to choose a first and second choice to elect the set of regional Assembly Members in a system that positively weights minority parties that do not hold other seats. The value of a voting choice is therefore different when a person has two choices than when a person only has one. Furthermore, by not including minority parties (such as UKIP and the Green Party) in their analysis, Scully and Wyn Jones possibly fail to capture some of the notions that Balsom *et al.* observed amongst voters when looking at the party of second choice (Balsom *et al.* 1983:313).

Intuitive knowing

Models are objects that emerge from and organize knowledge; they are both emplaced and relational. Although models, by this reckoning, are always emergent, what emerges is always a product of a much broader context, a set of circumstances that are outside the scope of the model, which is itself by necessity abstract (Hastrup 2004:457–8). It follows, then, that the knowledge that models express is interchangeable or portable. As alluded to above, Balsom's model maps very closely on rather more conceptual knowledge about Wales, its languages and identities. This is the generalizing notion that Welsh-speaking and Welsh nationalism are confined to mid and north-west Wales.

Although not citing the 'three Wales' model directly, Dorling (2019) illustrates just how entrenched the model of a divided Wales (or at least a Wales of multiple identities) is, a Wales that references both regional and ethnolinguistic identities as the ultimate basis for Welshness. Recently, commentators and academics have sought to understand why Wales, a net beneficiary of EU funding, voted in the majority to leave the EU. According to Dorling, it was retired English migrants to Wales who swung the EU referendum results across Wales in favour of leaving the EU (see Leake and Horton 2019). Dorling argues, 'If you look at the more genuinely Welsh areas, especially the Welsh-speaking ones, they did not want to leave the EU ... Wales was made to look like a Brexit-supporting nation by its English settlers' (ibid.).

Aside from some discrepancies between Dorling's perspective on migration and recent statistical reports on migration trends in Wales, which I shall return to below, Dorling's statement at once begs the question, what does it mean for an area of Wales to be more 'genuinely Welsh'? As noted, while Balsom's model is not explicitly referenced by Dorling, or indeed in the book that Dorling's talk was based on (2019), there appears to be an element of received wisdom about Wales and Welshness. A similar conflation of geography and identity occurs across simple binaries such as rural/urban, Welsh-/English-speaker and indeed Welsh/British. The notion 'genuinely Welsh' is highly problematic of course, and not exactly a notion that Balsom's model put forward, yet it becomes clear that in scholarship, and popular opinion, West Wales is distinct from the east and the south, and that distinction is primarily ethnolinguistically cultural. The following sections explore how ethnic identity and language are quantified in Wales, as opposed to how these categories may be popularly understood.

Knowing migration

The vote in 2016 to leave the EU is an example of historical circumstances that have brought into view a version of Wales-as-object, and a somewhat uncomfortable one. Despite benefiting financially from EU membership, a majority of voters in Wales voted to leave. Dorling and Tomlinson (2019) trace Britain's 'immigrant origins', debunking the very concept of 'Britain', origin myths about indigenous Anglo-Saxons and their place in current nationalist rhetoric, and they argue that the 'non-English' regions of the UK did not vote for Brexit (ibid.:47). The authors believe that the failure to decolonize the English school curriculum was an important reason for the referendum result, which was produced in the so-called 'home counties'. In other words, Brexit was produced through a lens of a romanticized colonial legacy that conservative Britain has never felt comfortable enough to let go (Dorling and Tomlinson 2019).While Dorling and Tomlinson are partially correct to note that the Remain vote in Wales was concentrated in Welsh-speaking areas, when cross-referencing their assertions with data from surveys of Welsh-language use, however, this assertion can be shown as a convenient gloss. Similarly, when Dorling and Tomlinson note the scale of migration into South Wales in the late nineteenth century as part of the anthracite mining industry, for them, the region became largely a non-Welsh-speaking area because of in-migration and settlement in the area by workers from other places (Dorling and Tomlinson 2019:100).

In contrast, Rosser and Harris noted that many migrant workers, such as their informant Mr Griffiths's grandfather, had come from rural Carmarthenshire, and that chapel life in Swansea was the locus of Welsh-speaking across generations (Rosser and Harris 1965:11). The decline in speaking Welsh vis-à-vis the decline of the importance of the chapel as a social institution is under-researched and may continue to be when dominant theories only reference the impact of migration on changes to Welsh culture. It is unfortunate that in the haste to paint Brexit as a colonial hangover, wrought by the English on the Welsh (and other regions), Dorling does not pause long enough to see how an oversimplified model of Wales and 'genuine' Welshness simply exemplifies the objectifying gaze of colonialism. A strong reprimand indeed, but migration data for Wales will be useful for expanding my critique, and I present data from two sources, Statistics for Wales (SfW 2013) and a report commissioned by the Bevan Foundation (Stone 2018).

In general, Wales experiences a net inflow of migrants every year, with most coming from other parts of the UK. Without in-migration, Wales's population would have decreased between 2016 and 2017. It is projected to decrease significantly by the year 2037 unless internal or international migration continues. This has relevance for the composition of the population too, which is projected to see a significant increase in the number of older people by 2037 (Stone 2018:21). The Bevan Foundation report is clear: securing a younger, or at least a more balanced, population for Wales depends on in-migration, and even slowing out-migration. Such messages seem to corroborate what the media reports of Dorling's research claimed: that it was wealthy English retiree in-migrants who voted for Brexit in Wales (Leake and Horton 2019). But does the data show this?

It seems significant, and is useful in clarifying Dorling's assertions, that the Welsh government has collected data about migration specifically between Wales and England, by age range and by local authority. On average, between 2007 and 2011, Wales experienced net in-migration of about 3,700 persons, yet most in-migrants were in the age range of 16 to 44. Over-65s were the least likely age group to migrate (the net gain being only 100 persons). A reading of data concerning migration to and from England, by age group and local authority, reveals a more complicated picture. While the 65-and-over age range was again the least migratory group, what might be termed pre-retirees, a group ranging from 45 to 64 years of age was the most migratory. Bearing in mind that when Dorling spoke of the more 'genuinely Welsh', Welsh-speaking areas in Wales not voting for Brexit, he was mainly referring to Ceredigion and Gwynedd, glossing over Cardiff and Monmouthshire as other Remain-voting local authorities. Yet in-migration to Wales from England by older persons (I have disregarded the 65-and-over group as the least migratory and focus on the 45 to 64 group) is relatively slight vis-à-vis the difference of over 80,000 votes between Leave and Remain in Wales.

The number of older English migrants to Remain areas, however, is large. Of the twenty-two local authorities in Wales, both Ceredigion and Gwynedd were in the top third of in-migration destinations for older migrants from England. Dorling's views do seem to accord with what is intuitively known about Wales and Welsh identities, but not perhaps what can be shown with recourse to migration data. The fact that such migration data are produced, however, indicates something of the salience of such fuzzy logic about in-migration trends.

Knowing the language

Welsh-language-use surveys are undertaken occasionally by the National Assembly for Wales. These are classed as national statistics produced using reliable methods. In the 2013–15 survey, the data were gathered to augment the 2011 census, which remains the primary source of data about the numbers of Welsh-speakers (SfW 2015). The 2013–15 report contains particularly useful comparisons with the results of the 2004–6 survey. The 2013–15 survey contains data about Welsh-speakers and fluent Welsh-speakers, which are two discrete categories. Around half of all Welsh-speakers are fluent, while among those aged 65 or over, the number of fluent speakers rise to 60 per cent.

The results show that fluency in Welsh has not changed much since previous surveys, though the number of non-fluent Welsh-speakers had increased by around 130,000. Some interesting trends emerge which point to changes in the composition of fluent Welsh speakers. What becomes clear is that Welsh-medium education has a positive effect on the number of fluent Welsh-speakers. While Welsh-speakers who learnt at home are more likely to be fluent, it is school, rather than the home, that is now the key location where fluent Welsh-speakers acquire the language. While Welsh language fluency is increasing, the composition of the category 'fluent Welsh-speaker' is clearly changing.

Further data from Welsh-language-use surveys contain useful information with regard to the 'three Wales' model. Although the highest concentrations of Welsh-speakers who speak Welsh daily are in the area that Balsom termed *Y Fro Gymraeg*, this area also contained the largest decrease in number of people speaking Welsh on a daily basis. This data matches the decrease in number of Welsh-speakers in the area found in the 2011 census. The number of non-fluent Welsh-speakers rose in every local authority area, and while the number of fluent Welsh-speakers declined in twelve of twenty-two local authorities, it is striking that all local authorities in *Y Fro Gymraeg* recorded a decline in the number of fluent speakers. At the same time, however, the most substantial increase in daily Welsh-speaking was found in Balsom's Welsh Wales, particularly in the Rhondda Valley and in Cardiff – perhaps Dorling was right after all.

This raises interesting notions about the part of South Wales (Monmouthshire, Newport, Cardiff and the Vale of Glamorgan) that Balsom referred to as British Wales and typified as British-identifying and not Welsh-speaking. It seems therefore that Welsh-speaking is increasing in that region, though surveys still record a weak concentration of Welsh-speakers, with between 0 and 15 per cent across the region, with only Cardiff at between 15 and 30 per cent. It is interesting, however, to cross-reference the number of Welsh-speakers with the number of fluent Welsh-speakers. Welsh-speakers in that part of 'British Wales' are recorded at between 30 and 45 per cent fluency, with the exceptions of Monmouthshire and Newport at less than 15 per cent.

Model migrants

I have engaged in ethnographic research in West Wales since 2010. For much of that time, and certainly initially, my research focus has been on migrants, where I was researching what the sociologists Karen O'Reilly and Michaela Benson have termed 'lifestyle migration' (O'Reilly and Benson 2009). I use the term 'green lifestyle migration' to describe an environmentally informed conflation of people engaged in downsizing, going 'back to the land' and living off-grid (see Forde 2015, 2016, 2017a, 2017b, 2019, 2020). Many of the people I have worked with over the years have been second- or even third-generation migrants. As will be seen, in this context, questions of identity are complicated by differing configurations of markers of Welsh identity, whether using the cultural attachment scale employed by Balsom *et al.* (1983) or factors like those that Bowie (1993) and Trosset (1993) have explored.

The context I describe is not particularly new, or freshly discovered. In 2014, Ceredigion Museum held an exhibition called *Into the West*. It described a 'hippy revolution' that took place in Ceredigion in the 1970s as a wave of young people from a range of backgrounds and social and economic classes moved into West Wales.[1] Contrasting this in-migration, mainly to take on rural smallholdings, with the decline in both population and employment on farms, which dropped by 70 per cent between 1911 and 1991, the influx was viewed positively as a renaissance of traditional skills and methods. Forty years later there is much more to be said about how this significant in-migration has shaped Welsh identities. With regard to Dorling's argument, Ceredigion was overall a 'Remain' constituency. We may say, therefore, that the hippy revolution described could not have produced the effect that Dorling highlights. It is also the case that the popular notion of West Wales as 'more genuinely Welsh' or *Y Fro Gymraeg* has endured despite in-migration patterns.

Clearly defined social worlds prevail in rural West Wales. On the one hand is *Cymru Cymraeg*, literally, 'Wales Welsh' (see Williams 1996:8), and members of this group live their lives almost entirely through the medium of Welsh. In rural areas, such people are often members, directly or peripherally, of the local farming community. It is quite commonplace for a person to introduce themselves as 'Jenkins Penbryn' or a similar amalgamation of family name and family-farm name. One of my informants, who used to be a farmer in West Wales, described how his identity became synonymous with that of his farm. For *Cymru Cymraeg*, social life and its institutions, such as chapel, are characterized by permanence and continuity, along with a sense of people and place as being inalienable from the land, a form of consubstantiation (Forde 2019; Halfacree 2007).

Much of my work in rural Wales examines another category of person, what I have provocatively termed 'welsh' (small w), to refer to those people who, after several generations of migration and settlement, were born and live in Balsom's *Y Fro Gymraeg* but who do not consider themselves ethnically Welsh and are not preferentially Welsh-speaking. At one point, not a single research participant identified themselves as culturally Welsh in any of the senses that have been outlined. Such people were part of a wider and non-place-specific alternative network. This fluidity and non-specificity of place sits at odds with rural Welsh conceptions of personhood rooted in the landscape (Forde 2016, 2020). Members of this extra category, which I have exemplified in my research on Green lifestyle migrants (but which could

---

1   See 'Migration'. Discover Ceredigion: www.discoverceredigion.co.uk/English/ more/story/Pages/Migration.aspx (accessed 17 October 2019).

equally include others, and anecdotally does so) might be third-generation 'incomers'. It soon became clear to me that the term 'incomer' was inadequate to describe people who had only ever known West Wales as their home and had taken on a 'welsh' identity. It must be noted though that it is very likely that local Welsh people would continue to think of such people as 'incomers' (see Bowie 1993; James 2003). One friend did concede, 'Well, I suppose they'll have to be called something'.

To clarify, I have appropriated the word 'welsh' in deference to the origin of the names 'Wales' and 'Welsh' deriving from the Saxon word for 'foreigner'. I argue that this category is distinct from Balsom's 'British Wales' in two important ways. First, it is spatially located within *Y Fro Gymraeg*, and secondly, members (by my reckoning) of this category may in fact be Welsh-speakers (of varying ability, but often, and especially in schoolchildren, fluent). This element of Welsh culture is not fully explained with recourse to any of the categories of Balsom's 'three Wales' model, although Balsom *et. al* (1983) make a tantalizing allusion to just such a category. The existence is noted in the data from the Welsh election study (WES) of a 'maverick' group of British-identifying Welsh-speakers. This information is not developed further, although Balsom does say it may be 'potentially interesting politically' (ibid.).

Evaluating the cultural attachment scale

Reading the work of Balsom and his colleagues (Balsom 1985; Balsom *et. al.* 1983) through an anthropological lens, one aspect that is particularly interesting and warrants further exploration is that of the measures used to enhance the explanatory power of the so-called Welsh perspective, the notion of 'cultural attachment' as described above. Cross-referencing my ethnographic data with the cultural attachment scale (CAS) reveals interesting findings.

The quotes I give are typical of the field – that is, they are a composite representation. We see that school, work and 'getting involved' are the principle motivations and opportunities for learning the Welsh language (*Cymraeg*). Others see *Cymraeg* as a bonus, something to cherish, perhaps as part of bucolic, Celtic-infused, neo-traditional, back-to-the-land discourses. One informant noted that, 'We can't change where we were born, although our son was born in Glangwili, but we do cherish the Welsh language and we have given our site a Welsh name'.

While presently this family demonstrate low cultural attachment, given the qualification about the son, it is conceivable that their children's generation will come to demonstrate more of these criteria. Learning Welsh is viewed as having a transformative potential on identities, and such migrants were likely to instil the value of *Cymraeg* in their children. One mother, who had acquired Welsh and usually spoke to her children bilingually at home, said: 'It's not the end of the world just to give it a go ... I have made a concerted effort. Rhian has been teaching me once a week. I can get more involved now'. At which point someone added, 'Yes, [she] can sit through a whole PTA meeting in Welsh now!'

Even though the family were relatively recent migrants to rural Wales (and bearing in mind that the WES data was self-defined), they might have scored a 4, while their children may score up to 6 since they both spoke Welsh at home and had received a Welsh-medium education. These examples would all figure as high cultural attachment in the WES results, but furthermore it is clear that the sense of Welshness is strengthened through generations.

Sarah and Jeff are the second generation of a three-generation migrant family. They were schooled in Welsh, as were their children. Jeff's parents are not around; however, Sarah's parents are, though they do not speak Welsh and were clearly among some of the least integrated into Welsh society. Sarah told me:

> All our boys speak Welsh and were in Welsh-medium schools ... We never spoke it in the home ... Jeff and I did both go to Welsh-medium schools. I can and I do speak a bit of Welsh, but Jeff can't really. He hated school and missed a lot ... It was different in the 1970s – kids at school could be very anti-English, anti-hippy. But that's school kids for you.

I spent a lot of time with this family, and it would be fair to say that according to the criteria of Balsom *et al.* (1983), they would score a 4, or even 5 on the CAS. A paper would not necessarily be read daily, though news would now be more likely read online, and the radio might be used in preference to the television. This family were very embedded in the local community, and I often learned that one of them had been called to help a neighbour with a farming or correspondence task for example.

Along with school, work is also seen to be a route towards greater and deeper Welsh belonging:

> Well, I am a more recent incomer if you like ... My wife has lived here her whole life, but she doesn't have much Welsh – none of her family do. I probably speak more Welsh ... I mostly learnt Welsh at work ... When people know you as a non-native they usually address you in English, so it can be hard to use Welsh ... It's important to keep the language alive, to support it if we can.

The role played by Welsh-medium schooling, something far more commonplace than in the late 1970s, becomes apparent. One research participant told me:

> I am Welsh, but some people don't see me as Welsh. I was born in Carmarthenshire, but home educated you see – lots of my friends were at the time, that's just what the hippies were doing ... My dad is from Cardiff, but my parents didn't speak Welsh, so I never really learnt to speak much of it. My kids go to a Welsh school ... I would like my kids to be able to speak Welsh. It would be a huge benefit to them even just as a second language wherever they end up ... I suppose I should learn more.

This family scored extremely low on the CAS, though again the children scored higher due to schooling. However, this illustrates one clear problem with the models applied to this case. If school and work are key locations for integrating into Wales and the Welsh language, it is not very surprising that slightly anarchic, self-reliant downshifters do not easily acquire, or make room to acquire, the Welsh language. Interaction with mainstream news media is a particularly irrelevant identity category. While not religious in tone, this kind of socio-political nonconformism chimes very well even with what Balsom *et al.* defined as a 'radical political tradition derived from a history of domination by English landlords and capitalists' (Balsom *et al.* 1983:304). My informants of English origin certainly expressed this concern! If the respondent above is Welsh identifying, born and bred in *Y Fro Gymraeg*, then where would they fit in Balsom's model? A further complication in this case is that the respondent was usually either a Green or a Plaid Cymru voter, something for which Balsom *et al.* do not fully account.

As well as unsettling the CAS, ethnographic data reveals a more nuanced picture of how notions of cultural attachment are intertwined with the constraints of real life, particularly with 'lifestyle' choices such as to home educate or not to watch television. The question remains then as to how well these migrants fit the model.

Rather than suggesting a 'four Wales' model, and while I do recognize the pluralistic nature of what it means to be Welsh, I am not sure that a model of division is an adequate way to describe the situation. Returning to Hastrup, she points out that a focus on what people know blurs the question of *how* they know it, and overlooks the question of what can be known in specific historical circumstances (Hastrup 2004:457). Bearing this in mind, I suggest that the Wales that Balsom sought to model in the early 1980s was a different Wales to the one that I have encountered. This is not only a predicament of subjectivity but one that means that one must consider the historical circumstances of devolution, which have changed Wales subtly but, I argue, deeply. This is nowhere more evident than in the case of the Welsh language.

One Wales, one model

A new turn of events has echoed but inverted Balsom's prognosis for the 'three Wales' model, and his predictions about how language would become a further strained and divisive element of Welsh identity. Welsh devolution, best viewed as a process beginning in 1997, has seen the incremental devolution of policy and decision-making powers to the National Assembly, now Y Senedd or Parliament. Since this has continued to promote pro-Welsh-language policy, the Welsh language is becoming decoupled from Welsh cultural identity, insofar as it is viewed as a technical skill that anybody, from any cultural background, can acquire. Osmond notes that the rise of Welsh-speaking institutions and media signal a new era for the Welsh language as a tool of inclusiveness among Welsh-speakers from all regions (Osmond 2002:75).

Y Senedd is one of the institutions that is based on the idea of a single Wales. Because of its privileged position in the education system of a devolved Wales, the Welsh language has ceased to be the 'hot potato' that it once was, as more young Welsh people from all regions and ethnic backgrounds learn to use the language in everyday settings (ibid.:75). The circumstances of devolution have allowed a far more singular model of Wales to become known. Planning, whether strategic or spatial, is one of the key areas in which Y Senedd has greater, and growing, autonomy from the UK Parliament. As a result, Wales's planning strategies differ markedly from those of England (Forde 2015).

One interesting policy context that exemplifies the idea that the Welsh language is a skill, not an inherent cultural trait, is that impact on the Welsh language is now a material consideration in planning applications. If Welsh is a technical skill, it no longer follows therefore that Welsh identity will correlate to language distribution in the sense that Balsom's model identified. Of course, this example illustrates precisely Hastrup's point about how particular historical circumstances shape the context(s) of knowing. Prior to devolution, it might have been inconceivable that speakers of the Welsh language could exist separately to some innate and 'genuine' Welshness. Certainly this may explain why Balsom *et al.* (1983) noted but did not explore the maverick group of British Welsh speakers.

The tenth edition of the Welsh government's planning policy states that, 'considerations relating to the use of the Welsh language may be taken into account by decision makers so far as they are material to applications for planning permission' (Welsh Government 2018:32), though it also cautions against any discrimination based on linguistic ability. Prior to revising this policy, Wales's language commissioner wrote to agree that spatial planning and language planning should be more closely intertwined. This interesting conflation of language and space is unlikely in practice to bring policymakers back to Balsom's model, but it is remarkable as an example that continues to use a model in which language is also a spatial object. This hints at the portability of this notion through a range of modes of knowing and ordering knowledge.

Conclusion: migrants in the model?

I have not argued that the popular notion about West Wales is necessarily incorrect; neither have I argued that Balsom's model is or was wrong (cf. Scully and Wyn Jones 2012). In terms of Balsom's model, I have tried to illustrate its portability, across disciplines, across modes of knowledge, to understand how models themselves can – and should – shift. Instead, what I have sought to put forward is a nuanced account of the 'three Wales' model that draws on different modes of knowing. The aim has been to illustrate ways that even casual observers or scholars of Wales' society and culture move away from ready classifications, derived from abstract models. As in so many things, a model is an abstraction, and must not be allowed to stand in for the real thing. Ethnography has of course assisted in this aim, with a focus on groups that had been muted in past research about Welsh language and identity. This element of contemporary rural Welsh culture is not fully explained with recourse to any of the categories of Balsom's 'three Wales' model, and challenges his view that language is the critical variable defining the intensity of ethnic identity (Balsom 1985:9).

At the same time it problematizes the question of Welsh identity as a combination of language and origin, and migrants to Wales have indicated a preoccupation with learning Welsh where language acquisition is key to initiating a process of becoming, if not 'Welsh', then certainly 'welsh' (cf. Dorling and Tomlinson 2019). Social life shifts and changes, as should the models by which we come to understand it. Balsom's 'Wales' is a socio-historical object, while today's devolved Wales is qualitatively different. Part of the reinvention of Wales as a devolved territory is its creation of new modes of knowing itself. However, although fresh 'one Wales' models will undoubtedly emerge, none are likely to endure quite as long or exist quite as diffusely as the 'three Wales' model.

References

Arensberg, C.M. 1937. *The Irish Countryman*. New York: Macmillan.

Balsom, D. 1985. 'The three Wales model'. In J. Osmond (ed.), *The National Question Again: Welsh Political Identity in the 1980s*, pp. 1–17. Llandysul: Gomer.

Balsom, D., Madgwick, P. and van Menchen, D. 1983. 'The red and the green: patterns of partisan choice in Wales'. *British Journal of Political Science* 13(3):299–325.

Benson, M. and O'Reilly, K. (eds). 2009. *Lifestyle Migration*. Farnham: Ashgate.

Bowie, F. 1993. 'Wales from within: conflicting interpretations of Welsh identity'. In S. Macdonald (ed.), *Inside European Identities*, pp. 167–93. Oxford: Berg.

Dorling, D. and Tomlinson, S. 2019. *Rule Britannia: Brexit and the End of Empire*. London: Biteback Publishing.

Emmett, I. 1964. *A North Wales Village*. London: Routledge.

——— 1982a. 'Fe godwn ni eto: stasis and change in a Welsh industrial town'. In A.P. Cohen (ed.), *Belonging: Identity and Social Organisation in British Rural Cultures*, pp. 165–97. Manchester: Manchester University Press.

——— 1982b. 'Place, community, and bilingualism in Blaenau Ffestiniog'. In A.P. Cohen (ed.), *Belonging: Identity and Social Organisation in British Rural Cultures*, pp. 202–21. Manchester: Manchester University Press.

Fabian, J. 1983. *Time and the Other: How Anthropology Makes Its Object*. New York: Columbia University Press.

Fernandez, J.W. 2000. 'Peripheral wisdom'. In A.P. Cohen (ed.), *Signifying Identities: Anthropological Perspectives on Boundaries and Contested Values*, pp. 117–44. London: Routledge.

Forde, E. 2015. 'Planning as a form of enclosure? The ambiguities of non-productive accumulation in the West Wales countryside'. *Focaal* 72:84–91.

——— 2016 'Permaculture: discovering materialities, designing nature'. In L. Steel and K. Zinn (eds), *Exploring the Materiality of Food 'Stuffs': Archaeological and Anthropological Perspectives*, pp. 118–30. London: Routledge.

——— 2017a. 'From cultures of resistance to the new social movements: DIY self-build in Wales'. In M. Benson and I. Hamiduddin (eds), *Self-Build Homes: Social Discourse, Experiences, and Directions*, pp. 81–95. London: UCL Press.

——— 2017b. 'The ethics of energy provisioning: living off-grid in rural Wales'. *Energy Research and Social Science* 30:82–9.

——— 2019 'Decolonising environmentalism'. Allegra Lab, 18 January: allegralaboratory.net/decolonising-environmentalism (accessed 26 October 2020).

——— 2020. *Living Off-Grid: Eco-Villages in Policy and Practice*. Cardiff: University of Wales Press.

Fox, R. 1978. *The Tory Islanders*. Cambridge: Cambridge University Press.

Frankenberg, R. 1957. *Village on the Border*. London: Cohen and West.

Halfacree, K. 2007. 'Back-to-the-land in the twenty-first century: making connections with rurality'. *Tijdschrift voor Economische en Sociale Geografie* 98:3–8.

Hastrup, K. 2004. 'Getting it right: knowledge and evidence in anthropology'. *Anthropological Theory* 4(4):455–72.

James, E. 2003. 'Rural communities and in-migration'. In C.A. Davies and S. Jones (eds), *Welsh Communities: New Ethnographic Perspectives*, pp. 49–79. Cardiff: University of Wales Press.

Jenkins, D. 1971. *The Agricultural Community in South-West Wales at the Turn of the Century*. Cardiff: University of Wales Press.

Leake, J. and Horton, I. 2019. 'Wealthy English blow-ins "swung Welsh Brexit vote"'. *Sunday Times*, 22 September: www.thetimes.co.uk/article/wealthy-english-blow-ins-swung-welsh-brexit-vote-r3qkpmnn3 (accessed 26 October 2020).

McKechnie, R. 1993. 'Becoming Celtic in Corsica'. In S. Macdonald (ed.), *Inside European Identities*, pp. 118–45. Oxford: Berg.

Mars, L. 1999. 'Celebrating diverse identities: person, work and place in south Wales'. In J.R. Campbell, and A. Rew (eds), *Identity and Affect: Experiences of Identity in a Globalising World*, pp. 251–74. London: Pluto Press.

Okely, J. 1983. *The Traveller Gypsies*. Cambridge: Cambridge University Press.

Osmond, J. 2002. 'Welsh civil identity in the twenty-first century'. In D.C. Harvey, R. Jones, R. McInroy and C. Milligan (eds), *Celtic Geographies: Old Culture, New Times*, pp. 69–88. London: Routledge.

Pearce, S. 2019. 'Young people, place and devolved politics: perceived scale(s) of political concerns among under eighteens living in Wales'. *Social and Cultural Geography* 20(2):157–77.

Rapport, N. 2002. 'Introduction'. In N. Rapport (ed.), *British Subjects: An Anthropology of Britain*, pp. 3–26. Oxford: Berg.

Rees, A.D. 1950. *Life in a Welsh Countryside: A Social Study of Llanfihangel-yng-Ngwynfa*. Cardiff: University of Wales Press.

Rosser, C. and Harries C. 1965. *The Family and Social Change*. London: Routledge and Kegan Paul.

Scully, R. and Wyn Jones, R. 2012. 'Still three Wales? Social location and electoral behaviour in contemporary Wales'. *Electoral Studies* 31:656–67.

SFW (Statistics for Wales). 2013. 'Migration statistics: Wales 2011'. Statistical Bulletin SB 28/2013. Cardiff: Statistics for Wales.

——— 2015. 'Welsh language use in Wales, 2013–2015': www.comisiynyddygymraeg. cymru/English/Publications%20List/Adroddiad%20-%20Y%20defnydd%20 o%27r%20Gymraeg%20yng%20Nghymru,%202013-15%20-%20Saesneg.pdf (accessed 26 October 2020).

Stone, L. 2018. 'Demographic trends in Wales'. Report, Bevan Foundation: www. bevanfoundation.org/wp-content/uploads/2018/11/Demographic-trends-FINAL.pdf (accessed 26 October 2020).

Trosset, C. 1993. *Welshness Performed: Welsh Concepts of Person and Society*. Tucson: University of Arizona Press.

Welsh Government. 2018. 'Planning policy Wales, edition 10': gov.wales/sites/default/ files/publications/2018-12/planning-policy-wales-edition-10.pdf (accessed 26 October 2020).

Williams, J. 1996. 'Globalisation in rural Wales: some dietary changes and continuities on Welsh farms'. In P. Caplan (ed.), *Concepts of Healthy Eating Food Research: Phases I and II, 1992- 1996, Phase II: Newport, Pembrokeshire,* User Guide. pp. 90–153: doc.ukdataservice.ac.uk/doc/5801/mrdoc/ pdf/5801uguide3.pdf (accessed 10 December 2013).

11

'I didn't even know that Wales existed'

European Union migrants' participation and belonging in Wales

TAULANT GUMA AND RHYS DAFYDD JONES

Introduction

> I didn't even know that Wales existed. They had a different language because they don't teach nothing about Wales in the school. Even our English that they teach us, it's American English. When I was here, when I first arrived in Wrexham, I was like, 'this is not English. I don't understand it'.
>
> —Branca

> I don't think I had any sort of perception of Wales before moving to this country, so no, it hasn't changed. From the first trip to the nearest cliffs I realized that I'm falling for Wales with its rugged beauty. Obviously learned a lot about the people and the culture, but it hasn't changed my perception either. It just made my connection stronger.
>
> —Emilia

The above comments highlight the limited amount or lack of knowledge that two of our research informants had about Wales on their arrival in the country, views that were widely shared among the migrants who participated in our study.[1] Such a perception of Wales (or rather lack of it) is perhaps unsurprising, as other studies have reported similar views that newcomers have about the country (Harris *et al.* 2012). As the first quote indicates, this partly relates to

---

1   All research participants' names have been altered to protect their anonymity.

the continuing domination of an 'Anglicized' view of the United Kingdom abroad, reinforcing its perception as an English-only territory, rendering invisible its cultural and linguistic diversity – that is, the fact that it is made of four different nations with ten indigenous languages (NicDhùghaill 2013). At the same time, what is also evident from the quotes above is the attachment and affection that these newcomers have come to have for Wales, against the backdrop of little previous knowledge or understanding of the country.

This chapter explores these attachments, connections and the sense of belonging that migrants come to develop to Welsh society, culture and nature. It draws on qualitative research conducted with EU migrants living in Wales between February 2016 and October 2017 as part of a study focused on these migrants' engagement in civil society in a range of localities across Wales.

By exploring issues of participation and belonging from the perspective of EU migrants living in Wales, this chapter contributes to the existing literature that critiques what Hall calls the 'migrancy problematic' (Hall 2015). This refers to prevailing discourses and narratives that problematize migrants' participation and belonging in the 'host society', depicting migrants as a 'threat' to national cohesion and questioning their ability and wishes to integrate into the national community. This preoccupation with the 'migrant problem' not only treats migration as an 'invasive process of change' (ibid.:854) but also overlooks migrants' role as active participants in the social, cultural and economic life of the 'host' society, and ignores their views and experiences of attachment and belonging in the new country. Foregrounding the agency and experiences of EU migrants living in Wales, this chapter brings to light forms of civil society participation and belonging that tend to be overlooked or rendered invisible by the ongoing preoccupation with the 'migrancy problematic'.

Belonging and migration

May defines belonging as a 'sense of ease with oneself and one's surroundings' (May 2011:368). It entails an identification with one's social as well as natural environments in which a person lives or feels connected to. While belonging relates to both people and places, when it comes to the mainstream literature it is the latter that has often played a far more prominent role, since belonging is largely seen as intimately connected with spatiality, an 'inherently geographical concept' as Mee and Wright (2009:772) put it. Thus, territorial belonging has been a major concern of scholarly attention, with researchers exploring the ways in which people come to develop attachment to places, especially at the local level (Savage *et al.* 2005; Tomaney 2014; Yarker 2019). Here, scholars have increasingly highlighted the complex relations between belonging and territoriality. For example, they have questioned the common perception that length of residence in one place is positively correlated to one's belonging to that place. As Gustafson (2009) has shown, mobility and belonging are not necessarily 'mutually exclusive'; mobile individuals are also able to develop place attachments and a sense of belonging.

This also applies to the case of EU migration, which has often been noted for its high levels of transnational mobility, movement and practices (Eade *et al.* 2006; Engbersen and Snel 2013; Favell 2008; Moskal 2013; Pollard *et al.* 2008; White 2011). This image has been reinforced by numerous surveys, showing that a significant number of (post-2004) EU migrants have no long-term intention of settling in the UK or are uncertain about their plans, leading some scholars to argue it would be more appropriate to consider them as 'temporary migrants' (Blanchflower and Lawton 2008). Yet empirical studies have also documented processes of settlement and belonging that take place amidst this mobility (Ryan 2018; White and Ryan 2008). Often focusing on Polish migration to the UK, researchers have explored the complex ways in which these migrants have developed attachment to British society – for example, through relationships developed at workplaces, parents' involvement in schools or encounters and interaction taking place at the neighbourhood level. Grzymala-Kazlowska (2018), for example, describes the processes of adaptation and settlement among her Polish informants as 'social anchoring', a process through which migrants established various 'footholds' in the UK while simultaneously maintaining links with Polishness and Poland. In similar ways, Ryan (2018) employs the concept of 'embedding' to explore her Polish informants' settlement and belonging in London over time.

Both these studies point to the temporal as well as spatial nature of belonging. They also challenge the 'integrationist' or 'assimilationist' perspectives that view migrants as remaining closely attached to their 'home' country and thus unable or uninterested in participating or settling in their countries of residence. These studies lend further weight to the existing research, which has shown that belonging is not only temporal but also multidimensional, as 'few of us feel a sense of belonging merely to one group, culture or place' (May 2011:370). This aspect of belonging has featured extensively in migration scholarship, where studies have documented the simultaneous and multiple attachments that migrants come to develop to localities both back 'home' as well as in their destination countries (Fortier 2000; Glick Schiller *et al.* 1995).

Moreover, belonging is not just an individual feeling; it is also political. Our sense of belonging to a group, place or country is linked to our rights as individuals. As Anthias (2016:179) notes, formal membership of one's country constitutes an important condition for individuals' effective participation in that society, as do informal and emotional elements of belonging. This is particularly relevant in the case of migrants who often have their rights restricted by immigration policies and legislation, leading to their exclusion from accessing social welfare, housing or employment, and more broadly from participating in 'host' societies (Breidahl 2012; Dwyer *et al.* 2018; Schierup *et al.* 2006). Migrants' experiences of belonging are further shaped by their societal reception, as some groups may be more negatively received than others by the 'host' population (Portes and Rumbaut 1996). For example, within EU migration to the UK, 'Eastern Europeans' have often been subject to ongoing hostility, stigmatization and racialization by British media and political discourses (Burrell 2010; Fox *et al.* 2012; Rzepnikowska 2018). Belonging is thus a contested issue; it entails struggles of classification (Bourdieu 1992) about who does and who does not belong to the national community. In other words, not everyone can belong.

In this sense, the EU referendum in June 2016 and the resulting Brexit process can be seen not only as threatening EU migrants' rights and entitlements but also their participation in and belonging to British society. Prior to the referendum, EU migrants enjoyed significant legal privileges and certainties that distinguished them from other, more traditional forms of migration. Unlike other migrant groups, EU citizenship afforded 'free movement' rights that enabled nationals to move freely within the European Union as they reduced or removed immigration barriers between member states. In theory, EU citizenship gave EU nationals rights and entitlements on a par with British citizens, although this did not mean that the former had the same rights or were able to receive those fully in practice (Guma 2020), as, for example, some restrictions on such things as residency requirements and voting rights still applied.

As a transnational form of governance, EU citizenship works by placing 'a thin layer of additional rights … on top of a thicker national citizenship' (Bauböck 2000:310). It thus entails a sort of integration 'by default' (Mügge and van der Haar 2016:82), offering a formal route that 'opened the entrance doors' (Wimmer 2002:251) to British society for EU nationals. As growing concerns surrounding the introduction of the so-called settled status scheme make evident (see Gentleman 2019), and as documented by an increasing literature in the field (Guma and Dafydd Jones 2019; Godin and Sigona 2019; Lulle *et al.* 2018; Ranta and Nancheva 2018), the outcome of the 2016 referendum has already affected EU nationals' rights and their lives in the UK, 'closing the entrance doors' to their participation in and belonging to British society.

Wales and immigration

Wales provides an interesting case with which to study issues around belonging and migration as it embodies a set of contradictions. Although a

distinct and devolved nation within the United Kingdom, Wales continues
to occupy a marginalized position within Britain in terms of popular media
coverage it receives both abroad and within the UK. As noted earlier, this
means that newcomers have often limited understanding of Welsh history,
culture and nature. Wales also attracts lower levels of migration than the UK
average: according to the 2011 census, 5.5 per cent of its population of 3 million
inhabitants were born outside the UK (compared to 12.7 per cent across the
UK), and 95.6 per cent of its population is white (compared to 87.2 per cent
across the UK). Meanwhile, around 80,000 residents in Wales hold citizenship
of another EU state (Welsh Government 2019a).

At the same time, Wales is keen to promote itself as a 'tolerant
nation' and as a 'welcoming place'; more recently, for example, the Welsh
Government introduced a plan, setting out its ambition to make the country
the first 'nation of sanctuary' in the world for refugees and asylum seekers
(Welsh Government 2019b). Yet empirical research shows that these positive
narratives and ideas tend to remain largely at the discursive and policy level,
failing to translate into actual feelings of welcome and belonging amongst
migrants and ethnic minorities living in the country, and numerous studies
have presented accounts of minority groups in Wales receiving hostility and
abuse (Jackson and Dafydd Jones 2014; Williams 2003). Indeed, Mann and
Tommis (2012) note the polarization of views towards immigration in Wales,
with a higher ratio of negative accounts than any other UK region. Moreover,
issues around migrants' participation and belonging are further complicated
by the fact that xenophobia in Wales is multidimensional, with anti-English
sentiment prevalent and widely accepted in casual settings (Williams 2003).
In addition, abuse towards immigrants and ethnic and religious minorities
outside the more diverse metropolitan areas surrounding Cardiff, Newport
and Swansea is well-documented (Crawley and Crimes 2009; Robinson 2003;
Robinson and Gardner 2004), although there is also empirical evidence of
more positive reception of immigrants and in-migrants in some parts of the
country, as exemplified by *Croeso* (Welcome) initiative (Dafydd Jones 2015).

The result of the referendum revealed another contradiction: Wales
voted to leave the EU by a similar margin to the UK as a whole, yet through
its member states' national payments the EU has contributed to economic
development. For example, West Wales and the Valleys received structural
funds because of their weak economy, and the single market is the destination
for 59.8 per cent of the country's exports (Welsh Government 2017). At the
same time, while areas that benefitted from EU funds tended to support
leaving, voting patterns did not conform to clear linguistic or urban/rural
divisions. Evidence presented by Wyn Jones (2017) suggests that those who
had both a strong Welsh identity and a strong British identity were more likely

to vote to leave the European Union, rather than those with simply a strong Welsh identity, who often place Wales in a multilingual, multinational Europe (Osmond 1995; Wyn Jones 2007).

This differs from England, where those with a strong English identity were most likely to vote to leave, and those with a strong British identity opted to remain. While it is surprising that most Welsh voters supported leaving the EU, one reason for the outcome may point to the absence of a strong public sphere in Wales, which perhaps meant that the specific Welsh impacts of leaving the EU were rarely addressed. Unlike Scotland and Northern Ireland, there is no Welsh version of British 'national' daily newspapers; the only two 'national' Welsh newspapers, the *Western Mail* and the *Daily Post* have low readerships (Thomas 2018), while the most widely read is the *Daily Mail* (Donovan 2019), noted for its negative portrayal of migrants, refugees and asylum seekers (Gerard 2016). Consequently, it is perhaps unsurprising that Wales exemplifies such contradictions: benefitting from EU membership but voting against it; promoting hospitable inclusivity but also hostile towards migrants.

Participating in Welsh society

This chapter is based on a qualitative study conducted with European Union migrants between February 2016 and October 2017. The study explored the various ways in which these migrants engaged in civil society organizations and groups in different parts of Wales, forming part of a wider research programme on civil society.[2] It adopted a broad conceptualization of civil society to include a diverse range of organizations and initiatives in the sample – that is, small and large, new and established online and offline groups. The chapter draws on interviews conducted with forty-two respondents representing or involved in twenty-five organizations and groups in a range of localities across Wales. Many of the informants came from central and eastern European countries, especially from Poland, although Portuguese nationals were also included in the sample.[3]

---

2   For further information on this research, see the website of the WISERD Civil Society Research Centre: wiserd.ac.uk/wiserd-civil-society-research-centre.

3   Of the 42 participants, 18 came from Poland, while others were from Slovakia, Czechia, Hungary, Latvia, Lithuania and Portugal. The sample included 23 women and 19 men aged between 22 and 68, although around half of respondents were in their 30s. The respondents thus consisted of a diverse group of EU citizens as regards nationality, ethnicity, age, gender, and class. The inclusion of Portuguese nationals was informed by fieldwork; we found organizations and groups which involved or catered for both central and eastern European and Portuguese-speaking migrants.

Among the research informants, several participated in existing third-sector organizations, working or volunteering as support workers or interpreters. These roles, involving the provision of front-line services and programmes to migrants around Wales, made up a crucial part of the charity and third-sector work and workforce in the country, linking migrants to service providers, enabling them to access these services as well as helping them to make sense of the way in which British bureaucracy and more generally society works. It is worth noting, however, that these roles were not necessarily highly paid or secure positions, and the migrants involved in them often had little or no say in terms of creating or shaping the services, projects or programmes that they helped deliver (see also Guma 2018). By contrast, other research participants played a leading role in the formation and running of new civil society organizations, groups and initiatives in Wales. Andrzej, the 39-year-old chair of a Polish organization in Cardiff in 2010, described how it was set up by a small group of migrants after a gathering at a Christmas party.

> We started just as a group of Polish people. The one event, that's how it started. Let's do something, and we realized that it was quite fun … We started. We've seen that the Polish people just need activities, and nobody is doing them. We started from *Mikolajki*, that's Santa coming to the kids … What's happened, we said, 'Okay, let's do that', and what we've don, we've got so many people, so this house was packed and we had to refuse most of them because due to the insurance we can only allow eighty people to get in this place. So, we've been really gutted but we've seen how such kind of activities are needed. After that when people find out what we're doing in there we opened an advice bureau.

Kamila, the 39-year-old director of a Polish Saturday school also based in Cardiff, explained how their school also emerged in a comparable way, when a small group of friends came together to form the school nearly ten years ago:

> I remember, like my friend Kasia, she's still with me there, and then a couple of other people … The main reason for us to meet and talk about things was because we wanted to start a school because I've got another son, he's fifteen now, but obviously in 2008 he was seven and she had a little daughter. So, we knew we must do something at least for our kids and maybe a couple of friend's kids to keep the language in kids. Some of them just come in and they start talking English straightaway. So, we thought, oh let's do something for kids.

What is evident from these accounts is the migrants' tenacity; these organizations emerged on an ad hoc basis, through the initiative of a few individuals. Differing from conventional third-sector organizations, they operated with little or no state or governmental funding and relied largely on a core group of volunteers/supporters for the continuation of their services and activities. Often, individuals involved in these groups worked in full-time, demanding jobs elsewhere (factory work, social care, hospitality) with little time for other activities. This was, for example, one of the reasons why these groups met on a Saturday, as their members were at work during the week. As one respondent put it, it required 'sacrifices' to keep the organization's services and activities going. This was, for instance, the case of a Portuguese-speaking organization based in northern Wales, which had managed to run for fifteen years largely based on a small core group of dedicated volunteers. A senior representative who helped set up the organization explained their frugal approach. For example, when talking about how they run one of their activities, Portuguese language classes, they made use of volunteers who had teaching experience back in Portugal. As 41-year-old Branca explained:

> So that's why I keep saying, okay, we don't need money for many things because all of us have a quality. All of us were born with something. I know Amanda – she used to be a teacher in Portugal. She was 'dying' there, working somewhere unconnected with what she wanted to do. Amanda would like to do two hours a week for free as a teacher, because she is all qualified, you see. She said, 'Yes'. So, we have Portuguese lessons … What she said, 'It's only £10 a week for the train [to get to where the organization is located]. It's not going to affect my family budget or anything. Branca, let's do it.'

These various initiatives began in response to a need that was identified among migrant populations. A lack of support services for migrants and concerns around loss of native language skills among migrant children were the two key issues that led to the creation of the groups outlined above. At first sight, such organizations appear migrant-focused, created by migrants to serve their own co-ethnics. Yet in practice their scope extended beyond an ethnically defined group to cover other migrant groups as well as local communities. Various participants representing Polish organizations, for example, mentioned how they also helped other migrants from central and eastern Europe. Andrzej noted how his Cardiff-based Polish organization offered help and support to other migrants such as Hungarians and Slovakians, not just Polish individuals. Maja, a 34-year-old Polish migrant who worked for a Polish organization in Llanelli, described the extended list of nationalities supported by her organization:

> Czech Republic we have, we have Czech Republic for … It's just because the
> Job Centre does not recognize the Slovak language and they send somebody,
> everybody to us, and they send us Czech or Russian or something. I can
> speak with Czech because I speak a little bit Czech but I cannot speak
> with Russian or something, but in [the main] office there's one Ukrainian
> or Moldavian – I don't remember, lady – and if we have Russian-speaking
> people she's coming to us to try and help so.

Maja's account also points to the significant role played by Polish organizations regarding service provision for marginalized groups and individuals. Because of the numerical advantage that Polish migrants have over that of the other groups, it was perhaps unsurprising to find a high level of civil society activities among this group in comparison to other research participants.[4] Of all the individuals involved in our study, nearly half were Polish; of the twenty-five groups and organizations studied, fifteen were related to Polish migration. Amongst them was also an initiative run by a group of Polish women that was specifically set up to offer information and support to a wider range of migrants who had recently arrived in and around the area of Bridgend. Joanna, the 32-year-old Polish chair of the initiative, explained how the initiative emerged from a lack of services in the area for this group of people and noted how the focus of their services was rather international, not just aimed at Polish or eastern European migrants:

> The reason why we were brought together was that we felt the need to
> help newly arrived migrants … Currently we are running the fortnightly
> drop-in, promoting Polish, other cultures and businesses as well as
> providing information, advice, support and guidance for people speaking
> other languages. [Our initiative] is the place where we meet with people
> of different nationalities to talk, help each other, share our experiences
> and learn English. Here we also make plans for multicultural events for
> food, dance, music, art. We work hard on improving our skills, confidence-
> building, helping people in finding employment and integrate into British
> society … We are gradually engaging more and more people with different

---

4   Statistical data show that Polish migrants represent the most numerous non-UK
     born group in Wales (BBC 2014).

nationalities through direct action, talking to the professionals, council, schools, etc., debates, speaking at events and providing and taking part in cultural events and festivals.

As noted above, the programmes and activities run by these migrant organizations included not just offering support to migrants but also engaging with local communities and authorities. In some cases, participation extended to wider, national events. Piotr, a 31-year-old informant who ran *Nasze małe* Cardiff ('Our little Cardiff') – an online group 'dedicated to the Polish community' living in and around Cardiff – noted how his group attended St David's Day parade regularly, a national event celebrating Welsh heritage and culture. He added that such participation was to show an appreciation for Welsh heritage but also to make a 'statement' that Polish migrants are also part of this culture – 'to say that we are here as well, we are part of this community of Wales'. Organizing multicultural events – whether it be *Mikolajki* (Polish Christmas parties) or nights of the Portuguese music tradition known as *Fado* – was another example of engagement with the local population. Branca explains:

> We did an event, *Fado* night, not long ago, the 4th of March. *Fado* is our traditional music. We arranged with small amounts from the fund that was given to us by Celebration. We had £2,000 to make an event. We tried to make it as big as we could, and then gather as many different people in. We had Polish. We had Welsh. We had all sorts of nationalities on that event.

The involvement of non-migrants in these organizations took other forms, too. Andrzej explained how his organization had 'Welsh and English people' who volunteered there. He added that some were married to Polish migrants and had thus developed a personal interest. Similar trends were noted by participants of other migrant communities, including the Portuguese one, as Branca relates:

> We're running Saturday school for children. Wednesday, we're going to start on the 2nd November, Portuguese for adults. Believe me or not, there's lots of adult people who are married with Portuguese. Polish, Welsh – they want to learn Portuguese because they go there on holiday, or they're planning to move there at some point one day, and they want to learn Portuguese, which is brilliant.

Connecting to Welsh nature

Migrants' connections to Wales emerged not only in relation to civil society but also to Welsh nature. As noted in the introduction, the Welsh landscape was something that left an impression on our research informants. Monika, a 39-year-old Polish respondent who lived in a small market town in West Wales, spoke of her 'shock' when she first encountered the rural area:

> When I came, lambs everywhere! Well cows, and I said, 'Oh my God' where
> I am, but I like now. I will not change that for anything, no. I will not move
> from Wales to go to England. Everyone who comes from England they
> say, 'My goodness, it's really nice. Wales is beautiful'. Up and down they do
> notice. Sheep everywhere, and near to the coast, to the sea. So, I like it.

Eventually, Monika came to appreciate the ruralness and ruggedness of Welsh nature and developed an affection for the country, which she said she now considers her 'home'. In the case of Emilia, a 38-year-old Polish respondent, such attachment had become even stronger. She spoke about her 'love' for the Welsh landscape and how she had 'fallen' for the country, so much so that she was keen to promote it to other fellow migrants. To this end, she co-created *Smok Walijski* ('Welsh dragon'), an online community aimed at encouraging Polish migrants to 'explore' the country:

> The idea behind *Smok Walijski* is to encourage Polish people to explore
> Wales. To get out and about, on their feet, on their bikes, in their cars. I
> believe that there's no better way to settle down in your new country than
> to walk it. To engage with its landscape, and through it with its history
> and culture. Myself and *Smok*'s co-founder have personally tested every
> destination, venue or attraction we have been writing about. The idea is to
> create the first complete guide to Wales in Polish.

Through creating a 'guide' and writing about Wales in Polish, the creators of *Smok Walijski* aimed to encourage the physical exploration of Wales, making migrants aware of key landmarks and places in the country, and providing a context for these places. Generating Polish-language content allowed information tailored to a specific national and linguistic context to be accessed. This act of 'translating' Welsh places and culture and making them accessible to migrants is important especially in the context where most tourist guides to Wales are written in English and for visitors from a UK or North American context.[5]

As Emilia explained, the aim of creating this 'guide' for migrants was to encourage encounters and interaction with Welsh/British people:

> I know from my own experience that if you get out and about you establish a connection between you and the new country. Your confidence will grow. Also, your British co-workers, neighbours will appreciate your passion for their country, which may help you to make new local friends. Which will obviously help you to integrate.

Learning about 'the new country', gaining local knowledge and demonstrating 'a passion' for it convey the image of 'good or active migrant', somebody who is interested in their surroundings and interested in its history, an image that counters commonly held constructions of immigrants in Wales and the UK more widely, which assume that migrants have no interest in such activities and remain within their own national or ethnic networks.

Albeit less explicitly, other groups also aided migrants' attachment to Wales. Stephan, a 38-year-old Slovak informant who ran the online group, *Slovaci a Cesi v Cardiffe* ('Czechs and Slovaks in Cardiff'), for example, noted that the group organized not only social get-togethers for Czech and Slovak migrants in the local area but also frequent trips to the Brecon Beacons National Park, a popular, mountainous destination in southern Wales, around 50 kilometres from Cardiff. In addition, the use of possessive pronoun 'our' in some of the migrant groups' names, such as 'Our little Cardiff' (*Nasze Małe Cardiff*) or 'Our Wales' (*Nasza Walia*), and references to Welsh symbols like the 'Welsh dragon' (*Smok Walijski*), further signified these groups' affection and connection to Wales.

Brexit Wales

The various links and attachments to Wales highlighted above were significantly disrupted by the result of the 2016 European Union referendum, which affected not only the respondents' rights and entitlements as EU citizens but also their participation in and sense of belonging to Wales. As described above, Emilia had developed a strong connection to Wales through travelling the country and creating an interactive guide for her fellow migrants, but Brexit made her feel uprooted again: 'I haven't felt like an immigrant for a

---

5   The *Crwydro Cymru* ('Wandering Wales') series of books focusing on each of the historic thirteen counties was published in Welsh in the 1950s and 1960s and remains the most comprehensive tour guides to Wales in Welsh.

while – the whole EU referendum hit back and made me feel a bit like one again'. Emilia had spent more than ten years in Wales and felt settled in the country. Along with her involvement in *Smok Walijski*, she listed a number of changes that she had undergone during this period, including getting a better job, finding a local partner and learning how Welsh/British society functioned, leading her to develop an attachment to the country.

The sense of uprootedness caused by Brexit was particularly strong in Branca's case, who found it extremely difficult to come to terms with the result in the days following the referendum:

> Personally, the first two days, I couldn't speak. Really, I was shocked. I was really … I don't know. It was worse than being raped and dumped in an alley. Really, that was the sensation I had. I remember that morning when I woke up, I already had interviews booked with the Portuguese media and BBC and blah, blah. I couldn't speak with the BBC, I was crying. Really, I couldn't believe my eyes. I was like somebody that you really … like imagine that you're stressed or … I don't know. I wasn't expecting that was really going to happen, especially because we are immigrants.

Having lived and worked in northern Wales since 2002, Brexit came as a sudden and dramatic shock for Branca, generating a great deal of anxiety in her everyday life and making her feeling rejected, abandoned or, as she put it, 'dumped in an alley'. She was also worried about the insecurities and uncertainties that the referendum had triggered for EU citizens, especially for those of the marginalized groups that her organization was helping and supporting.

> I fear there is going to be lots of panic here, because nobody is prepared to move. These people that came with me fifteen years ago, they're much older than I am. They're in their sixties. More, sixty plus. Some of them are now disabled, become disabled, ill. Lifelong term illnesses and they cannot go to work. If they have their benefits stopped, they're going to die, because my country is not prepared to have all of us back there. So where are we going to go? What's going to happen?

Luciana, another Portuguese informant who volunteered for the same organization, expressed her anger and sadness about the impact of the referendum on migrants' civil society engagement and participation, which threatened to 'undo' much of integration and community work that she and others have done over the years.

I spent so many years in this country. Gave so much to this country. Help with community. It's not all mine, but theirs too. I've done a lot of charity, and to be forced to go to home with the possibility that my husband can't come with me, because that is starting from zero again. I don't know. I don't know if I will like to do that. It makes me kind of sad.

Married to an Englishman, the 34-year-old has been living in an Anglo-Welsh border town for sixteen years and has a daughter who 'speaks only English and doesn't know any Portuguese'. While she previously felt 'half British and half Portuguese', Luciana could no longer identify herself in this way and was worried that the referendum would have an impact on her family life. Strong emotional reactions to Brexit were expressed by other respondents too, especially in the immediate aftermath of the vote, thus confirming the 'affective impact' of Brexit that has been documented elsewhere (Lulle *et al.* 2018; New Europeans 2017; Quinn 2017; Henley 2017). This was evident in the expressions used to describe Brexit such as feeling 'sad' or 'angry', being left 'speechless', being 'hit' by it or feeling completely 'shocked' or even 'panicked'.

Moreover, the unsettling effect of Brexit also manifested itself in everyday life in the form of increased hostility. Some respondents gave examples of incidents that they or their family had experienced, including verbal abuse, physical violence and vandalism. Monika, who owned two Polish delicatessens, described how one of her shops was attacked following the referendum:

Here [in the town] I had a broken sign ... That was destroyed one week. The next week ... all the flowers were taken out from the big tub which is in front of the shop. All the soil and everything was on the floor. Further down there was a few metres and they didn't touch those flowers because they're a solicitor. They only destroyed ours.

Resident in Wales for eleven years, Monika felt that her shop was being targeted as a visible manifestation of reactions to EU migration. Here the shop sign served as a 'marker of difference' (Rzepnikowska 2018), and the insecurity generated by these attacks affected not only Monika personally but also her customers. The shops that she owned were in rural areas in western Wales, a region which has attracted Polish and other (European) migrants due to employment opportunities offered by factories located in the vicinity (Jones and Lever 2014). In the absence of services offering information and support, the shops have become a key focal point for migrants living in this rural region, and she often helped migrants/customers with whatever problem they faced. It was in this context that, as Monika noted, one of her shops was often referred to as the 'Polish Centre' by the local population.

In her account, Monika juxtaposed this increased hostility with a growing sense of solidarity among those who opposed the rhetoric associated with the Leave campaigns. Although little acts of solidarity were also mentioned by other participants, with residents offering messages of support and welcoming statements to migrants and organizations working with them, overall our informants did not explicitly talk about Wales as being a welcoming or tolerant country. By contrast, a recent study of EU citizens living in Scotland found that in the context of Brexit their informants specifically highlighted the country as more welcoming than other parts of the UK (Godin and Sigona 2019).

Importantly, our respondents also highlighted experiences of hostility in Wales as a long-standing and ongoing issue. Krzysztof, a 38-year-old Polish respondent who ran an angling association promoting sustainable and ethical fishing practices, was particularly upset at the verbal abuse his children had received in school well before the EU referendum took place:

> It's all the people, some nasty people, who say 'Go back to your country' ...
> Lots of times they call my boys, 'You Polish twat' or something like that.
> Lots of comments, and sometimes the school will do nothing with that.
> Three or four times they do that, so we go straight to some ladies group
> who run the school. We told come down the policeman and try and explain,
> but it's happened again and again and again.

The distress caused by the abuse his children received was compounded by frustration that despite these incidents recurring frequently, the authorities had failed to take any action and tackle the issues. Marcel, another Polish informant, also told of similar experiences that his children had encountered at school. These two informants shared similar accounts despite living in distinct parts of Wales; Krzysztof lived in a small and relatively isolated town in mid Wales, whereas Marcel resided in Cardiff, a city highlighted for its diversity and multiculturalism.

The impact that ongoing anti-immigration sentiment and hostility had on migrants' sense of belonging can be illustrated by Tomek's example. Reflecting on the referendum vote, the 34-year-old Polish informant expressed more concern about the overall negative atmosphere in Britain, influenced by coverage of immigration in the British tabloid newspapers than the actual result. Unlike other respondents, Tomek had applied for and gained British citizenship well before the referendum, thus following a more formal route to settlement in the UK. He applied for citizenship after considering its benefits – for example, being able to vote in general elections or setting up a business. Yet rather than feeling secure in the context of Brexit, the referendum outcome had made him 'regret' becoming a British citizen.

> To be honest, when we went to the referendum recently, I'm very close to
> enough is enough. You know I find it very close and I said to a friend of
> mine, I said, 'Do you know despite I'm actually a British citizen and I really
> regret it now'. So, it made my decision very difficult because if I wouldn't be,
> I would just pack my bags and go back. Seriously, this is where I am now.

It is in the context of the ongoing hostility that the referendum had prompted Tomek to rethink his stay in the country. Thus, despite having a secure legal position in the UK and British citizenship, he clearly felt like he no longer belonged there. His sense of being uprooted felt particularly poignant given that his ongoing civil society engagement had been about promoting integration and community cohesion. Since 2010, he had been a key player in an initiative aimed at bringing together local and migrant anglers, a project which became remarkably successful and was expanded and rolled out throughout the UK. The project involved organizing events to bring migrants and locals together, consulting with relevant authorities to inform and educate both migrant anglers about UK laws and regulations and British authorities about legal and cultural contexts in central and eastern Europe.

Conclusion

This chapter has explored European Union migrants' experiences of participation and belonging in Wales. Amongst the different forms of participation highlighted, one involved research informants working or volunteering in existing third-sector organizations, helping with the provision of front-line services and programmes to migrants around the country. At the same time, others played a more leading role in civil society, creating and running new organizations and initiatives in various parts of the country. While these migrant-led initiatives emerged in response to a need among migrant populations, a key finding of the research is that these groups served and engaged not only with migrants but also with local populations, communities and authorities. Another form of participation, migrants' online groups, were noted as significant in facilitating migrants' connections and attachments to Welsh nature and more generally to Welsh society. Initiatives such as *Smok Walijski* further demonstrate the multidimensional nature of belonging, showing how migrants can develop strong connections with 'host' countries, not just with their 'homeland'.

Our analysis has further shown how the links and attachments developed by our research informants were severely disrupted by the result of the 2016 EU referendum. On the individual level, this occurred in various ways, with the Brexit vote triggering uncertainties around respondents' legal rights and formal participation in society. It also unsettled their everyday lives due to an increase in hostility and physical and verbal abuse, and affected their emotional attachments, identity and sense of belonging in Wales. At the same time, with all participants involved in civil society organizations and initiatives, the referendum result also undermined their ongoing engagement and contribution to Welsh civil society, threatening to 'undo' the incorporation, integration and community work that these migrants had done over the years. As May (2011) notes, belonging (and participation) is not a given but rather achieved through active processes, and as such any significant disruption caused to it may take time and effort to be remade. In this sense, whatever the outcome of subsequent Brexit negotiations between the United Kingdom government and the European Union, the result of the 2016 referendum itself impacted not only on the entitlements of EU citizens but also civil society and, more broadly, community relations and solidarity in Wales.

References

Anthias, F. 2016. 'Interconnecting boundaries of identity and belonging and hierarchy-making within transnational mobility studies: framing inequalities'. *Current Sociology* 64(2):172–90.

Bauböck, R. 2000. 'Dual and supranational citizenship: limits to transnationalism'. In T.A. Aleinikoff and D. Klusmeyer (eds), *From Migrants to Citizens: Membership in a Changing World*, pp. 305–11. Washington, DC: Brookings Institution Press.

BBC 2014. 'Wales' foreign-born population rises by 82% in 10 years'. BBC News, 4 March: www.bbc.co.uk/news/uk-wales-26423124?print=true (accessed on 23 November 2020).

Blanchflower, D. and Lawton, H. 2008. 'The impact of the recent expansion of the EU on the UK labour market'. IZA discussion paper No. 3695: ftp.iza.org/dp3695.pdf (22 November 2020).

Bourdieu, P. 1992. *Language and Symbolic Power*. Cambridge: Polity Press.

Breidahl, K.N. 2012. 'Immigrant-targeted activation policies: a comparison of the approaches of Scandinavian welfare states'. *Social Policy Review* 24:117–36.

Burrell, K. 2010. 'Staying, returning, working and living: key themes in current academic research undertaken in the UK on migration movements from Eastern Europe'. *Social Identities* 16:297–308.

Crawley, H. and Crimes, T. 2009. 'Refugees living in Wales: a survey of skills, experiences, and barriers to inclusion'. Swansea: Centre for Migration Policy Research, Swansea University: cronfa.swan.ac.uk/Record/cronfa8207 (accessed 22 November 2020).

Dafydd Jones, R. 2015. 'Mwslemiaid yn y Gymru wledig: datgysylltiad, ffydd, a pherthyn'. *Gwerddon* 19:9–27.

Donovan, O. 2019. 'The Welsh media III: where are people getting their news?' *State of Wales*, 28 August: stateofwales.com/2019/08/the-welsh-media-iii-where-are-people-getting-their-news (accessed 22 November 2020).

Dwyer, P.J., Scullion, L., Jones, K. and Stewart, A. 2018. 'The impact of conditionality on the welfare rights of EU migrants in the UK'. *Policy and Politics* 47(1):133–50.

Eade, J., Drinkwater, S. and Garapich, M. 2006. 'Class and ethnicity: Polish migrants in London'. Centre for Research on Nationalism, Ethnicity and Multiculturalism, University of Surrey: doc.ukdataservice.ac.uk/doc/6056/mrdoc/pdf/6056uguide.pdf (accessed 27 October 2020)

Engbersen, G., and Snel, E. 2013. 'Liquid migration: dynamic and fluid patterns of post-accession migration'. In B. Glorius, I. Grabowska-Lusinska and A. Rindoks (eds), *Mobility in Transition: Migration Patterns after EU Enlargement*, pp. 21–40. Amsterdam: Amsterdam University Press.

Favell, A. 2008. 'The new face of East–West migration from Europe'. *Journal of Ethnic and Migration Studies* 34(5):701–16.

Fortier, A.M. 2000. *Migrant Belongings: Memory, Space, and Identity*. Oxford: Berg.

Fox, J.E., Moroşanu, L. and Szilassy, E. 2012. 'The racialization of the new European migration to the UK'. *Sociology* 46:680–95.

Gentleman, A. 2019. 'Rise in EU citizens not getting UK settled status causes alarm'. *Guardian*, 30 August: www.theguardian.com/politics/2019/aug/30/eu-citizens-uk-settled-status-alarm (accessed 22 November 2020).

Gerard, L. 2016. 'The press and immigration: reporting the news or fanning the flames of hatred?' *SubScribe*, 3 September: www.sub-scribe.co.uk/2016/09/the-press-and-immigration-reporting.html (accessed 22 November 2020).

Glick Schiller, N., Basch, L. and Szanton Blanc, C. 1995. 'From immigrant to transmigrant: theorizing transnational migration'. *Anthropological Quarterly* 68(1):48–63.

Godin, M. and Sigona, N. 2019. 'EU families feel more welcome in Scotland than they do in the rest of the UK'. *LSE Blogs*: blogs.lse.ac.uk/europpblog/2019/10/10/eu-families-feel-more-welcome-in-scotland-than-they-do-in-the-rest-of-the-uk (accessed 22 November 2020).

Grzymala-Kazlowska, A. 2018. 'From connecting to social anchoring: adaptation and "settlement" of Polish migrants in the UK'. *Journal of Ethnic and Migration Studies* 44(2):252–69.

Guma, T. 2018. 'The making of a "risk population": categorisations of Roma and ethnic boundary making among Czech- and Slovak-speaking migrants in Glasgow'. *Identities: Global Studies in Culture and Power* 26(6):668–87.

——— 2020. 'Turning citizens into immigrants: state practices of welfare "cancellations" and document retention among EU nationals living in Glasgow'. *Journal of Ethnic and Migration Studies* 46(13):2647–63.

Guma, T. and Dafydd Jones, R. 2019. '"Where are we going to go now?": EU migrants' experiences of hostility, anxiety and (non-)belonging during Brexit'. *Population, Space and Place* 25:e2198.

Gustafson, P. 2009. 'Mobility and territorial belonging'. *Environment and Behaviour* 41(1):490–508.

Hall, S. 2015 'Migrant urbanisms: ordinary cities and everyday resistance'. *Sociology* 49(3):853–69.

Harris, J., Lee, S. and Lepp, A. 2012. 'England, Whales and Princess Diana: a case study of US students' perceptions of Wales'. *Journal of Hospitality, Leisure, Sport and Tourism Education* 11(2):87–92.

Henley, J. 2017. '"A bit of me is dying. But I can't stay": the EU nationals exiting Britain'. *The Guardian*, 28 July: www.theguardian.com/politics/2017/jul/28/brexit-the-eu-nationals-exiting-britain-a-bit-of-me-is-dying-but-i-cant-stay (accessed on 23 November 2020).

Jackson, L. and Dafydd Jones, R. 2014. '"We'll keep a welcome in the hillsides"? Proximity, distance and hospitality towards migrants in Wales'. *Contemporary Wales* 27:82–104.

Jones, L. and Lever, J. 2014. Migrant Workers in Rural Wales and the South Wales Valleys. Cardiff: Wales Rural Observatory: gov.wales/docs/wefo/report/1403 28migrantworkersreporten.pdf (accessed on 23 November 2020)

Lulle, A., Moroșanu, L. and King, R. 2018. 'And then came Brexit: experiences and future plans of young EU migrants in the London region'. *Population, Space and Place* 24:1–11.

Mann, R. and Tommis, Y. 2012. 'Public sentiments towards immigrants living in Wales'. Wales Institute of Social and Economic Research, Bangor University: wiserd.ac.uk/sites/default/files/documents/TommisPublicSentimentsTowardsImmigrationinWales_0.pdf (accessed 27 October 2020).

May, V. 2011. 'Self, belonging and social change'. *Sociology* 45(3):363–78.

Mee, K. and Wright, S. 2009. 'Guest editorial'. *Environment and Planning* 41(4):772–9.

Moskal, M. 2013. 'Circulating capitals between Poland and Scotland: a transnational perspective on European labour mobility'. *International Migration and Integration* 14:363–79.

Mügge, L.M. and van der Haar, M. 2016. 'Who is an immigrant and who requires integration? Categorising in European policies'. In B. Garcés-Mascareñas and R. Penninx (eds), *Integration Processes and Policies in Europe: Contexts, Levels and Actors*, pp. 77–90. Amsterdam: Amsterdam University Press.

New Europeans 2017. '"On 23rd June I became an alien." Brexit—The voice of EU citizens'. European Parliament Hearing, Briefing, 11 May. A moral case and legal case for unilateral guarantees: www.europarl.europa.eu/cmsdata/118364/new-europeans.pdf (accessed on 23 November 2020).

NicDhùghaill, R. 2013. 'Don't neglect the UK's indigenous languages'. *Guardian*, 20 October: www.theguardian.com/education/2013/oct/29/dont-neglect-uks-indigenous-languages (accessed 22 November 2020).

Osmond, J. 1995. *Welsh Europeans*. Bridgend: Seren.

Pollard, N., Latorre, M. and Sriskandarajah, D. 2008. 'Floodgates or turnstiles? Post EU-enlargement migration flows to (and from) the UK'. Institute for Public Policy Research: www.ippr.org/files/images/media/files/publication/2011/05/floodgates_or_turnstiles_1637.pdf (accessed 27 October 2020).

Portes, J. and Rumbaut, R.G. 1996. *Immigrant America: A Portrait*, 2nd edn. Berkeley: University of California Press.

Quinn, B. 2017. 'Sleepless, anxious, depressed: EU citizens in the shadow of Brexit'. *The Guardian*, 24 July: www.theguardian.com/politics/2017/jun/24/eu-citizens-shadow-brexit-sleepless-anxious-depressed (accessed 23 November 2020).

Ranta, R. and Nancheva, N. 2018. 'Unsettled: Brexit and European Union nationals' sense of belonging'. *Population, Space and Place* 25(1):1–10.

Robinson, V. 2003. 'Exploring myths about rural racism: a Welsh case study'. In C. Williams, N. Evans and P. O'Leary (eds), *A Tolerant Nation? Exploring Ethnic Diversity in Wales*, pp. 160–78. Cardiff: University of Wales Press.

Robinson, V., and Gardner, H. 2004. 'Unravelling a stereotype: the lived experience of black and minority ethnic people in rural Wales'. In N. Chakraborti and J. Garland (eds), *Rural Racism*, pp. 85–107. Cullompton: Willan Publishing.

Ryan, L. 2018. 'Differentiated embedding: Polish migrants in London negotiating belonging over time'. *Journal of Ethnic and Migration* Studies 44:233–51.

Rzepnikowska, R. 2018. 'Racism and xenophobia experienced by Polish migrants in the UK before and after Brexit vote'. *Journal of Ethnic and Migration Studies* 45:61–77.

Savage, M., Bagnall, G. and Longhurst, B. 2005. *Globalization and Belonging*. London: Sage Publications.

Schierup, C.-U., Hansen, P. and Castles, S. 2006. *Migration, Citizenship, and the European Welfare State: A European Dilemma*. Oxford: Oxford University Press.

Tomaney, J. 2014. 'Region and place II: belonging'. *Progress in Human Geography* 39(4):507–16.

Thomas, H. 2018. 'Newspaper circulation figures decline by up to 28 per cent'. *BBC News*, 1 March: www.bbc.co.uk/news/uk-wales-43246321 (accessed 22 November 2020).

Welsh Government 2017. 'Regional investment in Wales after Brexit: securing Wales' future': gov.wales/sites/default/files/publications/2018-10/regional-investment-in-wales-after-brexit.pdf (accessed on 23 November 2020).

——— 2019a. 'Nation of sanctuary: refugee and asylum seeker plan': gweddill.gov.
        wales/docs/dsjlg/publications/equality/190128-refugee-and-asylum-seeker-
        plan-en.pdf (accessed 27 October 2020).

——— 2019b. 'Package of support for EU citizens living in Wales announced'. Press
        release, 9 July: gov.wales/package-of-support-for-eu-citizens-living-in-
        wales-announced (accessed 27 October 2020).

White, A. 2011. *Polish Families and Migration since EU Accession*. Bristol: Policy
        Press.

White, A. and Ryan, L. 2008. 'Polish temporary migration: the formation and
        significance of social networks'. *Europe–Asia Studies* 60(9):1467–1502.

Williams, C. 2003. 'Claiming the national: nation, national identity and ethnic
        minorities'. In C. Williams, N. Evans and P. O'Leary (eds), *A Tolerant
        Nation? Exploring Ethnic Diversity in Wales*, pp. 220–34. Cardiff: University
        of Wales Press.

Wimmer, A. 2002. *Nationalist Exclusion and Ethnic Conflict: Shadows of Modernity*.
        Cambridge: Cambridge University Press.

Wyn Jones, R. 2007. *Rhoi Cymru'n Gyntaf: syniadaeth, Plaid Cymru*. Cardiff:
        University of Wales Press.

——— 2017. 'Brexit a hunaniaeth genedlaethol'. *Barn* 656:11–14.

Yarker, S. 2019. 'Reconceptualising comfort as part of local belonging: the use of
        confidence, commitment and irony'. *Social and Cultural Geography*
        20(4):534–50.

12

Voyages around fathers

Class, community and mobility
in industrial South Wales

CHRIS HANN

Introduction

My credentials for contributing to a volume exploring social anthropologies of the Welsh are not the strongest. I was born in Cardiff and spent the first seventeen and a half years of my life in a new town twenty miles away. But although the names of places and streets in this town were mostly Welsh, it was entirely English-speaking. Croesyceiliog Grammar School abandoned normal lessons to hold an *Eisteddfod* on St David's Day (1 March), but it was never easy to find a Welsh-speaking bard among the pupils. I had a gifted languages teacher called Idris Jones, who would undoubtedly have liked to teach us his native Welsh. In the mid nineteenth century, Welsh was apparently still spoken in this valley, but then a gradual demise was accelerated through repression.[1] The headmaster in Croesyceiliog in the 1960s was a chemistry graduate of Oxford University who took the view that Welsh was a dying language that had no place in our curriculum. Idris Jones therefore taught me only German and Italian.

Then I moved away. I learned to speak other European languages, and eventually family and friends joked that my accent in English betrayed more traces of Hungarian or Polish than of Welsh. But I have never ceased visiting family in Pontnewydd, Cwmbrân, where my father, born in Cardiff in 1924, still lives in the house he purchased in 1960. Reg is my main source of information

---

1   Although schools in the valley of the Afon Llwyd used only English, it seems that at least some chapels continued for some time to hold services in both languages. See Harwood *et al.* (1996:233).

for this chapter. Before turning to some empirical data, I shall elaborate a little on the concepts of class and community with reference to the ethnography of Wales. After the empirical discussion, I shall return to these concepts in a broader framework, with reference to my ongoing work in Hungary, to Brexit, to human mobility and to what Raymond Williams termed the 'idea of settlement' (Williams 2016:119ff.). My aim is to pose questions with respect to Wales that have wider implications: for Britain, for the European Union, even for our shrinking and overheated planet.

Community and class in the anthropology of Wales

When social anthropologists began to expand the horizons of their discipline in the middle of the last century, they realized the need to abandon a static antiquarianism and place the objects of research in historical time. Bronislaw Malinowski's self-critical appendices to the last of his Trobriand monographs set the tone – for example, when he regretted his failure to integrate the impact of colonial pearling into his accounts of the natives he observed (Malinowski 1965:479–81). Not long afterwards, Max Gluckman went much further when he famously proclaimed that 'An African townsman is a townsman, an African miner is a miner: he is only secondarily a tribesman' (Gluckman 1960:57). The assumption was that theoretical tools developed for the analysis of industrialized societies in the advanced states of Europe should be operationalized around the word as 'social change' unfolded. The implication remained that these societies had been in effect stagnant prior to the impact of colonialism and capitalism.

James Ferguson (2019) has recently questioned the implementation of this research agenda by scrutinizing the concept of the 'proletariat'. He points out that its meaning for Marx and Engels was entirely different from what it connoted in the Roman society from which we derive the term. Roman proletarians were not the dispossessed class characterized by Marx and Engels, obliged to sell their labour power to exploiting capitalists. They were citizens, with various rights and claims on imperial redistribution, though they mostly lived in what, in today's parlance, might be called precarious informality. Ferguson argues persuasively that to grasp the situation of the urban poor in contemporary South Africa, the original Roman sense of proletarian may be more pertinent than the Marxist sense that has prevailed in Euro-American social science theory.

But my focus is Wales, where the fit with Marxist concepts seems more promising. Thanks to mining and manufacturing industry in the valleys of South Wales from the late eighteenth century onwards, Wales became the world's first industrial nation (the census of 1851 recorded that more households were earning their living in industry than in agriculture). Yet when

Max Gluckman, in another innovative step, called upon social anthropologists to apply their insights from tribal Africa and other colonies to their home countries, he did not follow the logic of his implicit philosophy of history.

When Ronald Frankenberg, one of his most talented students, was prevented (for reasons to do with his radical left-wing politics) from undertaking research in the colonies, it was decided he should collect data for his doctorate in Wales instead. But Frankenberg worked not in the heavily industrialized south but in the settlement that he called 'Pentrediwaith', a village easily accessible from Manchester, where he loyally operationalized Gluckman's ideas about conflict and integration in a face-to-face community divided by religion as well as language and ethnicity (Frankenberg 1990). The other major study of that generation, by Isabel Emmet (1964), was also located in the north. Both authors addressed social change explicitly. They highlighted tensions and conflict, as well as community-building and the overcoming of antagonistic class relations at the local level. But if anthropologists were now permitted to work at home and encouraged to address the entire range of human societies in time and space, it is surely surprising that industrial South Wales was overlooked by these pioneers – slate received more attention than coal and steel.[2]

This pattern persisted in the next generation. Anthony Cohen's research on the Shetland island of Whalsay is an outstanding example of fine-grained British ethnography (1987; see also Cohen 1982). By now the bias towards the rural meant a focus on the 'symbolic construction of community', and the aims of the original Manchester School to engage with conflict and hostility had slipped out of focus. Perhaps this trend should not be surprising. Whether or not they use and theorize the concept of community, anthropologists have by and large been more at home with holistic analyses that prioritize questions of identity and belonging than they have with the study of class and structural antagonism.

Class, regardless of whether it is defined in Marxist terms with reference to ownership of the means of production or in a more diffuse Weberian sense, where it is given by 'market situation', is primarily a term for the sociologist. Of course, we are not entirely lacking ethnographic analyses of class relations, or of the historical emergence of class consciousness in a specific class. Equally, there is no shortage of sociologists who have deployed 'community' in one way or another. But the disciplinary bias seems undeniable. Whereas other social scientists readily identify *Klassen an sich* ('classes in themselves') according to

---

2   The major exception was Kenneth Little's study of 'negroes' in Butetown, Cardiff, one of Britain's first black ghettos (Little 1948). The book's curious title was an indication that the Welsh dimension was of no interest to the author.

various objective criteria, the social anthropologist has a propensity to report on the basis of field research that members of the class in question do not in fact share a common consciousness of its predicament and historical mission; in other words, it does not become a *Klasse für sich selbst* ('class for itself'), to employ the familiar Marxist distinction.

Sometimes, the concepts of class and community are creatively combined. When a common relationship to the means of production is complemented by the solidarities of households and associations, religious as well as secular, we may recognize 'working-class communities' (e.g. Kalb 1997). Countless historians, geographers, sociologists and others have shown that the South Wales Valleys were dominated by such communities following industrialization, and that they had a high degree of class consciousness in the familiar Marxist sense. It is enough to consider the militancy of the miners, all the way down to the failed strikes of the 1980s, the 'final paroxysm of classic proletarianism' (Day 2002:123). Nevertheless, in the following section I shall draw attention to certain limitations of the classic Marxist approach.

From 'council class' to Brexit

Let me begin the empirical discussion with family detail. Since both my parents were born in Cardiff and large extended families were rooted there, I visited continuously throughout my childhood. We generally headed to my mother Kathleen's parents, who lived in a terraced house in Australia Road, Heath. In the mid 1960s they moved to a socially superior semi-detached house in Beatty Avenue, close to Roath Park Lake. My mother's father hailed from the mining village of Gwaun-Cae-Gurwen, from a family that sold and repaired boots and shoes and had formerly farmed. He was the only Welsh-speaker among my four grandparents. The Protestant Alfred Mark married the Catholic Agnes McClean, whose father John, a ship plater, was born in Sligo and moved to Cardiff around 1890. Of course, these two Celts could only communicate in English. When relatives from Gwaun-Cae-Gurwen came to visit in the 1930s, my aunt recalls how the guests were shunted off into the kitchen to speak Welsh with her father. To this day, my middle-class relatives in Cardiff disapprove of the Welsh language requirements that have changed public life in the city during their lifetimes. They consider themselves Welsh but do not greatly value the language and culture. A solitary cousin who chose to study Welsh and became a Plaid Cymru activist is the sole exception.

My father's side was less present in my childhood. Reginald Hann was born at his maternal grandparents home in Bertram Street, but at this point in early 1924 his parents Alfred and Lucy had already purchased their own home, 176 Moorland Road, Splott. To me, as a child, this seemed a different kind of community, more working class (a vocabulary I could not have used at the time). Both my paternal great-grandfathers were born in Somerset. John Hann was a postman. One of his five sons set up a successful plumbing firm. My paternal grandfather was employed for almost all his working life (after military service) by Cardiff City Council, and he rose to be a supervisor in the Waterworks Department. It was the security of this job that enabled him to take out a mortgage and become a property owner in Moorland Road, in the parish of Roath. Recent conversations with Reg have helped me to realize that, though Splott was known as a tightly-knit working class community, very significant social differences existed along this long street: the children might all attend the same primary school, but the kids from the riff-raff area near the docks and steelworks belonged to a different milieu if not a different class from the kids of homeowners such as Alf Hann. When I pushed my father recently to describe his class background, he reflected and declared he grew up as 'council class'. This referred primarily to the fact that Alf's wages were secure throughout the years of the Great Depression, while the fathers of some of my dad's school friends were vulnerable to redundancy and hardship.

The differences were consolidated at secondary school level. Reg Hann passed the eleven-plus examination with grades good enough for Cardiff High School and completed his education there five years later. This was a big change, not least because it meant abandoning the passion Alf had inculcated in his son for the 'round ball' in favour of rugby football, the only game that mattered at Cardiff High. After leaving school aged sixteen, my father was recruited by the city council but his career there was interrupted by four years in the Royal Navy, which he joined on his eighteenth birthday. It is not clear to him or to me whether this experience influenced the choice he made to work for Cwmbrân Development Corporation, when it was decided in 1949 to build a new town under this name in the eastern valley of Monmouthshire. Certainly, the war years expanded my father's horizons. He needed little encouragement to obtain his qualifications in civil engineering through evening classes in the late 1940s (when again living at home with his parents in Moorland Road). Cwmbrân seemed to exemplify the new Wales that so many hoped for. Reg Hann worked for the Development Corporation for five years. Then in 1955 he was appointed surveyor to the Urban District Council. He remained in that post for the best part of two decades, during which Cwmbrân was a veritable boomtown.

It did not mushroom from nowhere in a virgin valley. In this respect and others, the Welsh new town differed from its counterparts elsewhere in Britain (Riden 1988). The history of ironmaking in Monmouthshire dates to the Romans. In the so-called eastern valley around Pontypool, exploitation of forest and mineral resources intensified in the early modern period under the aegis of the Hanbury family. Pontypool became famous for its japanware, emulating techniques pioneered centuries earlier in East Asia to produce luxury goods. This valley was a microcosm of Welsh industrialization throughout the nineteenth century, when the focus shifted from consumption to production goods. Forges, coal mines, tinplate factories and brickworks transformed the farming country along the banks of the Monmouthshire and Brecon Canal.

The population of Cwmbrân expanded, but its precarity was graphically demonstrated when it contracted significantly during the Great Depression. The small town, with over 40 per cent unemployment, then benefited from the Special Areas Reconstruction Act of 1936. Slum clearance programmes were implemented to alleviate poor health conditions, overcrowding and destitution. Alongside these public investments, during the late 1930s and the first half of the 1940s private industry returned to the valley, including large firms such as Lucas Girling (with a labour force in excess of 5,000 at its peak), Saunders Valves and Weston's Biscuits. After the Second World War, the Spencer Steelworks at Llanwern was founded not far away in Newport, and British Nylon Spinners colonized a large site adjacent to Pontypool.[3]

The logic behind locating Wales's only new town in this valley was thus the need to provide housing for the workers of factories that were already thriving, both in the designated area and close by. My father is sure that a high proportion of the immigrants hailed from declining settlements in the west and north of the county.[4] Most brought only their unskilled labour. They were accommodated on vast new housing estates, selecting their houses at affordable rents from the Development Corporation (3,000 new homes were built by 1958, rising to 8,000 by 1977 – see Riden 1988 for a fuller history). Council houses were also desirable and slightly cheaper, but these were generally allocated to natives of the town rather than new arrivals. I observed the construction of the town centre on green fields, which by the end of the 1960s also featured a solitary high-rise block.

My family did not live on a new estate but in Pontnewydd, formerly a separate village, and a commercial and industrial hub on the canal since the early nineteenth century. Our neighbourhood was known as the Lowlands, just up the hill from the cenotaph, five minutes' walk from what is still referred to locally as 'the village', and twenty minutes from the modern town centre. In Tynewydd Avenue, the first street to be built by the development corporation and the first home I can remember, my best friend was Kevin at number 18.

---

3   For description and analysis of Cwmbrân's industrial history, including the painfully slow replacement of earlier rural parish structures with new models of urban administration, see Harwood et al. (1996).

4   These points are confirmed in a survey conducted by Stephen Dorman (n.d.).

Like me, he was a Catholic, and our community was defined to a significant extent by religion. We played together in the Catholic football team, went to cubs and even to Ireland one summer with the altar boys. But I became aware of a social difference around the age of ten, when I was spoiled with expensive Christmas presents and he received just one football annual in his stocking. This embryonic awareness of class intensified when we moved out of the rented corporation house into the home my father purchased – for £2,850 – just around the corner from Tynewydd Avenue in 1960. With the benefit of hindsight, I can see that we moved into a small bourgeois enclave in a predominantly working-class community.

My class consciousness deepened after I passed the eleven-plus. Most boys with whom I played football did not. At Croesyceiliog Grammar School, just across the valley, relatively few pupils lived in the wards of Pontnewydd and Upper Cwmbrân. These children mostly attended the secondary modern school, which shared the same campus. A fence divided the two schools and there was virtually no interaction (apart from snowball fights in winter). The kids at the secondary modern school played round ball, while at the grammar school rugby football had a monopoly. When Kevin's family left the town, his place in my universe was taken by Tony, whose father had moved across from Caerphilly to work at Girlings. Tony was the only pupil in his year at the primary school in Upper Cwmbrân to pass the eleven-plus. Most of my classmates lived in the visibly more prosperous wards to the east of the Afon Lwyd: Llanfrechfa, Llanyravon and Croesyceiliog itself. These had been left largely untouched by the industries that had created a working class to the west of the river. The new town was supposed to transcend these distinctions, but it never quite managed to do so.

Fast forward to the 1980s and then to the present day. I realized recently, when googling the places that I still visit regularly, that Pontnewydd and Upper Cwmbrân are nowadays classified among the most deprived 10 per cent of all micro-administrative units in Wales.[5] The big factories of this valley declined under the governments led by Margaret Thatcher. Both coal and steel had disappeared by the end of the 1990s. Equally dramatic in these years was the privatization of the town centre and most of the housing stock built up by the corporation and local council. This new town, by now containing over 50,000 inhabitants (the original target was 35,000), shifted in a few years from predominantly public to predominantly private in its ethos. Despite continuities in politics and in the local shops of 'the village', it seems

---

5   According to the Welsh Index of Multiple Deprivation, 2019: www.torfaen.gov. uk/en/AboutTheCouncil/StatisticsCensusInformation/WIMD/WIMD-LSOA-Profiles.aspx (accessed 20 November 2020).

to me that a radical change took place in the decade of the 1980s. By the time the Cwmbrân Development Corporation was wound up, its main brief was no longer to build houses but to attract new industries to the town in order to create jobs for a local population once again struggling to cope with unemployment (Riden 1988).

No doubt Cwmbrân experienced the impact of neoliberalism less dramatically than most of industrial South Wales. Whereas communities further up the valley of the Afon Llwyd such as Blaenavon and Pontypool fell apart, the new town was more resilient. Easy access to the new motorway facilitated commuting, but was also conducive to investments in small businesses on scattered light-industrial estates. Of course, the number of employees in these units was small in comparison with the giants which dominated the pre-1980s 'Fordist' labour market.

My father identifies a paradoxical transformation of the original goals. The housing estates of the new town were designed so that workers would not have to travel in from elsewhere to work in Cwmbrân; but half a century later the town is dominated by its shopping centre and thousands of its inhabitants travel elsewhere to work – to Cardiff twenty miles away, and even across the River Severn to Bristol. Some estates that my father helped to plan are nowadays decidedly shabby, including the densely concentrated houses of Northville, with their low flat roofs, immediately adjacent to the town centre. Social problems are very visible here, as they are more widely in Pontypool and Blaenavon, the other major units of the county borough known since 1974 as Torfaen. All the old industrial hamlets of the valley are victims of the success of the new town, since mobile purchasing power inevitably gravitates south.[6]

At school, when studying O-level Welsh history, we were taught about the Chartist march through this valley to Newport in November 1839, and the heroics of Henry Vincent and John Frost. But silence reigned concerning the conflicts that persisted in the following generations. By the time of my childhood in the new town, working-class politics had become invisible. There was no significant party-political contestation. Local councils were dominated by the Labour Party from the First World War onwards. This did not change

---

6   Blaenafon has benefited from heritagization (it has featured on UNESCO's World Heritage List since 2001, the principal attraction being 'Big Pit', opened in 1880 and closed exactly 100 years later). But the numerous smaller industrial settlements have waned, along with the old civic and commercial centres of Pontypool, where the high street is now dominated by charity shops and a plethora of invitations to volunteer for the community.

with the foundation of the new town.[7] Cwmbrân was traditionally part of the parliamentary constituency of Pontypool (nowadays Torfaen), represented until his death in 1946 by Alderman Arthur Jenkins.[8] The main political causes of the colourful Cardiff solicitor Leo Abse, MP between 1958 and 1987, had little to do with class and community in his constituency. Abse was replaced by a local councillor of working-class origin, Paul Murphy. When Murphy retired in 2015, he was followed by a barrister, Nicholas Thomas-Symonds.[9] But no parliamentarian, either in Westminster or in the new assembly in Cardiff, could stem the haemorrhaging of jobs in the old industries.

To grasp social relations today in this region of South Wales, which the new town has failed to dislodge, I turn now to the research of Samuel Strong (2017). Strong, who is a geographer by training and not an anthropologist, conducted a year's fieldwork in 2014–15 in what used to be termed the western valleys of Monmouthshire. He chose to work in Blaenau Gwent because of this county's notoriety in recent years. No matter how you construct the deprivation indexes, Blaenau Gwent comes out top. It has the lowest gross value added, the lowest percentage of people of working age in work, the highest proportion of job seekers; it has terrible health and education statistics; car ownership is low and the bus services inadequate; at just 70 per cent, passport ownership is also remarkably low. Strong points out that 'numerous children [have] never left the county, yet alone Wales' (ibid.:258–9).

The main causes of this predicament are obvious: some 27,000 manufacturing jobs have disappeared in this part of Wales in recent decades. Strong explores the neoliberal political economic context and cautions against simplistic accounts of state withdrawal at the local level. In fact, there has been quite a lot of intervention – from Cardiff, London and Brussels.

---

7   As surveyor to Cwmbrân Council, Reg Hann had to attend many meetings and knew the local political scene very well. It was always dominated by the Labour Party. An exception was Bill Waters, a councillor who represented the Communist Party. This largely self-educated man, employed by the county council as a road sweeper, was for many years the only effective opposition to the Labour majority. (Waters began his long political career in the 1930s when he served as secretary of the local Labour Party; see Harwood *et al.* 1996:177).

8   At school we heard nothing about the imprisonment of Arthur Jenkins (father of Roy, vice-president of the South Wales Miners Federation) for inciting workers to riot in the wake of the General Strike of 1926. See Harwood *et al.* (1996:218).

9   My father was sceptical when he heard of this recent transition: 'Never trust a socialist with a double-barrelled name!' he quipped. Thomas-Symonds held the seat for Labour at the 2019 general election, albeit with a greatly reduced majority – the Labour vote was 16 per cent down on 2017. In the absence of a Brexit Party candidate, who obtained over 15 per cent, Labour would probably have lost a seat considered ultra-safe to the Conservatives.

But none of the new investments have even begun to compensate for the industrial jobs that have been lost. In the case of Blaenau Gwent, because they have been concentrated in the centre of the valley (Ebbw Vale), the more remote settlements have lost out relatively, and even in absolute terms. Strong documents how poverty is produced and reproduced, how public problems are converted into private character faults and how shame functions as 'affective governmentality' when thousands of citizens are compelled to make use of food banks (see also Strong 2021).

As a geographer, Strong is particularly interested in questions pertaining to place. He pours scorn on the rhetoric of Blairism, with its celebration of 'aspirational citizens'. The alternative is to be abject, a 'welfare queen', a scrounger and a cheat. Strong finds aspiration to be a slippery 'placeless concept' (2017:194). Precisely because the barriers to mobility away from these valleys are so high, residents formulate strong attachments to place. Strong describes the views of Irene, who has lived in Tredegar all her life and is irritated by the negative images of her home region incessantly purveyed by British (including Welsh) popular media. Irene 'depicts a sense of community that has long been lost elsewhere in the country, even other places proximate to Blaenau Gwent' (ibid.:69). She explains to the ethnographer how the local people are all friendly, open and honest: 'only Valleys people are like that. It's totally different in Abergavenny, that's only ten miles away... It's probably because there's too many English there!' (ibid.:70). For Irene, Blaenau Gwent 'is home, definitely. You know that you are coming home when you start going uphill! I've had opportunities to move away and live near my daughters. I do love going there, but I love coming home more'. Crucially, Irene's Blaenau Gwent is one that is characterized by her own fond memories of the area, from her childhood all the way through to the present day, and through which Irene articulates her deep local pride:

> In the summer holidays, you get all the mothers outside with their kids. That's the way it was when I grew up here. Mother used to sit out there with a table and a plate of Welsh cakes and the biggest pot of tea you've ever seen ... And it's not just Cefn. You can go to Waundeg, Sirhowy, it's the same. It's the community ... It's only really Blaenau Gwent that's like that.
>
> (ibid.:70)

Similar revealing testimony is drawn from younger persons who participated in focus groups that Strong organized with schoolchildren. The youngsters were invited to represent the range of their social contacts in cartographic form. George, year 10, is talented at rugby and popular music. He aspires to succeed, but not to leave his 'sports-heavy' community:

I don't think I could leave Ebbw Vale ... I mean, just, so much memories
here. Everything is so close, I mean, family, friends, everywhere. Cuz, it is
such a close community, I mean, all my friends are a walk around the corner.
My family is up the road. It's just so much easier and is so much nicer.

(ibid.:215)

Meanwhile, Jess, aged thirteen, would like nothing more than to find
work as a waitress in Newport or Cardiff. Although Geraint fantasizes about
becoming a scientist in Florida, the dominant tenor seems to be conservative:
kids do not want to leave, and thus there is an 'aspiration gap'. Strong concludes
that this makes perfect sense when one understands the context:

emigrating would mean forgoing what students expressed as particular 'ties'
to Blaenau Gwent. This was most frequently articulated through the notion
of family and can be seen by how common it is for several generations
of the same family to remain proximate on students' maps. Meeting this
model of aspiration and leaving the Valleys is not only incredibly difficult
financially and socially – it would also appear irrational to forgo these forms
of familiarity and safety.

(ibid:211)

One statistic that Strong fails to report is that, even here, in this most
deprived county, over 60 per cent of households own the houses in which
they live. This is far from being a propertyless proletariat of the Marxist sort.
Strong maintains nonetheless that, despite the policies of New Labour, and the
diagnoses of individualizing, atomizing social change proffered by sociologists
such as Ulrich Beck and Anthony Giddens, class is still central: 'rather than
these shifts leading to the disappearance of class, they have instead led to its
recasting' (ibid.:30). This theme remains undeveloped in his study. He does,
however, reflect carefully on the outcome of the referendum of June 2016, in
which both Blaenau Gwent and Torfaen voted 60 per cent for Brexit. Why
should these relatively deprived valleys, which have been the recipients of
substantial subsidies from the European Union, vote to bite the hand that
has fed them? Did they simply follow the incendiary headlines of Rupert
Murdoch's newspapers? Why did UKIP (the United Kingdom Independence
Party) consistently poll better in these places than Plaid Cymru? It seems
implausible to blame racism or anti-East European sentiment, since very few
recent immigrants are to be found here.

A century ago, immigrants dominated in the South Wales melting pot, as
the example of my own family history shows. Many came from rural parts of
Wales, but others came from England, some from Ireland. For all the friction,

by the early twentieth century these ethnic and religious differences had been largely transcended by the formation of a distinctive regional working class. How do we explain why so many members of this Welsh working class vote with Boris Johnson and other Tory Brexiteers, while their own Labour members of parliament tend to opt for Remain?[10] In the next section I probe these questions (which certainly warrant additional ethnographic investigation) by raising issues of comparison with developments I know well through my research in Eastern Europe, and with some stimulus from Raymond Williams (and his father).

Mobility, settlement and schools

The working-class communities of the South Wales coalfield were formed by diverse immigrants according to the logic of capitalism. The new town of Cwmbrân, conceived in the middle of the twentieth century, did not break the mould. Capitalism continues in the new century. Its logic of uneven development dictates that all communities are precarious. Industrial settlements must be open to change, just like the rural communities that exported their labour to the booming valleys in their heyday. This is the logic of Norman Tebbit's 'on your bike' remark in the 1980s. Hayekian economists deny that the state has any responsibility to sustain populations in places that have lost their economic *raison d'être* according to the logic of capitalism.

Despite the modest redistribution that takes place through regional development transfers ('cohesion'), Hayekian principles are dominant in the neoliberal EU, in the form of the 'four freedoms' (freedom of movement for capital, goods and persons, plus the freedom to supply services). For some free marketeers, this is not enough: they argue that the EU remains a restrictive regional trading bloc, and that the United Kingdom is better off pursuing free trade on a global basis. For such economists, a 'no deal' Brexit is desirable because it will hasten the accomplishment of long-term optimal solutions as determined by factor endowments and the laws of comparative advantage. Such economists view human beings not as the members of communities but as a factor of production, 'labour', which they expect, like other factors, to respond elastically to market signals.[11]

In recent years, the rural populations of Hungary and Poland, which I first studied more than forty years ago, have had to adapt to the logic of capitalism. They have become highly mobile (mainly thanks to cars and cheap airlines

---

10 I have, however, heard complaints in Pontnewydd about Polish drivers who steal jobs from local men because they are willing to work for half the wages.

11 A well-known economist of this type is Patrick Minford, Emeritus Professor of Economics at Cardiff University. See Minford 2015.

rather than bicycles). They have entered the British labour market in large numbers, a process facilitated sometimes by their qualifications (Pontnewydd now has a Polish dentist) but more commonly by their willingness to work hard for lower wages than native British workers. Obviously, few of these post-peasants from Eastern Europe have found their way to the valleys that concern me in this chapter. Wales, so diverse a century ago, is nowadays one of the least diverse parts of Britain. This brings me back to the puzzle as to why so many voters in these valleys opted for Brexit in June 2016.

At first glance, the Great Hungarian Plain could hardly present a greater contrast to the topography of the South Welsh Valleys, social as well as physical. But the more I reflect on the work of Samuel Strong, the more I see parallels and analogies with what I have observed in and written about rural Hungary. The settlement of Tázlár, where I began research in 1976, has undergone a demographic evolution that resembles that of the South Wales coalfield. The zone between the Danube and the Tisza was resettled by diverse migrants from the last quarter of the nineteenth century. Most lived on scattered farms and the population continued to swell until the 1940s. By the middle of the twentieth century most German and Slovak immigrant families had changed their surnames to Hungarian-sounding variants. Four decades of socialist industrialization intensified the social homogenization. In places such as Tázlár, many left their isolated farms to move either to a town or the village centre, where all modern conveniences were available. I have theorized the micro-level rural developments as the formation of a new and more cohesive community, a 'socialist civilization' (Hann 2015).

With the collapse of the socialist agrarian synthesis after 1990 it became clear very quickly that relatively large rural populations would be unable to maintain their standard of living. Young people, guaranteed work in or close to their home settlement under socialism, now had little choice but to move elsewhere. Many families have children working in London or other economic magnets. Those who remain in the homeland line up quite solidly behind Viktor Orbán, whose anti-immigrant rhetoric has been the foundation of his hold on power. His strategy in the 2019 EU election campaign was once again based on an 'idea of settlement' in the sense of Raymond Williams (2016).

German politicians accuse Orbán of hypocrisy because he accepts subsidies from Brussels (paid for in large measure by Germany) while castigating the EU in his nationalist rhetoric. But here I confess to feeling some sympathy with the megalomaniac Orbán. I think it is essentially the same idea that leads people in South Wales to reject the system that brings them some subsidies and prestige projects adorned with blue EU insignia, but which does not provide citizens with satisfying jobs and life chances. After sixteen years of maximal EU support, Samuel Strong found that Ebbw Vale had acquired a kind of imitation Canary Wharf on the site of the old steelworks; but the number of jobs had continued to fall and the local authority was too indebted to continue operating public lavatories.

The popularity of neo-nationalist politics in the villages and small towns of the Great Hungarian Plain is a consequence of the relative decline they have experienced during capitalist transformation since 1990. They have lost the benefits that brought them prosperity in the last decades of socialism (Hann 2015). Large numbers of people who previously flourished in places like the village of Tázlár, where both ecological and economic environments are unfavourable, have become surplus to requirements. This is basically the same fate as that experienced by the Welsh communities that have lost the basis of their economy not once but twice in the course of the twentieth century. The irony is that when the state or the EU attempts to stabilize these communities, their redistributive interventions to promote regional development seem to stimulate even more vigorous populist resentments. Population decline can be mitigated or even averted, but a high price is paid in terms of pathologies of waste and blame.

The comparison I am making between deindustrialization in South Wales and decollectivization on the Great Hungarian Plain would not have surprised Raymond Williams, who was born and raised in rural Pandy, just fifteen miles up the railway line from Cwmbrân. The whole argument of Williams's *The Country and the City*, first published in 1973 (Williams 2016), is to transcend simplistic stereotyping by drawing out the interrelations and similarities between urban and rural sectors, whose causes are ultimately to be found in the capitalist mode of production. More specifically:

> There is a visible qualitative difference between the results of farming and the results of mining, but ... [t]he effects on human settlements, and on customary or locally self-determined ways of life, are often very similar ...
> An immensely productive capitalism, in all its stages, has extended both the resources and the modes which, however unevenly, provide and contain forms of response to its effects.
>
> (ibid.:421–2)

Williams would have expected social anthropology to concern itself with the study of the people whose lives are transformed by these processes: people in the sense of *populus* rather than *ethnos*. The emergence of a Welsh identity in the sense of a nationality or ethnic group is certainly an important topic for anthropological investigation. But, for me at least, it is even more vital to study the people in the sense of the masses, in both their settlements and their mobilities, in their communities and in their relations to dominant classes.

In his cultural criticism and forays into political economy, Raymond Williams combines critique of nomad capitalism with the rejection of the 'idealization of settlement' (ibid.:120–3). He acknowledges the deep 'structure of values' that binds human beings to their 'native places' but he scorns the acts of settlement and the poor loans that formerly bound relief to residence in a parish, where the poor could be controlled and exploited. For Williams, mobility is 'inevitable and natural' (ibid.:119); by contrast, 'what is idealized as a moral economy' (ibid.:121) is rigid and repressive. His discussion is based on analysis of literary texts written in the early phases of agrarian capitalism in England.

Can these arguments be applied to the post-industrial communities of South Wales centuries later? It seems to me that Raymond Williams's position, however justified and persuasive in the light of British social history, and both logical and honest given his own trajectory from Pandy to Saffron Walden, is inadequate for the globalized world of the twenty-first century. The unprecedented mobility of Eastern Europeans in recent decades has contributed significantly to accentuating populist sentiments both in their home countries and in the UK, even in places where few if any Poles and Hungarians are to be found. So I have trouble in siding with Williams when he ends up, paradoxically, endorsing the stance of the free-market ideologists. It is unsurprising that no members of his family are to be found in Pandy today. Yet more needs to be done to enable people to remain and fulfil their potential through work in their home communities, in Wales and everywhere else on the planet.

An alternative view, espoused by countless reformers over the years, is to seek solutions to the conundrum through education, in the hope of enabling spontaneous forms of desirable social mobility in much the same way that spontaneous markets generate economic optima. Williams himself was an outstanding pupil who was recommended to Trinity College, Cambridge, by his headmaster at King Henry VIII Grammar School in Abergavenny. A generation later I was given a Welsh Foundation Scholarship by Jesus College, Oxford. But those grammar schools no longer exist. The proportion of pupils who now proceed from Croesyceiliog and Cwmbrân High School (the town's other large secondary school) to the 'top' universities that form the Russell Group is almost certainly smaller than the proportion that made this move half a century ago.

At Croesyceiliog Comprehensive School, where the fence between the old grammar and secondary modern schools was torn down shortly after I left in 1970, some horizons have contracted. Idris Jones, were he on the staff today, would be able to teach me Welsh, but not Italian, or even German, which was dropped from the curriculum a decade ago. The buildings erected sixty years ago are about to be demolished. They are being replaced, but my old school is losing its sixth form as a result of the decision to incorporate a Sixth Form College in a new 'Learning Zone' adjacent to Morrisons supermarket in the town centre, to serve the entire valley.

From 2021, the only other sixth form in Torfaen will be at Ysgol Gyfun Gwynllyw. This is a Welsh-language secondary school that opened in 1989 in Trevethin, a hilltop estate just north of Pontypool with magnificent views across to Mynydd Maen. Trevethin is one of the three most deprived micro-units of the county (the others being Upper Cwmbrân and Pontnewydd). All subjects except English are taught in Welsh. There is a price to pay for the targeted bilingualism; only Spanish survives as a foreign language. Like Cwmbrân High School, this school has attracted criticism from government inspectors (the watchdog Estyn) in recent years. Yet, in line with Welsh government policy, Ysgol Gyfun Gwynllyw is expanding and will admit pupils from year 1 from 2021 (Cooke-Black 2019). With this transformation to form a complex educating up to 1,100 pupils between nursery age and nineteen, the head teacher is optimistic that more local children will attend her school.[12] At present the school estimates that only 4 per cent of pupils come from Welsh-speaking households. Most are bussed to this inaccessible location from all over the county borough, and from Monmouthshire to the east and Blaenau Gwent to the west. Monmouthshire pupils are less likely to stay on for the sixth form because the local authority does not cover the transportation costs of pupils older than sixteen. The Welsh government intervenes through deprivation grants and the Seren Network.[13] Staff work hard to nurture talent and there is a flourishing cooperation with Wadham College, Oxford. Nevertheless, Cardiff and other universities in Wales are by far the most popular destinations for higher education.

Obviously, the educational mobility facilitated by the grammar schools benefited only the few. That system may have reinforced class distinctions and entailed costs for the community. But what has replaced it? What is the thinking behind the ongoing investment in a Welsh-medium school in Trevethin at a time when no major initiatives have been taken to bring jobs back to this part of the valley? Will this school and Cwmbrân's new Learning

---

12   Interview with Elan Bolton at Ysgol Gyfun Gwynllyw, 15 August 2019.

13   See: gov.wales/seren-network. 'Seren' is Welsh for 'star'. This network was established in 2015 with the aim of stemming the decline in applications from Wales to Oxford, Cambridge and other 'top' universities in England (in practice the Russell Group). It is too early to assess its impact. At Ysgol Gyfun Gwynllyw the 'Brilliance Club' depends on separate funding related to deprivation indexes. This is used in part to defray the costs of pupil visits to universities.

Zone enable the young people of Torfaen to become more mobile factors of production? The return of the Welsh language to a highly anglicized part of the country looks like a remarkable success story, but the challenges remain formidable.

At Ysgol Gyfun Gwynllyw, only the supporting staff are local. Most teachers have awkward commutes from Cardiff, Abergavenny and other locations with thriving Welsh-language communities. They do not move to Torfaen because it lacks such a community, and they leave for more desirable jobs as soon as they can. Does this mean that the valley of the Afon Llwyd is destined to suffer the worst of all worlds: dismal prospects of attractive secure employment within the valley, diminishing opportunities to escape from it via educational mobility, and long-term absence of a Welsh cultural infrastructure? Can the expansion of Welsh-language teaching and of higher education options within Wales compensate for the fact that the most prestigious higher education institutions of the UK have become harder to access? Or must one accept what the new head teacher at Ysgol Gyfun Gwynllyw refers to as a 'lack of aspiration' among working class parents? As Strong found in Blaenau Gwent, parents do not want their children to move away from the valleys, and these values and preferences are absorbed by many young people themselves. Perhaps their commitment to settlement, to what the Germans know as *Heimat* and the Welsh as *bro*, deserves more respect and should determine the agendas of policymakers.

Conclusion

In this chapter I have indicated some of the difficulties of the concepts of proletariat and class with reference to my own family history in Cardiff and Pontnewydd, Cwmbrân, together with Samuel Strong's recent urban geography of the neighbouring county of Blaenau Gwent. Strong (2017, 2021) documents deep bonds of community. He does not use the language of class analytically and it does not figure in the vernacular discourses he cites from this deindustrialized county. He declares with Henri Lefebvre that the politics of place must be a politics of class conflict, but this remains somehow formalistic. The geographer also asserts the continuing validity of Raymond Williams's original conceptualization of the 'structures of feeling' associated with class and its cultural, symbolic and social operations (see Morgan and Preston 1993). This is surely an invitation which the social anthropologist cannot afford to decline.

Williams as cultural critic employs the language of class regularly. He distanced himself from romanticized notions of the face-to-face community. Class is present in his border country near Abergavenny, just as it forms part of the context of Frankenberg's border village near Llangollen (Frankenberg

1990). Unlike Glyn Ceiriog (Pentrediwaith), the dispersed houses of Pandy did not constitute a conventional nuclear settlement. 'Knowable communities' come in many shapes and scales. But when Williams as novelist seeks to capture the changing social relations of the only settlement in which he was truly at home, a problem emerges. The hero Matthew Price has built his London academic career in economic history on a study of the migratory processes that populated the South Wales Valleys in the nineteenth century. But Matthew has lost his enthusiasm for dry scholarship. His father's stroke takes him back to his roots.

Matthew, or Will as he is known in the community, has complex relationships not only with his taciturn Labour Party-loyalist, trade-unionist parent Harry but also with the loquacious entrepreneur Morgan Rosser, who represents the more aspirational side of Williams's own father (and according to some readings of the novel might be Will's biological father). Morgan, too, in his own way, is a decent man at home in his community. How are we to interpret the final conversation between Matthew/Will and his dying father when they reflect enigmatically on the changing nature of work, human beings 'growing away, from what used to be real', being of 'one kind' and 'living through' social and kinship relations? When Harry stresses the generational shifts, Matthew/Will is puzzled, and asks: 'Leaving class out of it, you mean?' Harry replies 'Aye, I hope you leave it out of it.' (Williams 2006:387–8).

References

Cohen, A.P. 1987. *Whalsay: Symbol, Segment and Boundary in a Shetland Island Community*. Manchester: Manchester University Press.

——— (ed.) 1982. *Belonging: Identity and Social Organisation in British Rural Cultures*. Manchester: Manchester University Press.

Cooke-Black, S. 2919. 'School expansion plans are approved.' *Pontypool Free Press* (19 June):1–2.

Day, G. 2002. *Making Sense of Wales: A Sociological Perspective*. Cardiff: University of Wales Press.

Dorman, S. n.d. [*c.*1973]. 'Cwmbran: new town or residential area for Gwent?' Unpublished, Department of Geography, St Mary's College (St Mary's University), Twickenham, London.

Emmett, I. 1964. *A North Wales Village: A Social Anthropological Study*. London: Routledge and Kegan Paul.

Ferguson, J. 2019. 'Proletarian politics today: on the perils and possibilities of historical analogy.' *Comparative Studies in Society and History* 61(1):4–22.

Frankenberg, R. 1990 [1957]. *Village on the Border*. Prospect Heights, IL: Waveland Press.

Gluckman, M. 1960. 'Tribalism in modern British Central Africa'. *Cahiers d'Études Africaines* 1(1):55–70.

Hann, C. 2015. 'Backwardness revisited: time, space and civilization in rural Eastern Europe'. *Comparative Studies in Society and History* 57(4):881–911.

Harwood, C., Voisey, K., Littlewood, K. and Philpotts, C. 1996. *Cwmbrân: Chapters in Its History*. Cwmbrân: Cwmbrân Community Council.

Kalb, D. 1997. *Expanding Class. Power and Everyday Politics in Industrial Communities, The Netherlands, 1850-1950*. Durham, NC.: Duke University Press.

Little, K. 1948. *Negroes in Britain: A Study of Racial Relations in English Society*. London: Routledge and Kegan Paul.

Malinowski, B. 1965 [1935]. *Coral Gardens and Their Magic, I: Soil-Tilling and Agricultural Rites in the Trobriand Islands*. Bloomington: Indiana University Press.

Minford, P. 2015. *Should Britain Leave the EU? An Economic Analysis of a Troubled Relationship*, 2nd edn. Cheltenham: Edward Elgar Publishing.

Morgan, W.J. and Preston, P. (eds). 1993. *Raymond Williams: Politics, Education, Letters*. London: Macmillan.

Riden, P. 1988. *Rebuilding a Valley. A History of Cwmbrân Development Corporation*. Huddersfield: King's England Press.

Strong, S.R. 2017. 'The production of poverty: politics, place and social abandonment in Blaenau Gwent, Wales'. PhD thesis. Cambridge: Cambridge University.

——— 2021. 'Towards a geographical account of shame: foodbanks, austerity and the spaces of austere affective governmentality'. *Transactions of the Institute of British Geographers* 46:73–86.

Williams, R. 2016 [1973]. *The Country and the City*. London: Vintage.

——— 2006 [1960]. *Border Country*. Cardigan: Parthian.

Contributors

Helen Blakely is Research Associate, School of Social Sciences and Wales Institute of Social and Economic Research and Data, Cardiff University.

Fiona Bowie is Research Affiliate, School of Anthropology and Museum Ethnography, Oxford University, and a member of Wolfson College, Oxford.

David Dallimore is Honorary Research Associate, School of History, Philosophy and Social Sciences, Bangor University.

Howard Davis is Professor of Sociology, School of History, Philosophy and Social Sciences, Bangor University.

Marta Eichsteller is Lecturer in Sociology, School of History, Philosophy and Social Sciences, Bangor University.

Elaine Forde is Lecturer in Business, School of Management, Swansea University.

Taulant Guma is Lecturer in Human Geography, Edinburgh Napier University, and formerly a post-doctoral research associate, Wales Institute of Social and Economic Research, and Data, Aberystwyth University.

Chris Hann is Professor and Director, Max Planck Institute of Social Anthropology, Halle, Germany, and Fellow of Corpus Christi College, Cambridge.

Rhys Dafydd Jones is Lecturer in Human Geography, Aberystwyth University, and an affiliate of the Wales Institute of Social and Economic Research, and Data.

Robin Mann is Senior Lecturer in Sociology, School of History, Philosophy and Social Sciences, Bangor University.

W. John Morgan is Professor Emeritus of Comparative Education, University of Nottingham; Honorary Professor, School of Social Sciences, and Leverhulme Emeritus Fellow, the Wales Institute of Social and Economic Research, and Data, Cardiff University.

John O'Connell is Professor of Ethnomusicology, School of Music, Cardiff University.

Elen Phillips is Principal Curator of Contemporary and Community History, National Museum of History, St Fagans.

Huw Pryce is Professor Emeritus of Welsh History, Bangor University.

Gareth Rees is Professor Emeritus of Education, and formerly Director, the Wales Institute of Social and Economic Research, and Data, Cardiff University.

Iwan Wyn Rees is Lecturer, School of Welsh, and Director of the Cardiff Centre for Welsh-American Studies, Cardiff University.

Marilyn Strathern is Professor Emerita of Social Anthropology, and formerly William Wyse Professor, University of Cambridge, Fellow of the British Academy, and Honorary Fellow of the Learned Society of Wales.

INDEX

Page numbers in **bold** refer to chapter authorship.